The Fall and Rise
of American Finance

The Fall and Rise of American Finance

*From J. P. Morgan
to BlackRock*

Stephen Maher

and

Scott M. Aquanno

VERSO

London • New York

First published by Verso 2024
© Stephen Maher and Scott Aquanno 2024

1 3 5 7 9 10 8 6 4 2

Verso
UK: 6 Meard Street, London W1F 0EG
US: 388 Atlantic Avenue, Brooklyn, NY 11217
versobooks.com

Verso is the imprint of New Left Books

ISBN-13: 978-1-83976-526-1
ISBN-13: 978-1-83976-527-8 (US EBK)
ISBN-13: 978-1-83976-528-5 (UK EBK)

British Library Cataloguing in Publication Data
A catalogue record for this book is available from the British Library

Library of Congress Cataloging-in-Publication Data

Names: Maher, Stephen, 1985- author. | Aquanno, Scott M., author.
Title: The fall and rise of American finance : from J.P. Morgan to
  Blackrock / by Stephen Maher and Scott M. Aquanno.
Description: London ; New York : Verso, 2024. | Includes bibliographical
  references and index.
Identifiers: LCCN 2023026393 (print) | LCCN 2023026394 (ebook) | ISBN
  9781839765261 (paperback) | ISBN 9781839765278 (ebook)
Subjects: LCSH: Finance--United States--History. | Capitalism--United
  States--History.
Classification: LCC HJ241 .M365 2023 (print)
| LCC HJ241 (ebook) | DDC
  336.73--dc23/eng/20230807
LC record available at https://lccn.loc.gov/2023026393
LC ebook record available at https://lccn.loc.gov/2023026394

Typeset in Sabon by Biblichor Ltd, Scotland
Printed and bound by CPI Group (UK) Ltd, Croydon CR0 4YY

Contents

For Leo
1945–2020

Preface

This book is about the role of finance in the making of American capitalism. It shows how, contrary to what has become received wisdom from practically all political corners, the rise of finance—so-called financialization—has not indicated the decline of manufacturing, the hollowing out of the corporation, or the collapse of US hegemony. Rather, financialization has facilitated the competitiveness and global power of giant multinational corporations. Finance was pivotal to the initial formation and rise of corporate capitalism in the United States and has remained essential for the growing mobility and internationalization of these firms across the twentieth and twenty-first centuries. At the same time, this book demonstrates how the increasing complexity of the financial system was in no sense merely the result of more "speculation," separate from production and the "real economy," but in fact remained integral to the functioning of the capitalist system.

The process of formulating the ideas and writing the text contained in this book is very much the product of two brains. Thanks to the wonders of modern technology, especially online document sharing and telecommunications, we were able to craft literally every sentence together in real time. The wording of each phrase was the result of a dialogue about how to express our ideas and arguments as clearly and accurately as possible. Countless hours over the past few years were spent discussing the analysis presented in the pages that follow. This analysis was enriched by the fact that we each brought to the process our own distinct interests, knowledge, and areas of focus, which proved perfectly complementary—and over the intensive process of writing this book, our distinct perspectives and ideas blended to become virtually indistinguishable.

Important for this compatibility was our common foundation of having worked closely with the late Leo Panitch. After having served as the supervisor for both of our doctoral dissertations at York University—itself a rare home for political economy, thanks in no small part to his efforts—Leo remained a close friend, mentor, and comrade until his death in 2020. That Leo passed away just as this project was beginning to get underway is an incalculable loss. On numerous occasions during the process of writing, debating, and thinking, we had the urge to reach out to him for the clarity and guidance he so often offered, whether one agreed or disagreed with him. Nevertheless, Leo's presence loomed large in the powerful example he offered of creative scholarship, grounded in a critical relationship to the Marxian tradition and committed to the fight for a better world. It is in honor of his example that we dedicate this book to him. Rest in peace, Leo.

Fortunately, we benefited from the assistance and support of the rich community of scholars with whom we are regularly connected. First and foremost among these is Sam Gindin, for whose generosity in providing comments on every version of the manuscript, let alone the hours spent discussing the ideas therein, we are immensely grateful. Greg Albo was also a formative interlocutor. His unique perspective and incredible wealth of knowledge have long been an indispensable resource for each of us. For their support and intellectual contributions, particular thanks are also due to Rafael Khachaturian, Clyde Barrow, Colin Leys, William Carroll, David Chen, Michael McCarthy, Kyle Bailey, Sarah Sharma, Kevin Skerrett, Peter Graefe, Herman Rosenfeld, Bryan Evans, Donald Swartz, Alfredo Saad-Filho, Dick Bryan, Michael Rafferty, and Melanie Panitch, as well as Martijn Konings, Amin Samman, and all our colleagues at the Finance and Society Network.

In addition, we are grateful for our discussions with the brilliant graduate students and colleagues at the Institute of Political Economy at Carleton University, where Stephen Maher was visiting professor in 2022, and where both of us now hold appointments. Special recognition is due to Justin Paulson, whose energy and leadership at IPE has been vital for cultivating a remarkable community of critical political economy scholars. We also wish to thank our colleagues at Ontario Tech University, especially Tanner Mirrlees, Toba Bryant, Alyson King, and Shanti Fernando. The editing and comments of Nicole Aschoff, as well as Asher Dupuy-Spencer, along with the work of all their colleagues at Verso who helped to prepare the book for publication and publicize it, similarly deserve special mention.

Finally, this book would not have been possible without the support of our partners, Safa Ali and Kim Aquanno. During the years over which we completed this project, we often spent more time talking with each other than we did with them. We are infinitely grateful for their patience, and for the love that nourished us along the way.

Stephen Maher and Scott M. Aquanno
Toronto, March 2023

1

The Latest Phase of American Capitalist Development

The 2008 financial crisis marked a fundamental change in American capitalism. As the crisis management efforts of the Federal Reserve and Treasury brought state power more deeply into the heart of the financial system, successive rounds of quantitative easing facilitated the unprecedented concentration and centralization of corporate ownership in a small group of giant asset management companies. In the wake of the crisis, these firms—BlackRock, Vanguard, and State Street—displaced the banks as the most powerful institutions in contemporary finance, accumulating ownership power of a scale and scope never before seen in the history of capitalism. These asset management firms became central nodes in a vast network that incorporated nearly every major firm from every economic sector.

This amounted to a historic transformation of corporate power. Since the New Deal, the separation of ownership and control had been a central feature of the corporation's organizational form: those who *owned* the firm (shareholders) were formally different from those who *controlled* the firm (managers). In the decades before the crisis, markets mediated the relationship between shareholders and managers: shareholders could "exit" by selling shares in underperforming firms. But with the rise of the Big Three after the financial crisis, the distinction between ownership and control broke down. As "passive investors," asset management companies could trade only to reflect the changing position of firms they owned on a stock index, like the S&P 500 or Nasdaq. Unable to simply dump shares at will, they turned to more direct means of controlling industrial corporations.

Such financial influence over industrial corporations hadn't been seen since the Gilded Age, when titans like J. P. Morgan dominated American capitalism. For more than a century, the concentration of ownership power was constrained by a basic trade-off: investors could own either a relatively small portion of a large number of companies or a large portion of a small number of companies. With greater diversification, in other words, stock holdings were diluted across many firms, limiting the control investors could exercise over any particular corporation. Investors could thus amass sufficient holdings to exert substantial power over only a relatively small number of companies. The rise of the giant asset management firms since 2008 has reversed this dynamic: the Big Three have become the largest shareholders in nearly every one of the largest and most important companies.

Today, the Big Three are collectively the largest or second-largest shareholders in firms that comprise nearly 90 percent of total market capitalization in the US economy. This includes 98 percent of firms on the S&P 500 index, which tracks the largest American companies—with the Big Three owning an average of more than 20 percent of each company. Equally remarkable is the rate at which this concentration took place following the 2008 crisis. From 2004 to 2009, State Street's assets under management (AUM) increased by 41 percent, while those of Vanguard increased by an even more substantial 78 percent. The unique significance of BlackRock within this power structure, however, is reflected in the explosion of its AUM by a barely believable 879 percent in these years, becoming by far the largest global asset manager by 2009.

The pace and scale of this shift heralded a new phase of American capitalism, defined by the unprecedented concentration of ownership, as well as the centralization of corporate control, around a small number of financial firms. Giant asset management companies now play a highly active, direct, and powerful role in corporate management—and they do so in relation to nearly every single publicly traded firm in the American economy. They have become "universal owners," managing the total social capital of the United States.

The Fall and Rise of American Finance

The close bond between financial institutions and non-financial corporations established after 2008 constituted a new form of the *fusion* of financial and industrial capital that Marxian political economist Rudolf Hilferding dubbed "finance capital" in 1910.[1] Though the term has been widely misused, finance capital does not refer simply to financial, much less bank, capital. Rather, finance capital emerged through the conjunction of financial and industrial capital, as a new form of capital established through their union—a synthesis that sublated the original industrial and financial forms (*aufhebung* in Hegel's terminology). Through this process, financial institutions came to play an active and direct role in the management of industrial corporations. By shaping the strategic direction and organizational structure of the corporations they controlled, financiers aimed to maximize the returns on their money-capital in the form of stock prices as well as dividends and other interest payments.

Finance capital is one specific form of financialized capitalism. In general, financialization refers to the process through which money-capital—or the circuit whereby money is advanced and then returned with interest—achieves greater dominance over social life and the economy. The expansion of money-capital was, as has often been observed, a major feature of the neoliberal period. This was reflected in the doctrine of "shareholder value," whereby firms afforded greater weight to rewarding investors through dividends and stock buybacks. Finance capital in its present form represents a far more concentrated form of financialization, and a much closer link between financial and industrial capital. A core argument of this book is that neither the broader trend of financialization nor the emergence of finance capital indicates the decline of capitalism, or the hollowing out of industry, as has often been claimed. Rather, financialization has been about boosting competitiveness, maximizing profit, and increasing productivity and the exploitation of labor.

Moreover, contrary to the many accounts that depict financialization as an abrupt rupture with a pre-neoliberal, non-financialized capitalism, we argue that the roots of financialization lie in the

3

postwar period—when it emerged as a *consequence* of state efforts to impose a "watertight" separation between finance and industry. Tracing the rise of financial power over the latter two-thirds of the twentieth century to the first two decades of the twenty-first, from the collapse of J. P. Morgan's empire to the rise of BlackRock, we present an alternative history of American finance that challenges popular accounts. In the arc we sketch, the history of financialization has four distinct phases: classical finance capital, managerialism, neoliberalism, and new finance capital. These phases form a cycle consisting of the decline and then the gradual, uneven, and contradictory rebuilding of financial power. Each phase is characterized by specific organized forms of state, corporate, and class power, with transitions marked not by sharp "breaks" but rather by both continuity and change.

Hilferding's theory of finance capital was derived from his study of capitalist development in Germany at the end of the nineteenth century; however, his analysis broadly applied in the case of the United States as well.[3] During this *classical finance capital period* (1880–1929), investment banks formed large corporations through the merger of smaller enterprises. The power of these banks hinged on their ownership of corporate stock and their ability to issue credit. As investment banks loaned large sums of money to industrial firms, the interests of the two became closely intertwined: while industrial firms depended on access to credit, investment banks sought to ensure loans would be repaid, and thus they monitored corporate operations to safeguard their investments. The banks' position as the largest stockholders secured their power over corporations, allowing them to acquire seats on boards of directors and establish "interlocking directorates" of firms they controlled.

These finance capital networks became looser with the growing fragmentation of shareownership over the first part of the twentieth century. A new stratum of professional managers exercised increasingly autonomous control of industrial corporations, with banks reduced to a mere supporting part.[4] The *managerial period* (1930–1979) was consecrated by the regulations enacted in the wake of the stock market crash of 1929, which formally separated banks from the governance of industrial firms and left "insider" corporate managers as the preeminent force in the economy. The absence of large blocs of shareholdings in this period allowed these managers to control industrial firms without facing a coherent challenge from investors. Yet at the same time, separating the banks from industrial corporations led the latter to internalize a range of "financial" functions, developing extensive capacities to raise and lend capital independently. The financialization of the non-financial corporation thus originated in the heart of the postwar "golden age."

The hegemony of industrial corporations in this period was supported by the New Deal state, which had three key attributes. First was its focus on *legitimation*. New Deal reforms, such as trade union rights and social security, aimed to demobilize the intense class struggles of the 1930s. These measures enhanced the legitimacy of capitalism and integrated workers into the structure of managerial hegemony. Second, these reforms led to a tremendous expansion of state fiscal expenditure, which was substantially financed by taxation. The New Deal state was thus a *tax state*, whose redistributive programs resulted in reduced levels of income inequality.[5] This also resulted from the success of largely apolitical trade unions in collective bargaining. Finally, industrial hegemony was supported by a *military-industrial complex*, which integrated the most dynamic corporations with state power—leading to the huge growth and diversification of so-called multinational corporations (MNCs), and spurring the development of the multidivisional conglomerate form of corporate organization.

As the postwar boom slowed by the late 1960s, union wage militancy increasingly squeezed corporate profits, leading to a growing contradiction between legitimation and accumulation: union rights and New Deal programs now posed barriers to accumulation. This was resolved through the formation of the *neoliberal authoritarian state*, which disciplined labor through an unprecedented spike in interest rates and a new round of globalization.[6] Elections and political parties became even less significant as state power was concentrated in agencies that were insulated from democratic pressures, especially the Federal Reserve. This authoritarian structure was reinforced by the fact that the neoliberal state was a *debt state*. As taxes were slashed to restore corporate profits, state programs were increasingly financed through debt, enhancing the discipline of finance over state budgets. This also contributed to growing inequality. Rather than paying taxes for redistributive programs, the wealthy now loaned the state funds to be repaid with interest.[7]

In the *neoliberal period* (1980–2008), the hegemony of industry was overtaken by a new form of financial power. In part, this resulted from the integration of global financial markets, which provided the essential infrastructure for corporations to circulate value across internationalized production networks.[8] Financial hegemony was also supported by the proliferation of worker pension funds beginning in the 1960s and 1970s, managed by professional money managers. A wave of concentration and centralization of corporate stock took place in these new "institutional investors," which came to wield significant power over industrial firms.[9] Yet this form of financial power was quite different from that of classical finance capital. Rather than individual banks exercising direct control over networks of firms, constellations of competing financial institutions exerted broad structural discipline.[10]

However, far from being imposed by outside investor pressure, financial hegemony initially emerged *within* the industrial firm itself, as an adaptive response to diversification and internationalization over the postwar decades. In fact, this was an intrinsic aspect of the multidivisional conglomerate form of corporate organization. Rather than being organized around one business, with greater diversification, large corporations came to comprise many different operations, which often had little or no direct relation to each other. Moreover, these operations were increasingly international in scope. The challenges this brought led conglomerates to decentralize operational management of business units, even as power over investment was centralized in the hands of top managers.[11] These so-called "general managers" did not manage a concrete production process, but rather money-capital itself; by the neoliberal period, they had become finance capitalists, sitting at the nexus of finance and industry.

With the development of capital markets within the industrial corporation, its financial units and functions became increasingly
dominant. This was most starkly registered in the transformation of
the corporate treasurer into the chief financial officer responsible both
for establishing "investor expectations" and carrying out the internal
restructuring necessary to meet them as the right hand of the CEO.[12]
The financial capacities of industrial firms also expanded as they
sought to manage the risks of globalization by engaging in derivatives
trading.[13] All this culminated in the emergence of the multilayered subsidiary form of corporate organization, through which MNCs
organized production by integrating their internal divisions with a secondary layer of external subcontractors to form highly flexible and
competitive global networks.[14] Apple's reliance on Foxconn is just one
prominent example of this.

The *new finance capital* was formed after the 2008 crisis, as the diffuse
financial power of neoliberal shareholder capitalism was centralized in
giant asset management companies. Amid the financial meltdown, regulators sought to enhance systemic stability by orchestrating bank consolidation. When the dust settled, just four mega-banks—JPMorgan
Chase, Bank of America, Wells Fargo, and Citigroup—dominated the
sector. Ironically, however, state intervention contributed to a move
away from banks and *toward* a group of asset management companies—namely, BlackRock, State Street, and Vanguard. As the formation of the *risk state* dramatically reduced the riskiness of stocks, asset
management firms facilitated a flood of money into these assets. Chan-
neling savings into stocks further reduced their riskiness and led to
continuous stock price increases—as well as equally continuous concentration and centralization of ownership by asset managers.

An important foundation of the concentrated ownership of asset
management companies are the pension funds and other institutional
investors, which increasingly delegated management of their portfolios
to these firms. By pooling the already massive pools of capital accumulated in these funds, asset management companies further centralized
financial power, gaining a degree of economic dominance unseen since
the days of J. P. Morgan. This was underpinned by a historic shift

toward *passive management.* Unlike active management, whereby highly paid money managers seek to maximize returns by "beating the market," passive funds hold shares indefinitely, trading only to track movement in a particular index—allowing them to offer dramatically lower management fees and, especially in the context of rising share prices, high returns. But these passive investors are very active owners. Since they cannot discipline industrial corporations by simply trading shares, they have pursued the more direct methods of influence that are characteristic of finance capital.

If the rise of the asset management firms was part of a historic shift in the organization of American capitalism, this revolved in particular around the preeminence of BlackRock. By 2022, BlackRock's assets under management had reached $10 trillion. If one includes the assets it indirectly manages through its Aladdin software platform, this number approaches $25 trillion. BlackRock is now among the major owners of nearly every major publicly traded US company. Never before has the concentration of capital reached such a staggering extent. Its power is reflected not only in the size of its assets under management, but also in its special connection to the state. Whereas George W. Bush chose Hank Paulson of Goldman Sachs to be Treasury secretary during his administration, Hillary Clinton and Joe Biden both considered BlackRock CEO Larry Fink for that post. Biden's top economic advisor, Brian Deese, is also a BlackRock executive. All this points to the growing power of a new fraction of finance capitalists.

A New Picture of Financialization

The analysis of the role of finance in the development of contemporary capitalism offered in this book is markedly different from that which is generally found in progressive policy platforms and critical scholarship. Indeed, there is today all but universal agreement, particularly in the years since the 2008 crisis, that finance is a corrosive and parasitic force on the "real" industrial economy. So, too, are the many evils of neoliberalism, from economic crises to social inequality, often attributed to "financialization." While progressives fear that American prosperity and competitiveness will be diminished without regulations to rein in the power of finance, Marxists, for their part, often see financialization as a symptom of "late capitalism" and a harbinger of American imperial decline. These ideas have animated political debates among socialists and progressives alike, as well as the platforms of political figures ranging from Hillary Clinton to Jeremy Corbyn.[15]

Many observers have followed Giovanni Arrighi in seeing financialization as an inevitable stage in a cycle of growth and decline in the capitalist world system.[16] In this view, the decline of hegemonic powers is intimately linked with the growth of finance. Arrighi, however, downplays the central role of finance in capitalism's early growth and dynamism. Investment banks were the key actors in the organization of the modern corporation in the nineteenth century, just as in the present moment finance remains integral to the current multilayered subsidiary form of corporate organization. Finance is the nerve center of contemporary global capitalism, constituting the infrastructure that makes possible the circulation of value through internationalized production systems. The increased prominence of finance points not to the decline of the US empire—rather, it highlights American centrality in the global economy.

Echoing this story of decline, progressives like William Lazonick and Greta Krippner contend that the rise of finance has led to the "hollowing out" of production. Rather than investing in long-term growth and prosperity, they argue, finance is concerned with "making a quick buck." The rise of finance has consequently imposed a "short-termism" on industrial firms, leading them to abandon investments in the "good jobs" that underpinned "middle class" living standards of the postwar era, as well as the R and D necessary for US corporations to maintain global leadership. Instead, businesses have diverted funds toward "unproductive" financial services and lined the pockets of wealthy shareholders. That top executives are compensated with stock options only enhances incentives for them to engage in such dysfunctional strategies, leading them to inflate share prices through stock buybacks in order to make windfall gains.[17]

Yet it was not the benevolence or far-sightedness of corporate managers, but the balance of class forces, and particularly the ability of unions to win wage gains, that was responsible for the lower inequality of the postwar period. As we'll argue, these distributional bargains were supported by the unique circumstances of the postwar boom, as well as the structure of world trade prior to the advent of free capital mobility. What caused the rising inequality and rollback of social programs associated with neoliberalism was not the rise of finance but the inability of capitalism to support these compromises. With the end of the postwar boom, union wage militancy squeezed profits, causing a decade-long crisis that was resolved only with the defeat of labor and the opening of vast low-wage workforces to exploitation through globalization. Financialization was therefore key to restoring profitability and resolving the 1970s crisis—leading to a second golden age of capitalism, albeit one not quite as "golden" as the first.

Furthermore, seeing finance as fundamentally short-termist ignores the fact that some of the biggest stars of contemporary capitalism attracted plenty of investment despite not being profitable in the short-term. For instance, Uber has consistently operated at a loss, yet it has been sustained by investors looking ahead to the development of self-driving car technology that will supposedly allow the company to become profitable at some point.[18] Tesla, too, has maintained its focus on the long-term development of an entirely new electric car infrastructure even as it loses money on vehicle sales.[19] And investors poured capital into Amazon for over a decade despite low or nonexistent profits—which *The Economist* described as "the biggest bet in history on a company's long-term prospects."[20] Similarly, industrial firms across many sectors willingly shouldered the considerable short-term costs of global restructuring during the neoliberal decades in order to secure their long-term competitiveness and profitability.

None of this is surprising. After all, why would financiers or corporate executives have an interest in destroying the long-run value of their own assets? Moreover, the assumption that paying out dividends or engaging in stock buybacks must come at the expense of new investment is unfounded. In the context of low interest rates, there was no necessary contradiction between investing in production and R and D on the one hand and undertaking buybacks and making dividend payments on the other, since corporations could borrow practically for free. In fact, corporate investment and R and D spending both increased as a proportion of GDP over the past four decades, as did dividend payments, alongside a sharp rise in profits. Despite returning large amounts of surplus cash to investors through buybacks, ongoing investments in R and D by tech giants like Apple, Microsoft, and Google have clearly been sufficient to maintain their positions as global leaders.

In addition to laments about the short-termist prerogatives of Wall Street, many Marxists have contended that "financialization" is rooted in a deeper—even fundamental—crisis of the capitalist mode of production. For Robert Brenner, Cédric Durand, and David Harvey, the falling rate of profit in industrial sectors beginning in the late 1960s led to the diversion of corporate investment from manufacturing into relatively profitable and fast-growing financial services.[21] They argue that this has created the illusion of economic growth by generating a series of speculative bubbles, which have only served to mask the underlying lack of industrial profitability. French economist François Chesnais links the political and economic centrality of finance to its role in international economic integration, yet he, too, argues that financialization is an aspect of a prolonged economic crisis characterized by overproduction and a falling rate of profit. For Chesnais, this four-decade-long "global slump" indicates the decline of the capitalist world system.[22]

These accounts draw on a certain interpretation of Marx's theory of "fictitious capital" according to which many forms of financial capital are "fictitious" and separate from "real" industrial capital. In this view, finance is largely seen as a passive recipient of a portion of the surplus value generated by industry through the payment of various forms of interest (which includes interest on loans as well as dividends and service fees). Framing everything from corporate stocks to derivatives as fictitious capital tends, at best, to downplay the role that these financial instruments play in the integrity of industrial capital; at worst, it conceives of finance as a cancer on the "real" economy, which would thus be better off without it. This opens the door for interpretations that can come quite close to the social democratic theory of "hollowing out"—albeit rather than saving capitalism by restraining finance, these theorists usually aim to demonstrate that capitalism is doomed.

Finance is not antagonistic to industry. As we'll show in the chapters that follow, it has historically been deeply entwined with capitalist production. Finance—both within and outside the non-financial firm—disciplines the extraction of surplus value, fosters competitiveness, and facilitates the international circulation and valorization of capital. The ability of MNCs to freely move investment around the world in the blink of an eye has been a crucial condition for them to structure and restructure flexible, dynamic, and globalized networks of production. Far from merely being a speculative "casino," derivatives in particular are essential for corporations to manage the risks of globalized production. Finance is also vital for corporate mergers and acquisitions, as well as to maintain consumption in the context of the stagnant wages of recent decades.

Radical economist Costas Lapavitsas avoids defining finance as separate from or opposed to industry, highlighting its structural role in capitalism.[23] However, in arguing that finance "exploits us all," he tends to minimize the important and very positive role finance plays in the production of value. Rather than merely being a rentier and extractive force in the economy, finance has been critical to enabling the competitiveness and dynamism of productive capital.[24] Additionally, he understands the financialization of the non-financial corporation largely in terms of changing asset mixes—that is, as a matter of industrial firms investing more heavily in financial services. The deeper transformation of the corporation, whereby money-capital became more prominent in its organizational structure, is left unexplored. Nor does Lapavitsas sufficiently interrogate the changing relationship between corporations and financial institutions, missing the defining features of neoliberal shareholder capitalism: the concentration of stock in powerful institutional investors, intensified investor discipline on the non-financial corporation, and the restructuring of corporate governance to reflect the empowerment of finance.

Perhaps most critically, Lapavitsas—like many Marxian and non-Marxian economists—largely ignores the central role of the imperial

American state in organizing the economic structure and political hegemony of finance. This omission has paved the way for interpretations, such as that of Robert Brenner and Dylan Riley, as well as Cedric Durand, that the state has today been instrumentalized or "captured" by a corrosive financial sector. One of the key arguments advanced in this book is that, on the contrary, the state's role in managing and structuring the financial system reflects what Nicos Poulantzas called its "relative autonomy" from particular capitalist firms and fractions in overseeing the general, long-term systemic interests of capitalism. As we emphasize, capitalism is not only an economic system, but also a political system, requiring the state to manage trade-offs and power conflicts between different fractions of capital within the power bloc— albeit always in the context of deeper economic contradictions and pressures.

As Leo Panitch and Sam Gindin have long argued, finance represents a challenge neither to production nor to American hegemony. Instead, it is a basic component of the American imperial order that has made globalization possible. For them, global financial integration represents the culmination of the project of "making global capitalism" undertaken by the American state since World War II. The American state's unique imperial responsibility for superintending the world system has, above all, been oriented toward securing the free movement of capital across borders, regardless of national origin—creating a truly *global* capitalism instead of distinct regional or national capitalisms.[25] As they show, the critical foundation for this was the integration of global finance. Though this meant that finance would become more powerful in the global economy, industrial firms were able to accept this precisely because they also benefited from it.

Panitch and Gindin draw out the interconnections between the unique imperial role of the American state, state institutional development, and the rise of finance. In doing so, they show how globalization was not the automatic result of economic "laws" but required the development of specific state capacities. This led to the centralization of state power in the Fed and the Treasury, and their insulation from democratic pressures. Such independence allowed these agencies to flexibly intervene in managing the contradictions of a globalizing capitalism, free from the arbitrariness of democratic accountability or direct "capture" by capitalists. The relatively autonomous state was therefore able to act on the *behalf*, if not at the *behest*, of capital. Financialization, globalization, and the development of a more authoritarian state were all part of "making global capitalism."

Finance has always been closely connected to the state—forming what David Harvey has termed a "state-finance nexus" whereby finance "integrates directly" with a part of the state apparatus.[26] One cannot understand finance without accounting for the central role of state power in supporting and protecting it; nor can one understand the structure of state power without accounting for its integration with the economy. Yet there have to date been few, if any, serious attempts to trace the historical development of the economic apparatus of the American state. As we'll show, the evolution of the financial system over the twentieth century depended on the continuous expansion of the state's economic functions, leading to the emergence *in* the democratic capitalist state of an authoritarian structure of power that is today a basic foundation of the new finance capital.

Sociologists and political scientists have also cataloged some of the major shifts in corporate capitalism over the twentieth century, including financialization. However, they often fail to situate institutional changes in relation to capitalism *as a system*, and are therefore unable to perceive how such shifts enable, and result from, the competitive restructuring of accumulation—even seeing economic concentration as leading to the suppression, rather than intensification, of competitiveness. Moreover, the focus on institutions in these accounts, rather than on the production and circulation of value, supports the perception that financialization emerged suddenly with the rise of neoliberal shareholder capitalism—thus ignoring the deeper and more complex interconnections that always exist between finance and production in what is fundamentally a monetary economy. So too do the dynamics of class struggle, which are so fundamental for understanding history, largely fade from view.

Sociologist John Scott showed how concentration by institutional investors since the 1970s generated a historic shift from the managerial firm, which was largely controlled by insiders, to the neoliberal firm, which was subject to greater investor discipline in the form of "polyarchic financial hegemony." Rather than individual investment banks directly controlling networks of corporations, as in classical finance capital, constellations of competing financial institutions established ephemeral alliances on corporate boards to exert broad influence and discipline on corporate "insiders."[27] Gerald Davis went further, claiming that asset concentration in mutual funds (especially Fidelity) had constituted a "new finance capital." However, he argued this concentrated *ownership* had not translated into *control* due to regulatory restrictions, conflicts of interest, the short-term nature of active mutual funds, and the fact that simply trading shares is easier than direct activism.[28]

Davis thus defines the new finance capital as a "historically unique combination of concentration and liquidity" that amounts to "ownership without control." However, Davis did not anticipate how these dynamics would be altered by the truly staggering concentration of equity in passive investment funds, such as those managed by BlackRock, Vanguard, and State Street. Davis saw the $1 trillion Fidelity fund as facing "difficulty in remaining limber in its investments," leading it to move into other lines of business. Yet BlackRock alone now has $10 trillion in assets under management. Moreover, unlike Fidelity, which as Davis observes is a relatively short-term investor, these passive funds are extremely long-term. As such, they wield power not by trading but through direct control. The new finance capital, like the old, is founded on concentration and long-termism, and is consequently defined above all by the fusion of ownership and control.[29]

Benjamin Braun has conducted the most important research on what he terms "asset manager capitalism," the new regime of corporate governance that he sees as having replaced neoliberal shareholder capitalism. However, despite the extensive concentration and diversification that defines this regime, Braun argues that the asset management firms have "no direct economic interest" in their portfolio companies.[30] This is because, as "fee-based intermediaries," they supposedly do not directly benefit from the performance of firms in which they hold stakes: all returns are passed on to their clients, and they make money only from fees. Consequently, he argues, their primary interest is in maximizing their assets under management, and they have little incentive to undertake costly interventions to enhance the performance of portfolio companies. This distinguishes asset manager capitalism from classical finance capital, in which firms were largely controlled by financiers.

Yet despite asset management companies' apparent lack of active control, Braun also suggests (somewhat ambiguously) that the centralization of assets in these firms has stifled competition.[31] Other researchers, such as Jan Fichtner, Eelke M. Heemskerk and Javier Garcia-Bernardo, have argued that although the Big Three are passive investors, they are not passive owners. Rather, they show that these firms enact coordinated and centralized voting strategies across the funds they manage, allowing them to wield substantial power over their portfolio firms. Perhaps even more significant, they suggest, is the "hidden power" these firms may bring to bear behind the scenes. Nevertheless, these scholars, too, see the centralization of financial power as leading to the suppression of competition. As giant asset management companies come to own all the competitors in a particular sector, these firms lose the incentive to compete, leading to higher prices and eroding the dynamism of capitalism.[32]

In fact, competition between the giant asset management firms compels them to intervene to maximize the competitiveness of their portfolio companies. Asset management companies compete with one another, as well as with all other financial institutions, to attract savings. This means that they must offer the most attractive returns to their clients as compared with other possible outlets. Moreover, as Braun recognizes, the fees these firms collect are calculated as a percent of the value of the assets they hold. If they have an interest in maximizing their fees, then they must also possess a similar interest in maximizing the value of their holdings. Given that they cannot trade, this gives them a direct incentive to intervene in corporate governance. The interests of asset management companies, and those of their clients, are all but identical.

The clear implication from these works is the need to "save capitalism from itself" by reining in finance and restoring competition. Like

Braun, Fichtner et al. see finance as parasitical, draining rent from industry, sapping competitiveness, and increasing prices to consumers while adding nothing to production or national prosperity. On the contrary, the new finance capital is intensely competitive, amplifying discipline to maximize exploitation and profits. The primary political task, then, is not to "restore competitiveness" by attacking finance, but precisely the opposite: we must create spaces that are shielded from competitive pressures wherein we can begin forming more cooperative and democratic forms of social, political, and economic organization. It is capital itself, not only finance, that must be confronted by those seeking to create a more just and sustainable world.

Rethinking Finance and the Corporation

Financialization is rooted in the evolution of capitalism as it works out its tensions and antagonisms. Since the contradictions of capitalism can never be fully resolved, it must change continuously to overcome the barriers and crises they generate—a process akin to Darwinian adaptation. Class conflict is the most important, but by no means the only such contradiction.[33] While the stock market crash of 1929 was certainly followed by waves of working-class struggle in the 1930s, it also revealed the profound instabilities of the bank-centered system of finance capital. This spurred the state to separate banks from corporate governance, in turn leading the industrial corporation to take on new financial functions. Subsequently, these firms adapted to the challenges of managing increasingly complex, internationalized, and diversified operations by reorganizing corporate planning as an internal financial market.

When working-class militancy squeezed corporate profits in the 1970s, financialization and globalization imposed class discipline and reduced labor costs, thus restoring profits and allowing accumulation to resume. The regime of financial hegemony that emerged from this was centered around banks, as well as a new group of institutional investors who held large concentrations of stock. These institutions were linked with a new system of market-based finance, which depended on a complicated chain of financial exchanges to generate credit. The

collapse of this system was at the core of the financial crisis of 2008—
the deepest crisis of capitalism since the 1930s. Subsequently, through
a range of drastic and unprecedented interventions, the state restructured the financial order. By providing extensive liquidity to stabilize
the system, the state inadvertently facilitated the consolidation of a new
form of finance capital centered around asset management firms.

By tracing the roots of contemporary financialization back to the very
moment when classical finance capital came to an end, we emphasize
the extent to which finance and industry are not antagonistic, but
fundamentally interlinked. Moreover, we illustrate how finance has
been essential for the health, dynamism, and competitiveness of
industry from the earliest days of corporate capitalism. Finance was
not a problem but a solution for the systemic contradictions of capitalism. This picture of how finance has been functional to capitalist
development differs sharply from the many accounts that see its
ascent as a sign of decay that emerged only at a relatively recent "late"
stage. As such, our analysis will reveal how misguided are the pre-
scriptions, implicitly or explicitly contained in these works, that aim
to return to a healthier, pre-financialized form of capitalism. It is
possible to distill from our analysis several key challenges to theories
of financialization:

1) Financialization is not new. Financialization is often considered a
specifically neoliberal phenomenon originating in the 1980s. As Hilferding already understood at the dawn of the twentieth century, forms of
financialization have been present from the earliest days of corporate
capitalism. For him, the key feature of the corporation was that it
allowed industry to be "operated with money capital."[34] The joint-stock
company replaced the personal ownership of industrial assets with
impersonal ownership of tradable shares—monetary instruments that
also afford control over industrial firms. Control over production came
to be reorganized around possession of money-capital, rather than
direct ownership of fixed capital such as machinery and factories. Consequently, during the classical finance capital period, the banks'
possession of concentrated pools of money and capacity to generate
credit allowed them to play the most active part in forming and
controlling corporations.

After the demise of the investment banks, a new form of corporate financialization emerged during the managerial period—often held up as the pinnacle of "pre-financialized" capitalism. During the postwar decades, industrial corporations increasingly became financial institutions. Very high profits and relatively weak investors left industrial managers in control of large pools of retained earnings, which they lent out on financial markets, entering into direct competition with banks. Meanwhile, these firms adapted to the challenges of internationalization, diversification, and the growing scale of production through the development of internal capital markets—in which top executives allocated money-capital across what they increasingly saw as a portfolio of competing financial assets. This process was already well underway by the time investor power reemerged in the 1980s, which has today taken the form of the concentrated ownership by asset managers.

2) *Finance and industry are not separate.* Control over capital is inherently financial: it depends on the ability to access money in a sufficient quantity to be set in motion so as to generate profit. The economic power of capital results above all from the ability to direct investment, which determines the use to which society's productive capacities are put. All capitalists are, in a sense, financiers, faced with the choice of investing in one thing or another and pursuing the most profitable opportunities. Nevertheless, capital is divided into fractions: finance plays a specific role in the overall structure of accumulation, competitively circulating investment across the various branches of production. Finance depends on industrial profits to receive interest, while industry engages with the financial system to raise investment and circulate capital. Even when not fused into finance capital, therefore, finance and industry are deeply interdependent.

Political strategies that aim to isolate finance as the cause of "bad" capitalism, as opposed to "good" manufacturing, are thus bound to fall short. For one thing, capitalists instinctively understand attacks on finance as challenges to capital as a whole. More fundamentally, this framing fails to appreciate the extent to which, in a very material way, the interests of finance and industry have become almost indistinguishable. It is not possible to separate a discrete group of industrialists who have been victimized by financialization from financiers who have benefitted from it. While the internal restructuring of the firm converted industrial managers into financiers, globalization has made finance even more essential for industrial production. And the distinctly long-term nature of the passive investment strategies that underpin the current form of finance capital have led to an especially close interconnection between financiers and industrial corporations.

3) *Financialization does not signify the decline of capitalism.* The growth and empowerment of finance are not signs that capitalism is collapsing. Indeed, if the financialization of the past several decades has been harmful for the system, capitalists would be most surprised to hear it. Financialization was critical for resolving the 1970s crisis, restoring industrial profitability and opening the vast low-wage labor forces of the global periphery to exploitation. Today, profits and managerial compensation are sky high. Investors, meanwhile, have been enriched through rising stock prices and dividend payments. None of this has come at the expense of corporate investment or R and D spending, both of which have also remained high. Finance continually establishes the conditions for American MNCs to remain the most dynamic and competitive in the world.

In fact, the problems of finance are the problems of capitalism. Financialization has enhanced competitive discipline on industrial firms and has provided managers with the tools to pursue new profit-maximizing strategies. Just as concentrated ownership of stock enabled investment banks to organize corporations in the nineteenth century, today it allows financial institutions to play an active and direct role in controlling industrial capital and restructuring the corporation. At the same time, the competitive reallocation of capital by the financial sector channels savings into the most productive and profitable outlets. In this way, financialization has facilitated the formation of dynamic, competitive, and flexible networks of global production and investment. That this has intensified exploitation and labor discipline is hardly a problem for capital, but rather signifies the success of these strategies.

4) *Financialization is not monopolization.* Seeing the financialization of the non-financial corporation in terms of its reorganization

around the allocation of money-capital points to the serious flaws in seeing large corporations as "monopolies." Capitalist development is often portrayed as beginning with a "competitive" phase, which was later overtaken by a "monopolistic" phase. This assumes a quantity theory of competition, according to which competitiveness is a function of the number of firms in any particular sector. According to this view, as the number of firms declines over with greater concentration and centralization over time, competition succumbs to monopolization as giant firms set prices and reap monopoly profits. However, financialization means that firms are not necessarily tied to particular sectors: they allocate their money-capital in whatever ways are most profitable across distinct operations, among different facilities and by entering entirely new sectors.

Capitalism generates tendencies toward concentration, centralization, and financialization. Competitiveness does not result from the number of firms in a market but from the mobility of capital: the process whereby it flows into those spheres yielding the highest returns, and away from those producing lower returns. Organizations that most effectively facilitate this movement are the most competitive. Insofar as finance makes capital more mobile, reducing transaction costs and facilitating the circulation of capital across sectors as well as geographic space, it makes capital more, not less, competitive. Growing capital mobility, in turn, exerts tremendous competitive pressure to maximize efficiency and profits as workers compete for jobs, states compete for investment, subcontractors compete for contracts, and corporations compete to develop and control technologies, intellectual property, and organizational forms.

5) The state never "retreated." The measures enacted to address Covid-19 have been seen as heralding the "return of the state." This assumes that the state had retreated during the laissez-faire neoliberal years. On the contrary, the growing complexity of capitalism has impelled the ever-deeper integration of state power into the economy. This has not occurred through the simple linear accumulation of functions. Rather, state forms emerge through a series of breaks, whereby not just the extent of its economic functions, but their qualitative form, is profoundly reshaped, and the relationship between the state and the economy redefined. During the managerial period, the hegemony of industrial corporations was supported by the military-industrial complex, as well as social programs that boosted effective demand. The neoliberal state concentrated power in the Federal Reserve and Treasury, which were more closely integrated with finance.

The difference between these state forms is not merely a matter of degree, but of kind. The neoliberal state was more directly and organically embedded in capital accumulation, but this did not simply represent "more" of what the New Deal state was doing. Rather, it was a qualitatively different institutional ensemble, which emerged through the process of class struggle as a reflection of, and support for, the hegemony of finance. The post-2008 risk state was even more deeply integrated with the financial system. This state radically internalized the basic foundations of the system of market-based finance that took shape during the neoliberal years, and further integrated the huge mega-banks with state power. Above all, it has been defined by the core practice of *de-risking*, or the deployment of state power to absorb or deflect financial risk. The asset price inflation this supported was essential to the development of the new finance capital.

6) Finance capital is distinct from neoliberalism. It is certainly true, as Adolph Reed has said, that neoliberalism is "capitalism without a working-class opposition."[35] Others, equally correctly, have identified neoliberalism as being synonymous with the state promotion of pro-market policies. The problem is not that these observations are wrong, but that, as definitions, they are far too general. Both are compatible with more than one regime of capital accumulation: while the capitalist state always reproduces market dependence in one form or another, there is certainly nothing distinctively neoliberal about the defeat of the working class at the hands of capital and the state. As a result, it becomes very difficult to determine how neoliberalism could ever come to an end, apart from a shift in the balance of class forces toward labor, which would (supposedly) lead to the enactment of something like what postwar "Keynesian" capitalism is imagined to have looked like.

Things become much clearer if we define phases of capitalist development by the distinct forms of corporate governance, state power, and class hegemony that characterize them. Even though the defeat of the working class has hardly been reversed, we can still observe that neoliberal shareholder capitalism has been replaced by a new finance capital dominated by asset management companies. The consolidation of the risk state, based on a range of new economic practices, also suggests a new period is underway. Nevertheless, the future of this new finance capital is uncertain. Indeed, the continued power of pro-austerity forces has prevented the formulation of a coherent new policy paradigm, despite calls for this from finance capitalists and policymakers. Whether the hegemony of this new class fraction can become consolidated, particularly in light of stock market volatility and rising interest rates, remains to be seen.

These arguments are developed by tracing the fall and rise of American finance from the 1880s to the present. The next chapter focuses on how the early development of the corporation and the banking system led to the consolidation of the classical form of finance capital centered around investment banks, concluding as this regime came to an end with the 1929 stock market crash. Chapter 3 covers the managerial period that followed, in which industrial corporations were hegemonic. It shows how industrial corporations gradually evolved into financial institutions in this period, laying critical foundations for the neoliberal period. Chapter 4 explores how the resolution to the 1970s crisis led to the return of financial hegemony in the neoliberal era. As it shows, despite the new competitive challenges to the banks that came with the formation of the shadow banking system, they remained at the center of this diffuse form of financial power.

The final two chapters turn to examining the new finance capital that emerged from the ashes of the 2008 crisis, showing how the new risk state formed out of this crisis became increasingly integrated with the ascendant shadow banking system—in which the Big Three asset managers were major players. Chapter 5 illustrates how state efforts to address the crisis led to the dramatic "statization" of the financial system, supporting the formation of a new form of finance capital in which a small group of asset management companies exerted increasingly direct control over nearly every US publicly traded corporation. Chapter 6 examines the maturation of this regime and addresses the new challenges and growing contradictions it faced through the Covid-19 crisis, rising inflation, and the intensification of market volatility. It concludes with some reflections on how the emerging interlocking form of state and financial power impacts the urgent project of democratizing finance.

2

Classical Finance Capital and the Modern State

Finance was essential for the emergence of larger-scale and more competitive forms of capitalist organization in the United States in the late nineteenth and early twentieth centuries. In this chapter we'll show how banks, rather than simply advancing money and passively collecting interest, became the dominant force in the US economy. The elevation of banks to the central role of coordinating flows of investment and controlling corporations amounted to finance capital—the fusion of financial and industrial capital. The class fraction of finance capitalists, epitomized above all by investment bankers such as J. P. Morgan, became the most powerful stratum of the capitalist economy at the turn of the twentieth century.

By tracing the emergence of finance capital, we show that far from being a feature of a supposedly "late" stage of capitalism, finance was in fact central to the early development and dynamism of American capitalism. Nor could finance be thought of as parasitic. The amassing of vast pools of money-capital in the banks, along with their ability to generate credit, allowed banks to organize accumulation on a massive scale by merging isolated enterprises into giant industrial firms. But these bank-controlled firms were not "monopolies." Instead, the emergence of the corporate form and the development of the financial system reduced transaction costs and increased capital mobility, intensifying competitive pressures. The result was the integration of a highly regionalized American economy into a national economy, dominated by investment banks and the corporations they owned and controlled.

The creation of finance capital involved a fusion between financial and industrial capital, but it also relied on a close connection between capital and the state. At the center of the transformation of the US economy was a series of increasingly large-scale state-led projects, from the building of the railroads—among the most ambitious initiatives ever undertaken by a capitalist state—to the even more colossal task of waging war on a global scale for the first time. Moreover, as capitalism expanded, so too did its crisis tendencies, calling forth new forms of state intervention that crystallized into permanent economic functions. As an expanding state economic apparatus became ever more closely integrated with the circulation and accumulation of capital, state power became more fundamental for structuring the relationship between financial and industrial capital themselves.

In what follows, we build on Karl Marx's unfinished analysis in volume 3 of *Capital*, as well as Rudolf Hilferding's *Finance Capital*, to examine how the emergence of the modern banking system and industrial corporation culminated in the formation of finance capital by the first decades of the twentieth century. Although Marx was largely analyzing the case of England, and Hilferding was focused on Germany, their analyses broadly apply to the United States as well. In particular, the American case generally followed the process whereby money-capital became independently organized in a banking system, which then came to serve as the basis for controlling industrial capital and organizing production on a massive scale through the formation of corporations. As we shall see, the bank-centered networks that resulted were unmistakably those of finance capital.

Financial Capital and Industrial Capital

The emergence of the modern banking system and the corporation transformed the capitalist mode of production, generating a new interconnectedness between financial and industrial capital. As Marx observed, the development of capitalism resulted in an increasingly complex division of labor in the capitalist class, such that "technical operations" related to finance came to be "performed as far as possible for the capitalist class as a whole by a particular division of agents or capitalists as their exclusive function, that these operations should be concentrated in their hands." As "a part of the industrial capital present in the circulation process separates off and becomes autonomous in the form of money-capital," financial capital emerged as a qualitatively distinct *fraction of capital*, differentiated from industrial capital even as it remained organically interconnected with it.[1]

Capitalism thus relied for its growth on the formation of an increasingly complex and specialized financial system, which pooled money-capital, generated credit, and allocated investment. Though they can never be "separate," industrial capital and financial capital are two distinct forms of capital: the former pertains to the sphere of *production*, and the latter to the sphere of *circulation*. Industrial capital is defined as the circuit whereby the capitalist starts with money, then buys labor power and means of production. By setting these commodities in motion in a labor process through "productive consumption," a commodity is produced. This commodity is then sold, realizing a greater value in money than what the capitalist began with. Marx summarized this process with the "general formula" $M\text{-}C\text{-}M'$, with money at the starting and ending point, and in a greater quantity at the end.

Yet where does this original M come from? How does the industrial capitalist come to possess it? And how does the commodity produced by the workers come to find the final M on the market that completes the circuit of industrial capital? All these matters lie in the realm of circulation, and they have a large amount to do with the role of the financial system in facilitating the flow of capital through the "veins" of capitalist society. Like the industrial capitalist, the financial capitalist sets capital in motion through a circuit that begins with money and ends with a larger quantity of money. But the financial capitalist does not directly enter into industrial production. Instead, they advance a sum of money (in the form of a loan) in expectation of a return (interest). Thus, for the financial capitalist, money "automatically" begets more money. Marx summarized this process with the formula $M\text{-}M'$.

Marx saw this division in terms of a relationship between an *active* industrial capitalist and a *passive* financial capitalist. While the "functioning" industrial capitalist actively organizes and manages production, financial capital adds nothing tangible to the production process, merely advancing a sum of money to the industrialist and awaiting its return plus interest. The financial capitalist is therefore the owner of interest-bearing capital, making profits merely by throwing money into circulation. As Marx says, interest is "a particular name, a special title, for a part of the profit which the actually functioning capitalist has to pay the capital's proprietor, instead of pocketing it himself."[2] The financier is separate from and outside of production, "the mere owner of capital," relying upon legal ownership rights as the basis for claiming a part of the surplus.

However, through this process banks nevertheless came to occupy a pivotal place in the structure of accumulation, taking on a range of specialized functions in "the management of interest-bearing capital": mediating financial transactions, generating credit, and distributing investment among industrial capitals. As Marx explains, this entailed

> concentrating money capital for loan in large masses in the bank's hands, so that, instead of the individual lenders of money, it is the bankers as representatives of all lenders of money who confront the industrial and commercial capitalists. They become the general managers of money capital.[3]

The banking system thereby became the central nervous system of American capitalism. It turned money into money-capital by concentrating smaller quantities of idle funds into vast pools it controlled, which could be loaned out to "functioning capitalists" in the form of industrial credit or invested in speculative activities. But banks did not just pool money; they also *created* money. One way they did so was by acting as a central clearinghouse for debts and claims—canceling out mutual debts, organizing final payments, and executing trades. In settling complex transactions between capitalists without the use of "real" money, banks created credit money, greatly reducing transaction costs and facilitating the mobility of capital.

In fact, credit money resulted from every bank deposit: the deposited funds appeared both as a number in a savings account, which could be withdrawn or disposed of via check at any time, and as a part of the bank's reserves, which supported other lending. Yet such customer deposits served as the basis for only a small portion of the actual credit generated in the national banking system that emerged by the time of the Civil War. More important for the American monetary system was the role of banks in extending credit by *creating deposits* for their customers—including merchants and, increasingly, industrialists—by making loans and purchasing (or "discounting") so-called bills of exchange.[4]

Bills of exchange were written promises to pay at a future date. Insofar as they canceled each other out, such bills functioned as money, as payment could thereby be made without actual currency ever needing to change hands. But in addition to this, banks also purchased these bills, supplying immediate cash to the lender by creating credit in the form of a deposit. Then, when the bill (or debt) came due, the bank would receive the payment. In this way, banks transformed bills of exchange into money before they were due. That banks purchased these bills at a "discount," or slightly below face value, meant that the seller of the bill accepted slightly less than the full value of the debt owed, but was able to get cash right away. Meanwhile, the bank made a profit from the difference between the discount rate it paid for the bill and its full value once it was repaid. Through such practices, the credit system was "expanded, generalized, and elaborated."[5]

With the development of the credit system, banking was not primarily a matter of gathering deposits and then lending them to others, but *precisely the opposite*: banks generated credit by creating deposits (that is, numbers in a bank account) for their customers. As Marx recognized, deposits were at the disposal of depositors, and so "in a state of perpetual flux" as some drew down their account balances while others added to them. Nevertheless, the "overall average fluctuates only a little in times of normal business." Given that the supply of deposits would always be restricted, banks could never have functioned on the scale necessary to compete only by lending money they actually possessed. This forced them to expand credit, while holding only a portion of deposits as a reserve.

It was the centralization of credit creation, more than the accumulation of pools of money, that was the foundation of the US banking system. While Marx spent most time in *Capital: Volume III* on the concentration of funds in the banks, he explicitly bracketed discussion of "credit in relation to interest-bearing capital as such" to chapters that, while often mere sketches, began to explore what he understood as "the greater part of banker's capital," bills of exchange and shares. These chapters aimed to examine how "with the development of interest-bearing capital and the credit system, all capital seems to be duplicated, and at some points triplicated." As he saw, "with the exception of the reserve fund, deposits are never more than credits with the banker, and never exist as real deposits." Later, he noted how even these reserve funds "actually boil down to" the credit-generating capacities of the central bank, which we shall explore below.[6]

The centralization of credit creation and money-dealing in the banks immensely eased the circulation of capital and gave lending a general social character. Since money is the independent form of value, it is the universal equivalent of not only all commodities but also all specific circuits of capital. The transferability of money-capital into any concrete form of capital means that, in money markets, "all particular forms of capital, arising from its investments in particular spheres of production or circulation, are obliterated." All capitalists are "thrown together" as borrowers, distinguished not by the concrete uses to which the money they are advanced will be put, but only by their ability to repay the loan. Consequently, Marx observed, "capital really does emerge, in the pressure of its demand and supply, as *the common capital of the class*." Money-capital had become "a concentrated and organized mass, placed under the control of bankers as representative of the social capital."[7]

The concentration of money-capital in the banking system led to the separation of ownership and control of capital: while *control* of the money-capital advanced by banks was transferred to the borrower, *ownership* was not. The loaned capital remained the property of the lender (the bank). The work of organizing and managing production could thus become superfluous to the owners of capital, who could passively collect profits by virtue of their property rights. This separation was significantly extended by the corporation, as professional managers who did not necessarily own any of the firm's capital were hired by its owners, who now took the form of associated shareholders, to supervise production. The corporation thus greatly reinforced the "tendency to separate this function of managerial work more and more from the possession of capital, whether one's own or borrowed."[8]

In this way, the development of the corporation led to the "transformation of the actually functioning capitalist into a mere manager, administrator of other people's capital, and of the owner of capital into a mere owner, a mere money-capitalist."[9] The evolution of the industrial capitalist into the "functioning capitalist" signified the dispossession of the industrialist from ownership of capital, as he now "merely" managed the capital of investors—either loaned by the banks or advanced by shareholders. Meanwhile, shareholders and financiers had become "mere owners," relying on pure property rights, rather than immediate control over the conditions of production, to collect a share of the surplus. The corporation thus affected a shift from *personal possession* to *impersonal possession*: rather than direct possession of fixed assets (factories, machines, and so on), ownership and control of the means of production were now established through credit relations and possession of tradable shares.

The corporation not only placed the money-capital of the firm's shareholders under the control of non-owning managers, it also allowed them to draw on the total monetary savings of society as a whole by raising capital on financial markets. The greater capacities of corporations for rational planning and risk management made them especially worthy recipients of credit, which fueled the fires of industrial expansion and concentration. The "private capital" of the individual owner had now given way to the "social capital" of the banker and corporate manager. This "socialization of capital" granted "the individual capitalist, or the person who [could] pass as the capitalist, an absolute command over the capital and property of others . . . and through this command over other people's labor." The separation of ownership and control therefore allowed for the concentration of capital far beyond what an individual capitalist could have directly owned.[10]

The stockpiling of money in the banks and the elaboration of the credit system were essential conditions for the development of corporations. The capital owned by any particular capitalist was now "simply the basis for a superstructure of credit," amalgamated with the social capital through corporations and the banking system—thereby granting them control over social labor.[11] Stock ownership constituted a credit relation that entitled owners to a future share of corporate profits, paid out in the form of dividends. Banks not only profited by underwriting share issues but also became themselves the major shareowners in large corporations, which they played the most active role in forming.

Ownership of the means of production was now traded on stock exchanges. The stock market created the opportunity for further concentration and centralization through "expropriation on the most enormous scale," which "now extend[ed] from the immediate producers to the small and medium capitalists themselves." While the origins of capitalism lie in the expropriation of the workers from the means of production,

> . . . within the capitalist system itself, this expropriation takes the antithetical form of the appropriation of social property by a few, and credit gives these few ever more the character of simple adventurers. Since ownership now exists in the form of shares, its movement and transfer become simply the result of stock-exchange dealings, where little fishes are gobbled up by the sharks and sheep by the stock-exchange wolves.[12]

The difference between "wolves" and "sheep," or between "sharks" and "fishes," was a matter of the capacity to command monetary power. This allowed banks to gain substantial control of large corporations, and to concentrate small companies into bigger firms through takeovers and mergers. Since banks were the primary shareholders in most major firms, and it was possible to exercise control over a corporation with far less than 100 percent share ownership—and even less than 50 percent—the stock market allowed them to further extend their control over the capital of others (that is, small shareholders). By the late nineteenth century, banks had become the "wolves of Wall Street," while smaller capitalists were the sheep, destined for the slaughter of expropriation and merger.

With corporate capitalism, therefore, *securities*—that is, stocks and bonds—came to constitute a substantial component of bank capital. Marx referred to such forms of money-capital as "fictitious capital" in that they are not directly connected to the production of surplus value. Unlike industrial loans, which amalgamate the circuits of industrial capital and are paid off over time out of the surplus generated in production, stocks are a legal claim on profits with no definite end. After the initial issue of shares, money spent on subsequent stock purchases does not directly flow into production, but rather to the seller of the stock. Since such securities are themselves exchanged as commodities, their value rises and falls independently of the underlying corporate capital. Two distinct circuits thus coexist: (1) industrial capital managed by the corporation, and (2) securities bought and sold on secondary markets. For Marx, the latter were "pure illusion."[13]

What made fictitious capital fictitious, according to Marx, was that it appeared to produce new surplus value when in fact that was not the case. Yet because money had, after all, become more money (M-M′), Marx argued that financiers had a systematic interest in expanding the realm of fictitious capital, which consisted of the major forms of profitable interest-bearing capital—and according to Marx, the majority of the banks' activities. Through the buying and selling of financial assets, financiers could reap huge gains (or rack up massive losses) despite the fact these markets had no direct connection to surplus value production. Nevertheless, this capitalized "fictitious" value constituted very real money power for financiers, especially insofar as gains realized in this fashion could be used to acquire "real" values.

One example of fictitious capital Marx offers is that of government bonds. In lending the state money by purchasing a bond, the buyer expects the loan to be repaid with interest in the future, thus generating a return on the initial investment. Marx claimed this circuit constituted fictitious capital because the state does not directly invest this capital in production, but rather spends it to finance consumption. While the interest paid on the loan made it *appear* as if new value had been produced as a result of the capital advanced, this was not the case: these returns were paid not out of new surplus generated but rather out of tax revenues. Moreover, government bonds were bought and sold on secondary markets, where they acquired a price that had no connection to the actual use to which the money raised by the state is put. Thus, Marx concluded that gains from trading bonds on these secondary markets are also "fictitious."[14]

At first glance, it may seem correct that government spending is wasteful from an economic point of view, especially in the case of things like warfare. Yet the development of the financial system and the corporation was the result of massive state-led projects to build railroads, to develop systems for electricity generation and distribution, and to win World War I. Railroads and electrical infrastructure—like the financial system itself—integrated the national economy, reduced transaction costs, and opened new territories for commerce and exploitation. At the same time, the technologies developed through these projects served as the basis for new production techniques, new products, and new sources of competitive advantage and profit. Moreover, the extensive protection and subsidization the state offered to private investors in carrying out these capital-intensive projects helped economic organization to take on staggering dimensions.

The problem with viewing state spending as simply "unproductive" only increased as the range of its economic functions expanded with time. Already by the 1970s, James O'Connor illustrated how the majority of government spending, from highways to the space program, must be seen, in some sense, as productive of surplus value.[15] If the former constituted a massive subsidy for the automobile industry— one purchased a car only because there were roads to drive it on—the latter represented a core element of US industrial policy, which was indispensable for the competitiveness of American MNCs. Even

financing the fighting of wars had been critical for technological innovation, not only impacting the profitability of military contractors but
also supporting the development of new product lines and leading to
the development of labor-saving technologies that boosted productivity
across the economy.[16]

Conceiving of finance as fictitious became more problematic as the
financial system became more complex and more directly entwined in
mediating the circuits of industrial capital. In the decades following
WWII, it became the norm for corporations to take loans in the form
of bonds, which are tradable assets that can be on-sold to others. In
Marx's framework, such bonds would be viewed as fictitious once they
are traded on secondary markets. Yet the creditworthiness of firms,
and thus their ability to raise "real" capital on bond markets, is determined by the prices established on these "fictitious" secondary markets.
One could not understand the functioning of "real" capital apart from
the fundamental impact of the "fictitious."

In practice, however, Marx's analysis of the financial system illustrated the blurred boundaries between real and fictitious capital, and
the fundamental impact of finance on industrial production. The development of the credit system was an essential condition for the emergence
of the corporation itself. The stock market then emerged as a venue for
organizing the power of capital and intensifying tendencies toward
concentration and centralization. The "stock-exchange wolves" that
gobbled up the smaller capitalist "sheep" gained very real control over
industrial assets, which they controlled and reorganized. These large
owners—the big banks—then came to possess a direct interest, and
play a primary role, in maximizing surplus value production. They
were no more fictitious than the corporate managers who were their de
facto subordinates.

Just as importantly, stock markets profoundly impacted the competitiveness of firms, including by shaping their ability to raise financing.
The stock market threw industrial capitals from across the economy
into competition with one another, allowing investors to assess the
relative strength of firms from every sector. As a form of money-
capital, stock "obliterates" the concrete differences between different
circuits of industrial capital, which came to matter only in terms of

their ability to generate profit over the long term (or to produce capital gains over the short term in the case of financial speculators). As we will see, investment bankers such as J. P. Morgan, as the largest owners and major controllers of corporations, came to possess an especially long-term interest in the profitability and competitiveness of industrial corporations from the late nineteenth century on.

From Bank Capital to Finance Capital

Clearly, the development of the banking system and the corporation represented a profound and irreversible transformation in the capitalist mode of production. Yet it is easy to forget that even when Marx died in 1883, corporate capitalism was still in its infancy. At this time, the modern corporation existed only in nascent form, primarily what were effectively quasi-public railroad companies. While a new group of investment banks leveraged the funds they amassed through deposits and their credit-generating capacity to organize and control these companies, most banks were still largely relegated to supporting small-scale capitalist operations in firms controlled by owner-entrepreneurs, who often raised funds through family and kinship networks.

It was only over the period from 1880 to 1929 that the regime that would become known as "finance capital," in which both ownership and control of industry were centered around large investment banks, truly came into its own. Finance capital was, above all, characterized by an organizational fusion between financial institutions and industrial corporations with the support and intervention of the state. The extensive bureaucratic organization of the new firms, which were functionally divided into specialized departments dealing with marketing, legal, engineering, accounting, and so on, facilitated the administration of nationally integrated business operations. These firms were able to assemble vast concentrations of capital through their close relationship to financial markets, and were thus especially competitive in the most capital-intensive sectors.

Critical for the formation of finance capital was the role of the state. The national banking system was created by the National Banking Act of 1863, conceived of by Abraham Lincoln to expand credit creation to finance the Civil War. The act also established the powerful Office of the Comptroller of the Currency within the Treasury department to oversee the new system of nationally chartered banks, as well as a uniform national currency that would replace the state-level bank notes of the "free banking" era. Under the law, the largest national banks were required to hold reserves equivalent to 25 percent of their liabilities. Once banks hit this minimum level of reserves, they were not permitted to extend additional credit unless they could borrow from other banks or attract deposits. As a result, those banks that were able to hold the reserves of other banks could generate the most credit—and make the most profits—driving immense concentration and centralization in the banking system.[17]

The 1863 act helped J. P. Morgan to attain a unique place at the very top of the commanding heights of the national banking system. It set forth three categories of banks: central reserve city banks, reserve city banks, and country banks. The system was designed so that the reserve city banks in New York, and in particular the largest ones—especially J. P. Morgan—acted as a de facto central bank by holding the reserve deposits of smaller banks throughout the system. Smaller city and country banks had to hold deposit accounts at the New York City banks to settle balances that emerged through the transfer of deposits from one bank to another. In this way, the big New York City banks acted as central clearinghouses for the rest of the system. The result was a pyramid structure whereby deposits were funneled from the smaller banks at the bottom up to the largest banks at the top.[18]

The state also extended substantial support to the railway companies and the financiers who formed and controlled them, not least by granting them free land on which to construct the new national rail system. Yet it was only with the New Jersey Corporation Act of 1889 that the patchwork system of state regulations related to corporate organization was replaced by a consistent national standard. The law allowed businesses incorporated in that state to operate nationally under its extremely liberal provisions, unleashing immense pressure on other states to follow suit. The result was the "privatization" of the corporation, as the prior model of states chartering firms to undertake specific public works tasks—especially building public infrastructure such as bridges, roads, canals, and so on—gave way to one in which the corporation was the primary form for organizing large-scale industrial capital.[19]

If this regulatory change opened the door for the further centralization of production in large corporations, this process was dramatically accelerated the following year when Congress enacted the Sherman Antitrust Act. While the act was passed in response to public anger over the cartels and trusts that had come to dominate the American economy, it in fact resulted in a major merger wave as smaller firms were combined and reorganized into giant national corporations. By outlawing cartels and trusts between firms, the act encouraged the consolidation of these arrangements into single large enterprises so as to avoid antitrust prosecution. The merger of federations of smaller companies into new centralized and consolidated firms, governed by large administrative bureaucracies, represented the true birth of the modern industrial corporation.[20]

While banks were already becoming increasingly powerful from the mid-nineteenth century onward, these legal changes consecrated their dominance and codified the system of finance capital. Investment banks now controlled networks of giant firms by virtue of their functions as commercial lenders and institutional investors. By the end of the 1890s, finance capitalists, especially J. P. Morgan, had formed hundreds of corporations, such as U.S. Steel, International Harvester, and General Electric, primarily by gaining control of and merging smaller firms. Some entrepreneurs resisted such takeovers, seeking to hold on to their personal possession of their enterprises. One by one, however, investment bankers wrested control of these assets and assimilated them to the system of finance capital. The merger of industrial capital with finance had sparked the corporate revolution.

The rise of the finance capital system produced a new fraction of capital. Marx had defined three distinct capitalist fractions: industrial capital, bank capital, and commercial capital. Yet the development of the banking system and the corporation in the late nineteenth century made the boundaries between these forms of capital less clear. This blurring was due in large part to the banks' role in managing production—not merely passively advancing interest-bearing capital, but playing the most active part in forming and controlling corporations. Bank capital could no longer be relegated to the sphere of circulation, nor clearly separated from "functioning capital." What had taken shape, rather, was a fusion of financial and industrial capital, and the formation of a new, hegemonic class fraction: finance capital.

Marx argued that while it predated the capitalist mode of production, interest-bearing capital had been "subordinated to industrial capital" in the period of large-scale industry, merely facilitating circulation and the realization of surplus value.[21] A half-century later, Rudolf Hilferding saw how the growing importance of the banks had resulted in their attaining hegemony over industrial capital as they became more intimately involved in organizing production. The result was nothing short of

a complete change in the position of the money capitalists. The power of the banks increases and they become founders and eventually rulers of industry, whose profits they seize for themselves as finance capital, just as formerly the old usurer seized, in the form of "interest," the produce of the peasants and the ground rent of the lord of the manor. The Hegelians spoke of the negation of the negation: bank capital was the negation of usurer's capital, and is itself negated by finance capital.[22]

For Marx, capital underwent "a completely different movement" in the hands of the industrial and financial capitalists, whereby "the one simply lends the capital, the other applies it productively."[23] Hilferding showed how these circuits had become tightly unified into finance capital. While banks were essential for corporations to secure financing through loans or stock issues, bank ownership of stocks and loans ensured that the surplus would flow back to its "rightful" owner. Stock ownership afforded banks the ability to directly take part in corporate management, forming "interlocking directorates" by placing individuals on the boards of directors of firms they controlled. Meanwhile, the power of the banks was bolstered by their ability to turn the credit spigot on or off.

At the peak of the finance capital era around the turn of the twentieth century, Morgan had 72 seats on the boards of 112 of the largest American corporations. Firms such as Kidder, Peabody & Co.; Kuhn, Loeb & Co.; First National and the National City Bank of New York; and Lee, Higginson, & Co. were also prominent in organizing and controlling the new giant corporations. From 1900 to 1910, every time a firm tried to raise more than $10 million, one of these banks participated—although "if Morgan did not think he should help a corporation raise money, money would not be raised."[24] These investment banks maintained close relationships with the industrial firms in which they invested, and their own financial success was tightly connected with these corporations.[25]

A new fraction of capital thereby emerged, defined by its position at the nexus of finance and industry, and supported by its ownership of both. Hilferding explains:

> A circle of people emerges who, thanks to their own capital resources or to the concentrated power of outside capital which they represent . . . become members of the boards of directors of numerous corporations. There develops in this way a kind of personal union, on one side among the various corporations themselves, and on the other, between the corporations and the bank: and the common ownership interest which is thus formed among the various companies must necessarily exert a powerful influence on their policies.[26]

An interdependent relationship thus developed between financial and industrial capital, in which the concentration of industrial production in the corporation, and the centralization of money power in the banks reinforced each other. This meant that "an ever-increasing part of the capital of industry does not belong to the industrialists who use it"; rather, industrialists "are able to dispose of capital only through the banks, which represent the owners." At the same time, banks had to "invest an ever-increasing part of their capital in industry" and thereby became "to a greater and greater extent industrial capitalists." It was this that, for Hilferding, marked the emergence of finance capital, which he defined as "bank capital . . . which is actually transformed in this way into industrial capital."[27]

Bank capital could be converted into industrial capital in one of two ways: through either providing credit or acquiring stock in an industrial enterprise. In practice, of course, the big investment banks relied on both methods. Both resulted in the distinctly *long-term* interconnection between bank and industrial capital that constituted finance capital. The volume of the loans banks issued to corporations was so great that their own stability came to be completely tied up with these corporations. Similarly, since stock ownership was a vital foundation for maintaining control over corporations, banks sought to hold shares indefinitely to avoid surrendering power to others.

Industrial-financial fusion and long-termism were, in other words, two sides of the same coin. The long-term commitment of the banks to the industrial firms they owned reinforced and deepened the fusion of finance and industry, as the banks sought to consolidate their control over the industrial assets with which their own interests were ever more deeply interconnected. Banks developed an enduring stake in monitoring and controlling the internal operations of corporations in which they invested. As Hilferding put it, "the bank acquires a permanent interest in the corporation which must now be closely watched to ensure that credit is used for the appropriate purpose," supervision which is "best done by securing representation on the boards of directors."[28]

The ability for banks to exercise control over industry was critically enabled by their concentrated ownership of stock. Aside from purchasing shares on the stock exchange, the unique role of banks in underwriting share issues allowed them to gain extensive control of corporate stock, and to remain the most significant shareholders in industrial firms across all economic sectors. Through the underwriting process, banks advanced all the credit necessary to establish a corporation, and then issued shares in the new firm on the stock market to recoup at least a portion of the credit they had advanced. This meant

41

that banks by default controlled all new shares issued by any corporation and could determine what percentage of the ownership stakes should be sold to others.

Since corporations could be controlled with far less than 100 percent ownership, banks were able to extend their de facto power over the capital invested by smaller shareowners, as well as all the loan capital made available to the corporation. Because all the firm's capital was in effect placed under the control of large shareholders, who possessed a "controlling stake," the corporation served as a vehicle for widening bank control over the social capital. Similarly, the ability to acquire shares on the stock market allowed banks "to impose their representatives even upon corporations which initially resisted." In this way, the "joint-stock system" enabled "a distinctive financial technique, the aim of which is to ensure control over the largest possible amount of outside capital with the smallest possible amount of one's own capital."[29]

That Morgan sat at the center of interbank networks also meant that the power to form new corporations, or gain control of existing ones, was similarly centralized in his hands. Smaller banks funneled deposits to Morgan, who was then able to use these funds to establish and control industrial firms. Additionally, Morgan could purchase corporate securities by creating deposits for the corporation in his own bank— thus not only gaining control of the corporate equity, but also maintaining control over the money expended to procure this equity. As Louis Brandeis, the foremost researcher of finance capital in the United States, put it, "J. P. Morgan & Co. achieve the supposedly impossible feat of having their cake and eating it too."[30]

This then laid the basis for the structure of finance capital—the conversion of banking capital into industrial capital and back again— as the corporation would recycle a portion of its surplus back to the bank in the form of deposits, interest payments, and dividends. Morgan therefore gained direct institutional control over the firm through concentrated share ownership, which afforded his allies power on the board of directors, as well as maintaining leverage through credit relations. When the firm needed a loan, it was Morgan it would turn to—and the ability to do so was a major competitive advantage over other rivals. Meanwhile, his control over the total surplus, and ability to expand credit, was enhanced by the fact that such firms held their deposits with Morgan.[31]

The desire to "spread their risks" also contributed to the "tendency for the banks to accumulate . . . directorships."[32] By diversifying their investments across the economy, banks minimized their exposure to losses in any one firm or sector. But diversification was not only about managing risk—it also enabled the banks to capture gains throughout the economy. It helped to stabilize fluctuations in returns from particular investments, smoothing out the boom-and-bust business cycle across sectors. Consequently, banks were able to reliably pay out high dividends to their own shareholders. Because banks invested so widely, dividends on bank shares were safer and more predictable than those of any single industrial firm, which would be subject to the business conditions in its sector as well as the vicissitudes of its own individual competitive fortune.

Because of the lower risk and relatively high yields banks could offer, many investors were inclined to purchase bank shares rather than invest directly in industrial corporations. In this way, the banks functioned as financial intermediaries, investing money they controlled and paying out gains in the form of regular dividends. The owners of bank shares were thus indirectly diversified across the economy. In addition to pooling and investing the idle money-capital of others (acquired through bank deposits), banks also invested their own capital (acquired through issues of bank shares). The ownership power of the banks was thus supported by their role as money managers, whereby they amassed capital and distributed it across financial assets, then paid out returns to investors after collecting their own profits.

Hilferding argued that banks would prefer to sell shares rather than take deposits, as this allowed them to permanently increase their own capital. Money raised through issues of bank shares did not have to be repaid but was integrated with the bank's own capital. Only a portion of the returns generated by investing this capital were passed on to holders of bank shares. The banks were thus free to invest this capital as they chose, without having to worry that depositors might suddenly withdraw their money at an inconvenient time. Such disruptive withdrawals could require the bank to sell assets (that is, corporate shares) to pay off the depositor, thereby jeopardizing their control over particular firms. The preference of banks for issuing bank shares rather than taking deposits was therefore rooted in their desire to secure and maintain long-term control over industrial corporations.

Finance Capital and Competition

The pivotal role played by equity markets in finance capital reinforces the importance of seeing money-capital not only in terms of cash but also of corporate stocks and other credit monies. All of these are forms of money in that they bestow upon their bearers the right to command the labor of others, or an entitlement to a share of the social product. They do so because they represent and express value, with varying degrees of independence from the universal equivalent form (that is, currency). While they can be circulated to a certain extent independently, the monetary character of stocks and other credit monies depends on their ability to be converted into and out of the universal equivalent form quickly and easily at a relatively stable rate. This relation to the universal equivalent guarantees their *liquidity*—the ability to be transferred into any number of forms.

A major effect of the development of the corporation and the stock market, therefore, was the penetration of money-capital into the sphere of production in a radically new way. Unlike the industrial capitalist, who had "tied up his capital in his enterprise" and could not "withdraw his capital unless he sells the enterprise," the shareholder was a money-capitalist in that he was "able to regain possession of his capital as money-capital at all times." It is important to emphasize that shares may or may not be frequently sold; what matters in their ability to function as money-capital is that the institutions exist—especially the stock market—whereby gains *could* be realized by redeeming these equities for currency at any time. It is this capacity, Hilferding understood, which "endows share capital . . . completely with the character of money-capital."[33]

Corporate shares are monetary instruments with very special properties—granting their owner the right to participate in controlling a corporation for an indefinite period. Share ownership allowed the money-capitalist to become an industrialist, while simultaneously converting the industrialist into a money-capitalist. In reality these were the same person: the class fraction that was finance capital had emerged from the convergence of the roles of industrialist and money-capitalist. The rise of the corporation meant that "industry [was] now operated with money capital" as a result of "the transformation of the industrial capitalist into a shareholder"—that is, "a particular kind of money capitalist." What's more, "there emerg[ed] a tendency for shareholders to become increasingly pure money capitalists," as shares were amalgamated with the rest of the money-capital managed by the banks.[34]

This historical development renders problematic the common notion that corporate shares are merely fictitious capital. Of course, like that of the industrial capitalist, the capital raised through corporate share issues *really is tied up in an industrial enterprise*. The issuance of new shares by corporations augments their existing capital with additional money-capital. The ability of corporations to raise capital through share issues rests in part on the determination of stock prices on secondary markets—that is, on the value of fictitious capital. The process of determining stock prices on secondary markets, which is premised on the ability of shareholders to profit from such trades, is not separate from, but integral to the ability of firms to raise investment through stock issuance and credit. Share prices play an even more important role in firm competitiveness today.

If the fusion of finance and industry that defined finance capital makes understanding where "real" capital ends and "fictitious" capital begins rather difficult, Hilferding's sophisticated theorization of equity and the stock market further highlights the inadequacy of the notion of fictitious capital to capture the dynamics of an increasingly complex financial system. Hilferding was forced into a series of arcane contortions in his attempts to explain how the banks continuously converted fictitious capital into real capital and back again in their intimate relation to industrial corporations. With bank shares, for example,

Hilferding was forced to argue that "fictitious capital has been doubled" since "money-capital assumes a fictitious form as shares in bank capital, and thereby becomes in reality the property of the bank; and this bank capital then assumes the fictitious form of industrial shares, and is converted in reality into the elements of productive capital."[35]

Concentrated ownership of equity was a cornerstone of finance capital—institutionalizing bank power, enabling the concentration and centralization of capital in giant corporations, and disciplining production. That share ownership was fundamental to bank control of the corporation meant that possession of fictitious capital translated into direct power over the structure and direction of "real" productive capital. If industrial firms required financing from the banks to commence production, and bankers came to directly control the subsequent allocation of this capital by industrial firms, then with finance capital, bankers became both owners *and* top managers of industrial capital. This not only problematized the relationship between real and fictitious capital, but also between the spheres of circulation and production, as well as between owners and managers.

If bankers had "become industrialists" with the development of finance capital, and stock was the means whereby capital they invested "rightfully" flowed back to them, this would seem to make shares utterly integral to the circuit of industrial capital. The same can be said for Hilferding's strikingly prescient analysis of the primitive derivatives markets of his time. As he saw, derivatives gave "manufacturers and merchants the possibility of avoiding the unforeseen consequences of price movements, of protecting themselves against price fluctuations, and of passing on the risks of price changes to the speculators."[36] If this was true at a time when futures markets were relatively small, and primarily concerned with agricultural products subject to the contingencies of weather and harvests, it has only become more significant in an era of globalized production and financial markets.

In fact, as Hilferding argued, even naked speculation itself could not be understood as strictly parasitic on industrial production, but was an essential function within the organization of finance capital. Unlike banks, which took a long-term interest in controlling firms, and which profited from share ownership primarily through dividend payments, speculative traders exploited short-term marginal changes in the prices of stocks and other financial assets with no concern for the underlying production of surplus value. Yet the presence of such traders also ensured the existence of a functioning market for such assets and was therefore essential to their liquidity, allowing them to be "reconverted into money at any time."[37] Speculation was thus integral to the functioning of stock and futures exchanges.

However, stock market liquidity did decline at the peak of the finance capital period. In the late nineteenth century, railroad companies accounted for most stocks traded on the market. By the first decade of the twentieth century, industrial and utility shares made up a clear majority. The concentration of ownership of these firms by investment banks was reflected in a dramatic decline in the volume of their shares traded on the stock market, from 109 million annual trades in 1906 to 39 million in 1913.[38] This pointed to the significance of finance capital in fueling the rapid industrialization of the American economy through its growing involvement in organizing and controlling vast national corporations. With this, the corporation emerged from its early form in the railroad industry to become the basic form of large-scale industrial property.

If the consolidation of finance capital accounted for this decline in stock market liquidity in the first decade of the twentieth century, the overriding tendency was nevertheless toward the expansion and liquidification of financial markets. As corporate capitalism continuously took on larger proportions, the stock market tended to grow with it. Indeed, despite the interruption at the very peak of the finance capital era, liquidity on the stock market steadily *increased* across the period from 1880 to 1929 overall. As share ownership became broader and less centralized, the networks of finance capital became looser.[39] Meanwhile, the increasingly complex industrial corporations formed in the structure of finance capital, and the increasingly specialized professional managers necessary to run them, became increasingly independent of their finance capital overlords.

All this indicated that finance capital had in no way reduced competition, which remained the driving force behind the dynamism and continual restructuring of accumulation. In fact, the formation of finance capital was a process of breaking down the economic, social, and political barriers that hindered the operation of competition. The banks and the corporations they controlled integrated the national economy, dramatically reducing the costs of circulating capital across space as well as among the various branches of production. Insofar as large-scale capitalist organization was about overcoming limits to the spatial and sectoral mobility of capital, it served not to hinder but rather to dramatically *intensify* competition while integrating previously far-flung regions into a single national economy. With concentration and integration, all economic sectors and territories were increasingly drawn into a direct competitive relationship with one another.

But the domination of the national economy by giant bank-controlled firms did lead to the perception that competition was being squelched. Hilferding himself thought this was producing a system of de facto economic planning he called "organized capitalism." He believed the banks would come to manage the entire economy, eliminating competition between monopolistic firms they assembled into gigantic trusts and cartels. Trustification and cartelization would proceed alongside concentration in the banking sector, serving to "eliminate competition among the banks themselves, and on the other side, to concentrate all capital in the form of money-capital, and to make it available to producers only through the banks." Eventually, "if this trend were to continue, it would finally result in a single bank or a group of banks establishing control over the entire money capital"—which would thereby "exercise control over social production as a whole."⁴⁰

With competition between banks themselves as well as among cartelized industries all but eliminated, the banks' possession of money-capital would serve as the basis for them to exercise centralized coordinated control over the economy. Hilferding even went so far as to suggest that

a fully developed credit system is the antithesis of capitalism, and represents organization and control as opposed to anarchy. It has its source in socialism, but has been adapted to capitalist society; it is a fraudulent kind of socialism, modified to suit the needs of capitalism. It socializes other people's money for use by the few.[41]

Hilferding's theorization of how the corporation and the banking system were laying the foundations for socialism is highly problematic. According to Hilferding, finance capital emerged through the concentration of ownership and the socialization of capital. The centralization of control over the largest part of the social money-capital led in turn to the centralization of control over social production, bringing together all economic sectors under the power of a small number of financial institutions. As a result, finance capitalists supposedly gained both an interest in restraining competition and the power to do so. This was enacted through the construction of a vast architecture of cartels and trusts centered around the banks, which would mean that prices would not be set through market competition, but fixed by financiers seeking to maximize profit and minimize competition.

The centralization and socialization of capital, Hilferding argued, would therefore lead the anarchy of the market to give way to the *conscious planning* of the economy in organized capitalism. The corporation and the banking system were effectively transitional forms to socialism: through their development, capitalism was *automatically* building the infrastructure for a socialist planning regime. Moreover, in addition to "creating the final organizational prerequisites for socialism, finance capital also [made] the transition easier in a political sense." Since finance capital had "already achieved expropriation to the extent required by socialism" by gaining control of the most important industries, all that was needed was to replace the capitalist planners, who ran this system in the interest of the oligarchic elite, with socialists, who would do so in the interests of society as a whole.

Hilferding's error lies in a fundamental misconception of the nature of the socialization of capital that occurred with finance capital. This socialization did not negate capitalist social relations, but rather took place on the basis of these relations. Indeed, the socialization of capital in the banks and corporations dramatically strengthened the private power of capital. The accumulation of social money-capital, and control over social production, in giant financial institutions in no way altered the fact that the power they expressed remained that of money-capital, now consolidated to an unprecedented degree. It is impossible to understand such institutions, whose function was the accumulation of private money-power and the intensification of the ruthless drive for profit that came with it, as constituting the "organizational prerequisites for socialism."

The formation of larger-scale units of capital does not reduce competition but intensifies it. The quantity theory of competition holds that competitiveness is a function of the *number of firms* in a given sector: as this number declines over time, competition is replaced by monopoly, as in the theory of organized capitalism.[42] In reality, competition is a function of *capital mobility*. This is because competition is not primarily over sales or market share, but over *profits*. It therefore takes the form of competition between investment opportunities: low profit rates lead to the withdrawal of investment, while high profits draw increased investment. The flow of financing depends on the rate of return in comparison with all other possible investment outlets. This dynamic exerts competitive discipline across all capitalist processes to maximize returns or face the withdrawal of investment.[43]

This mechanism was the core of the theory of competition that Marx elaborated in volume 3 of *Capital*. As he argued, the mobility of capital draws different economic sectors into competition with each other, tending to equalize rates of profit to a general average. This was greatly lubricated by the development and centralization of the financial system, which gave lending a general social character and enabled the circulation of money-capital across economic spheres in pursuit of the highest returns.[44] As a result, Marx held, competitive pressures become stronger, not weaker, with capitalist development:

> What competition brings about, first of all in one sphere, is the establishment of a uniform market value and market price out of the various individual values of commodities. But it is only the competition of capitals in *different* spheres that brings forth the production

price that equalizes the rates of profit between those spheres. The latter process requires a higher development of the capitalist mode of production than the former.[45]

Due to its abstract nature, money-capital is never exclusively tied to any particular sector of use-value production. The liquid and abstract qualities of money-capital mean that it is the most *mobile*, and most competitive, form of capital. It confronts the entire range of possible investment opportunities as different *concrete* forms that it could potentially take in its quest for profits. Money-capital therefore disciplines every moment of production to maximize returns in the form of abstract exchange value (that is, money). As the domination of exchange over use, and of the abstract over the concrete, became greater with the concentration and socialization of money-capital by the banking system, competitive discipline also became more intense.

The role of finance in amplifying the competitiveness of capital gives rise to a tendency in capitalism toward financialization. Capital becomes more competitive with the emergence of technologies and organizational forms that increase the geographical and sectoral mobility of investment, allowing money-capital to circulate more easily across space and between economic spheres. Large firms were *more* competitive because they were the most mobile, able to cheaply move investment to whichever operations or facilities were most profitable. Similarly, the socialization of capital within banks broke down sectoral barriers as they competitively allocated capital across firms. Banks themselves also competed for access to capital. This discipline compelled *all* firms to implement organizational forms that further increased mobility, profitability, and competitiveness.

Not only did the fusion of financial and industrial capital not lead to the elimination of competitive pressures through monopolization, but it had precisely the opposite effect. Insofar as finance capital entailed the greater dominance of abstract money-capital in the structure of accumulation and evolved through the development of institutional forms that increased the mobility of investment, the discipline to generate returns in the form of money was intensified. The socialization of capital in the banks was therefore a process of breaking down barriers to the ruthless application of the coercive laws of competition across all enterprises and sectors. The orientation of finance capital toward profit maximization was not a result of the conscious decisions of those who sat at its center, but a basic consequence of its institutional structure.

By the first decade of the twentieth century, the institution of a uniform national currency and national banking system had produced an integrated national economy dominated by giant investment banks. Yet the capacity of these banks to act as monopolies was continuously undermined by the very competitive pressures that resulted from and drove forward processes of concentration and centralization. The formation of corporations and the broadening of the stock market and financial system also challenged financial and non-financial firms to continuously adapt by devising new organizational, administrative, and technological innovations. That this regime in no way amounted to a stable "organized capitalism" was clear above all from the fact that it was plagued by repeated financial crises, with especially major breakdowns in 1898 and 1907. These crises would impel the development of an increasingly significant role for the state in managing capitalism.

State Power, Class Power, and Crisis

Finance capital arose not only from the convergence of financial and industrial capital but also through a connection with state power. Navigating the contradictions of an increasingly complex, violent, and global corporate capitalist system propelled the rapid growth of the state's powers. By the 1940s, it was clear to Hilferding that the bank-centric phase of capitalist development was passing into a new stage, marked by the tremendous centralization of power in a modern capitalist state. In a 1941 manuscript he was working on at the time of his death in a Nazi prison, he observed that the state had become "a power in its own right, with its own agencies, its own tendencies and its own interests." This amounted to a "change in the relation of the state to society, brought about by the subordination of the economy to the coercive power of the state."[46]

While this was perhaps an overstatement, it was certainly true that the rapidly increasing involvement of the state in the capitalist economy had profoundly transformed how the system operated. The first half of the twentieth century saw the development, through two world wars, the Great Depression, and the New Deal, of a muscular bureaucratic state. Tendencies toward the centralization of power within the state administration, already apparent in the project of "building a new American state" beginning in the late nineteenth century, sharply accelerated over the twentieth.[47] The birth of the modern capitalist state in this period saw the enactment of new economic regulations, which drastically redefined the relationship between financial and industrial capital—and ultimately brought an end to finance capital.

By its very nature, finance is particularly dependent on the state. The state establishes a national currency that serves as the universal equivalent form of value. As a result, the state must also manage the circulation of currency and defend its value. Moreover, because of the systemic impact of financial failures, both the state and capital are especially sensitive to financial breakdowns. Consequently, state power has continually been extended to support the financial system. A growing range of state capacities and functions, thereby become foundational components of the architecture of the financial system. As finance evolved and became more complex, the state economic apparatus grew as well, becoming ever more integral to its functioning.

Especially important for the development of the economic apparatus in this period was the formation of the Federal Reserve in 1913, relieving the Treasury Department and the private banking system of full responsibility for managing crises. The Treasury had responded to the series of financial crises over the 1890s, culminating in the panic of 1907, by effectively writing J. P. Morgan blank checks and relying on him to dispense the necessary liquidity to stabilize the system. This was a fraught process, however, not least because the state's relative autonomy was jeopardized by virtue of its close relationship to one particular capitalist. In the crisis of 1907, the Treasury counted on Morgan not only to distribute bailout funds but also to augment these by raising tens of millions of dollars from Wall Street's top bankers "within ten or twelve minutes"—which he successfully did.[48]

The tenuous nature of these financial rescues highlighted the need for far greater and more direct state management of the financial system. For his part, Morgan found the development of such state capacities deeply worrying, in no small part because he had increasingly become a target of a rising tide of populist politics. Indeed, the congressional Pujo hearings, which ultimately led to the formation of the Federal Reserve, zeroed in on Morgan's vast economic network, fueling populist demands for "trust busting." However much the formation of the Fed may have contributed to the devolution of financial power away from Morgan himself, it was nevertheless foundational for securing the stability and integrity of an increasingly complex, large-scale—and still crisis-prone—financial system, as well as the broader corporate capitalist order of which it was a part.

As a bank, the Fed had the power to create money, liquidity, and credit. However, the money it created was distinct in that it was backed by the full faith and credit of the state and was legal tender—meaning that it could be used to settle "all debts, public and private." The intent in creating the Fed was to support the liquidity of bills of exchange held by banks. This meant that, like other banks, it would generate credit by discounting bills of exchange—but instead of buying them from consumers, it would purchase them from banks. While private banks supplied credit to merchants and industrialists by discounting bills of exchange, the Fed was to supply liquidity to the banks themselves by *rediscounting* bills of exchange. In the process, it would generate new state money out of thin air, creating deposits for banks held at the Fed that could be used to pay their own obligations to other banks. As a *central bank*, the Fed was to become "the bankers' bank."

The capacity of banks to issue credit was thereby completely entangled with the power of the central bank to manage the flow of credit and support bank balance sheets. The money issued by private banks was now integrated with the state money issued by the central bank.

By extending credit though the creation of deposits, banks supplied customers with money, which these customers then used. As borrowers circulated this money across the economy (that is, by writing checks), at the end of the day, deposits had to be transferred between banks to settle liabilities. This ultimately occurred through the formal transfer of state money between banks. The money created by the Fed was therefore central to the capacity of the banking system to generate deposits and credit. The balance sheets of private banks were now permanently integrated with the balance sheet of the central bank, which replaced the big New York banks as the pivot of the national banking system.[49]

This highlighted the extent to which the credit-money issued by private banks had become *hybrid money*, in the sense that its money-ness depended upon its relationship to state money. Customers would make deposits, or accept bank credit-money, only insofar as such credit-money and deposits could be exchanged for commodities. Since market exchanges did not take place only among those with accounts at the same bank, the circulation of credit depended upon the ability of banks to gain access to state money to settle balances between them on the inter-bank payment system. Thus, the monetary quality of the various forms of credit-money flowed directly from the central bank, bestowing upon them the capacity to function as a stable store of value, a means of payment, and a means of exchange in various degrees depending on their relationship to the universal equivalent form.

While the Fed was designed to support commercial lending through the rediscounting of bills of exchange, its functions dramatically changed during the First World War. As the Fed and the banking system supported war finance by purchasing US Treasury bonds, by the 1920s banks were holding very large quantities of these assets. Consequently, the Fed turned to purchasing Treasury bonds as the primary mechanism whereby it generated state money. This meant that the money issued by the Fed was no longer backed by private assets, in the form of bills of exchange, but was now backed by the debt of the US state itself. The Fed in this sense was not just supporting commercial lending, but state borrowing. Fiscal policy therefore became integrated with monetary policy; and both were integrated with the private banking system. The state had become a fundamental organ supporting the socialization of money-capital and the centralization of credit creation.

To be sure, at this point the Fed was hardly the centralized organ of macroeconomic management that it would later become. Its functions were decentralized to regional banks, and primarily oriented around supporting the banking system, as they would remain until the New Deal regulations of the 1930s granted it greater power to influence general economic performance. Nevertheless, with the creation of the Fed, a deep transformation in the logic of banking and money began to take hold. The establishment of the central bank integrated the banking system with state power in a new way, blurring the relationship between the private credit-money generated by banks on the one hand and state money on the other. The capacity of private banks to generate credit became ever more linked with the Fed's own liquidity-creating powers.[50]

If the formation of the central bank was a critical element in the development of the state economic apparatus in the finance capital period, it was not the only element. From the building of the railroads and the almost equally capital-intensive project of national electrification, to the fighting of the First World War, the state took a leading role in organizing large-scale public works projects that also provided the critical investment outlets for finance capital. The War Industries Board and War Finance Corporation, which coordinated the production of war materiel, were largely run in collaboration with Wall Street. At the same time, through the war, the scale and capacities of industrial corporations developed tremendously, as state investment financed industrial expansion and a new stratum of professional managers filled expanding corporate bureaucracies to help formulate and implement war production plans.

The growth of this layer of professional managers in the incubator of finance capital served to increase the independence of industrial firms from the investment banks. The challenges of managing larger and more complex industrial firms, and the need for expertise in law, finance, engineering, administration, and other areas, contributed to the growth and professionalization of corporate bureaucracies. The increasing complexity of these operations placed a premium on insider knowledge, enhancing the autonomy of corporate managers. After the war, these managers confidently proclaimed the arrival of a "New Capitalism," which would supposedly be free of the speculative pro-clivities of the old financiers. In its place would supposedly be a scientifically planned corporate economy. Yet it was only after the 1929 stock market crash and subsequent Great Depression that the modern bureaucratic state dealt the coup de grace to finance capital by finally separating the banks from industrial corporations.[51]

The period following the 1929 crash saw the complete implosion of the system of finance capital that had developed over the previous half century. Naturally, the investment banks that were at the center of this regime were also at the center of the crisis. The overaccumu-lation of money-capital in the banks with the ending of a series of state-led financial booms was exacerbated as the dramatic increase in exploitation that resulted from the crushing of the nascent labor movement led to declining effective demand. As the industrial lend-ing that was at the heart of finance capital no longer provided an adequate outlet for bank investment, banks pivoted toward lending to investors seeking to capitalize on stock appreciation through "margin accounts." The long-termism so characteristic of finance capital gave way to speculative finance, producing a massive stock bubble.

Ultimately, the bubble burst. As the stock market bonanza that banks had helped drive crashed, the banking system crashed with it. By 1933, with stock prices about 90 percent below their 1929 peak, one-third of US banks collapsed. The result was the destruction of the money-capital socialized in the banks, and the sharp contraction of credit. The crumbling of the banks had a devastating effect on all eco-nomic activity, spiraling outward and contributing to the Great Depression. The destruction of social money-capital also meant destroying personal savings, leaving tens of millions destitute as unem-ployment rose to 25 percent. Meanwhile, unprecedented deflation from the flatlining of investment and cratering consumer demand led to a sharp increase in the cost of repaying debts, further restricting economic activity.

As capital had become organized on a larger scale, its crisis tendencies and volatilities had by no means been eliminated—quite the contrary. Indeed, the implications of a financial crisis now took on immediate national dimensions. This pointed to the extent to which finance had become pivotal to the national economy. Yet even the explosion of what was by far the largest crisis in the history of capitalism could not simply undo what had been built over the previous half century. American capitalism had been revolutionized in these years, as it came to be dominated by giant, highly mobile, and intensely competitive corporations, supported by an increasingly broad-based and national-scale financial system.

Indeed, behind the dramatic events of 1929 lay a longer-term evolutionary process. If the collapse of 1929 and its tragic aftermath signaled the end of finance capital, the networks of the great financiers— especially Morgan—had already become looser and more diffuse by that time. The financial system, and the capitalist class itself, had also broadened, no longer centralized around a handful of financiers. This was not least the result of the tremendous expansion of state institutional capacities over the early twentieth century, including massive state intervention in running the war economy. That state officials largely turned to the new managerial elite in intervening to restore accumulation, and to organize a new class compromise around the reforms necessary to demobilize intense waves of class struggle from below, indicated the transformation of class power that was well underway.[52]

The reforms enacted during the Depression marked a transition to a new and far more interventionist form of capitalist state. The New Deal state, which would persist throughout the managerial period, took on a substantial range of new economic and political functions. New Deal regulations would reshape the structure of the financial system, as practices that had been concentrated in the banks were dispersed across a range of financial institutions. This destroyed what had previously been the hegemonic fraction of capital—finance capital—and imposing a watertight separation between distinct categories of "financial" and "industrial" capital. On this basis, the state would organize an unstable equilibrium of compromise under the hegemony of a new, broader class fraction, represented by the managers of the industrial corporations.

3

Managerialism and the New Deal State

By the 1930s, bank-centered finance capital networks had been restructured into autonomous, centralized corporations controlled by professional managers. In the managerial period that followed, the separation of banks from industrial firms by New Deal regulations, the fragmentation of share ownership, the accumulation of large pools of retained earnings, and the development of a military-industrial complex all served to limit the power of outside investors over internal managers. External control of the industrial corporation by bankers gave way to internal control by professional managers. As the investment functions that were so foundational for finance capital were severed from the banks, a new model of commercial banking emerged in a regulatory architecture that supported bank profitability and financial stability.

As this chapter shows, the same dynamics that led industrial firms to become more autonomous from banks also generated tendencies toward corporate financialization. The accumulation of pools of money-capital in industrial firms allowed them to finance new investment without relying on external financiers. This tended to convert managers from industrialists, concerned with managing concrete processes of production, into financiers, searching for profitable outlets for pools of abstract money-capital. Indeed, non-financial corporations actually became net *lenders* to capital markets in this period. This was reinforced as industrial firms diversified, partly as a result of their integration with an expanding military-industrial complex. Corporations were transformed from systems of production into systems of investment, allocating money-capital on internal capital markets among divisions with international operations.[1]

The separation of finance and industry by the New Deal state was thus beset by contradictions. Far from emerging through a sharp "break" in the neoliberal period, financialization finds its roots in the very heart of the supposedly pre-financialized "golden age." Crucially, the reemergence of finance in this period was an indication not of the failure or decline of capitalism, but the exact opposite: it resulted from, and reinforced, the profitability and competitiveness of what were now called "multinational" corporations, facilitating their diversification and internationalization. Moreover, the regulations imposed in the wake of the 1929 collapse were aimed not at weakening the banks but at restoring the financial system to health. Within just a few short decades, finance would strain against this incubator, setting the stage for the return of financial power as the accumulating contradictions of managerialism generated the next great crisis of capitalism.

Remaking Capitalist Finance

The end of finance capital brought a fundamental transformation of the relationship between financial and industrial capital, as well as a broad restructuring of the banking system itself. This was substantially affected by the dramatic expansion of the state's economic functions, marking a qualitative shift toward a far deeper entanglement of state power and capitalist finance. While new state regulations and the growing capacities of its economic apparatus limited the activities of finance, they also helped to consolidate an entirely new financial architecture. This "state-finance nexus" became increasingly central both for the operation of capitalism and for the institutional organization of the state.[2] The muscular, bureaucratic New Deal state constrained the scope of financial power, even as it supported and stabilized a new financial order.

The foundations of the new financial regulatory architecture were the banking acts of 1933 and 1935, which separated banks from the governance of industrial corporations. The sections of the 1933 act commonly known as Glass-Steagall sealed commercial and investment banking into watertight compartments. Banks were given one year to declare whether they would become "commercial" or "investment" banks. Commercial banks would be prevented from underwriting or dealing in corporate securities—or even being connected to investment banks, which would now be "principally engaged" in such activities. Investment banks, meanwhile, were barred from taking deposits and deprived of the credit-generating capacity of commercial banks. More-over, since they were not regulated as banks, investment banks were separated from the liquidity-providing mechanisms of the Federal Reserve. Commercial banks would henceforth collect deposits and make loans, while investment banks would underwrite and deal in securities.

This led directly to the "dismemberment of the House of Morgan," and severely limited the money power of both investment and commer-cial banks.[3] While they could continue to hold equity, the fact that investment banks could not take or create deposits prevented them from gaining the control over industrial firms they had during the finance capital period. Meanwhile, although commercial banks could still potentially exert some leverage through their capacity to extend credit, they could no longer hold concentrated blocs of equity or under-write shares. Limiting the convertibility of bank capital into stock in these ways prevented the banks' role as general managers of money-capital from translating into direct control over industry. State power had divided the functions of the banking system into two different institutional forms.

Investment banks certainly continued to exist, and to play an important role in the issuance of corporate stocks and bonds. But the old model of investment banking that had been so central to finance capital had come to an end. This was reflected in the transformation of the underwriting process. In Hilferding's time, investment banks created and purchased corporate stocks and bonds, and they sold some portion of them to other buyers. They remained long-term hold-ers of corporate equities, and their interests were deeply and indefinitely interconnected with the industrial firms they controlled. With the end of finance capital, investment banks became inter-mediaries, supporting the issuance and sale of corporate securities to other buyers. Moreover, since these banks increasingly did so in syndicates of investment firms, their ability to concentrate ownership was blunted, as each bank in the syndicate held only a small portion of the issues.

While the bank acts imposed strict limits on the activities and powers of investment banks, as well as on the investment functions that could be conducted by commercial banks, they also extended substantial support to commercial banks. This drove the restructuring of the entire banking industry around commercial banking, and left investment banks relatively small and marginal. Even J. P. Morgan itself opted to become a commercial bank, spinning off its investment banking operations as Morgan Stanley in 1935, which later became Morgan Guaranty in 1959 through a merger with the much larger Guaranty Trust. There could hardly have been a clearer indication of the extent of the remaking of American finance than the transformation and decline of the House of Morgan, which had been the central pillar of finance capital less than a generation prior.

State support for commercial banking perhaps most importantly included Regulation Q. While this rule limited the interest banks could pay on savings accounts, and eliminated all interest on checking accounts, it also served as a major prop for the profits and stability of commercial banks. Competition for consumer deposits among banks during the 1920s had resulted in high interest rates, which meant that banks had to pay higher costs to access such funds. The necessity to offer higher interest rates on deposits in turn drove banks to pursue riskier—but potentially higher-yield—investments. Limiting such competition allowed banks to make healthy profits on safer investments. The new regulations also made it more difficult to charter a new bank, thereby further capping competition for deposits. All this led to the so-called 3-6-3 model of commercial banking: pay 3 percent on deposits, lend money at 6 percent, and be on the golf course by 3 o'clock.

In addition to imposing new rules and regulations, the 1933 act also significantly expanded the capacities of the state, which became integrated with the financial system in more significant ways. Although bankers initially opposed such state encroachment, the new state powers ultimately served to support and stabilize the financial system, consolidating the position of the big banks. Most important in this regard were the dramatic increase in the capacities of the Federal Reserve and the creation of the Federal Deposit Insurance Corporation (FDIC). The FDIC guaranteed deposits up to a certain maximum level in return for a fee paid by the banks. The state therefore backstopped a large portion of the deposit base of the commercial banks, increasing public confidence in the financial system by preventing the bank runs that had occurred during the Great Depression. Meanwhile, big banks were also brought under closer supervision by the Fed.

The creation of the FDIC deepened the interconnection between state power and the banking system, expanding the state support for private money that, as we saw, constituted a "hybrid" form of public-private money.[4] The emergence of hybrid money had initially resulted from the integration of the central bank with the credit-generating functions of the private banking system. As such, the capacity of private banks to create credit became completely bound up with their relationship to the Federal Reserve. With the FDIC, deposits were backed by public assets, ensuring that these deposits could be exchanged on demand with state money at a set rate—thus guaranteeing a one-to-one exchange relationship between private bank credit-money (the deposits) and state money up to a certain amount. In effect, the FDIC made unsecured private credit into public credit, thereby merging the market price of one with the other.

The 1933 and 1935 banking acts also laid the basis for the modern Federal Reserve system. Prior to the acts, the Fed's control over monetary policy had been decentralized at the regional level. Interest rates were set in a largely uncoordinated way, with different rates prevailing in different regions. The creation of the Federal Open Market Committee by the 1933 act, and the further centralization that resulted from the 1935 act, allowed the Fed's central board in Washington to implement a single, coherent, national monetary policy. The 1933 and 1935 acts centralized the Fed's control over the supply of credit and short-term interest rates, which are foundational powers of modern central banks. At the same time, the acts increased the Fed's independence from the executive branch, and insulated it from the pressures of electoral democracy, by removing the Treasury secretary and the Comptroller of the Currency—both political appointees—from the Federal Reserve Board of Governors.[5]

The Fed now had the ability to set reserve requirements for national banks, which extended its power beyond maintaining the solvency of certain banks to affecting the performance of the entire economy. Setting reserve requirements enhanced the stability of the banking system by ensuring banks maintained a capital buffer to draw on during times of instability. But it also provided the Fed a key lever of macroeconomic management, allowing it greater control over the amount of credit that banks could create. In addition, the acts increased the Fed's powers to expand or contract bank reserves by undertaking "open market operations," or buying and selling government bonds to and from private banks.[6] This determined interest rates on inter-bank markets, and influenced credit conditions throughout the economy. Moreover, the 1935 act enhanced the Fed's role as "lender of last resort" by centralizing control over the rates at which it could lend to troubled institutions (often at a premium) through the "discount window."

The Fed had acquired the basic powers of a modern central bank: managing macroeconomic growth and financial stability by regulating the money supply, in addition to providing emergency funding to deal with crises. It had emerged from the rubble of finance capital as the primary institution capable of generating liquidity and coordinating its provision across the financial system—functions that had been fulfilled by Morgan during the harrowing rescues of the nineteenth and early twentieth centuries. While the Fed had become increasingly important over the 1920s, its centrality as a bedrock of the financial system took on new dimensions with the formation of the New Deal state. A single institution now established a consistent, across-the-board national framework for all member banks, no matter what state they were chartered in, for accessing capital, providing emergency liquidity, and determining reserve requirements and interest rates for deposits.

The close relationship between the commercial banks and the Fed was further reflected in the fact that the prohibition on commercial banks dealing in securities, which had been so important for ending the system of finance capital, *did not* apply to government bonds. The formalization of open market operations in 1939 through the "recognized dealer" system, forerunner of the modern "primary dealer" system, required a handful of large commercial banks to coordinate with the New York Fed on a daily basis to maintain desired market conditions by buying and selling state bonds.[7] Allowing these banks to continue trading in government bonds was thus essential for the Fed's ability to implement a coordinated national policy, just as it supported the profits of commercial banks. Meanwhile, the state was afforded privileged access to financing from the commercial banking system.

This close interconnection between commercial banks and the Fed allowed the state to funnel massive investment into industrial firms, leading to the doubling of output during the war, as well as to support postwar industrial expansion and the construction of a new "informal empire" spanning much of the globe. In fact, commercial banks absorbed more than 30 percent of government war debt, while the Fed itself held almost 15 percent.[8] This meant that the US state-finance nexus absorbed nearly half of the almost quarter trillion dollars of debt issued from 1940 to 1945. By the end of the war, the commercial banks alone held half of *all* existing marketable Treasury debt.[9] Subsequently, the Fed's monetary policy was built around encouraging banks to use this Treasury debt as collateral to access cheap capital through the discount window—fueling bank profits and encouraging lending on highly favorable terms.

Commercial banks thus made interest by funding the war risk-free, and then were allowed to transfer those government war bonds into cheap liquid funds that would finance industrial expansion and consumer spending after the war. That FDIC-insured banks were at the center of this process meant that the state effectively insured its own stream of debt finance. In this way, the development of the state economic apparatus served as a critical support for the historic postwar boom and was pivotal for the remaking of capitalist finance. The integration of this apparatus with the financial system served to fundamentally restructure banking organization and practices—the effect of which was to restrain the power of finance, and to consolidate a system of commercial banking that would support the economic expansion and hegemony of industrial corporations.

Particularly important for the postwar boom was the role of the state-finance nexus in supporting the expansion of cheap consumer credit. This helped drive the transformation of the banking system from the investment-focused finance capital model into the vast new architecture of consumer banking. Over the two decades from 1944 to 1964, consumer credit as a percentage of GDP increased by about 400 percent—a historic shift that reflected the emergence of an entirely new financial regime. This restructuring was partly rooted in the fact that consumer lending was one of the main business areas in which banks were allowed to participate under New Deal financial regulations. The resulting diversification of banks away from the strict interconnection with industrial corporations also played a major part in the explosion of consumer credit in the postwar decades.

Despite the new powers it had gained from the 1933 and 1935 acts, the Fed still largely remained captive to the fiscal policy implemented through the Treasury Department, which set interest rate targets for the Fed to meet. In this period, the Fed supported fiscal expansion by holding down interest rates on government bonds, thereby facilitating debt finance for state spending. This began to change after the war, when the Fed abandoned interest rate pegs—first for short-term government debt in 1947, then for long-term debt through the so-called Fed-Treasury Accord of 1951. The latter brought about the "liberation of monetary policy" by granting the Fed the independence to control interest rates and the money supply, greatly enhancing the Fed's ability to regulate inflation and economic growth.[10] The accord thus marked another important step in the formation of the modern Fed, further entrenching its independence.

The growing power and independence of the Fed were especially important for the new imperial role the American state assumed after the war, a central component of which was the international centrality of the dollar. The Bretton Woods global monetary and trade regime established after the war sought to promote trade and growth by establishing a framework of capital controls and fixed exchange rates. All national currencies were pegged to the dollar, which in turn was pegged to gold. The Fed played a central role in this system, especially by establishing swap lines of credit with other central banks to manage exchange rate pressures. In this way, the Fed supported central banks by absorbing the dollars they purchased to relieve pressures on their own currencies. It also provided dollar swaps to the Bank of International Settlements, which were used to support liquidity in offshore dollar markets—which, though unregulated, were crucial for the international operations of US financial institutions and industrial corporations alike.[11]

The global centrality of the US dollar was a pillar of the new American "informal empire," composed of formally independent states.[12] Motivating the creation of Bretton Woods was a desire to avoid the competitive currency devaluations that had undermined international trade during the 1930s by establishing a legitimate and stable global financial order under American hegemony. By limiting the movement of finance internationally, capital controls blunted competition between states for investment. This allowed for a degree of fiscal expansion by individual states, while also permitting central banks significant autonomy in setting monetary policy to support this. Bretton Woods thus established the conditions for economic growth and a stable investment climate, while deepening the integration of capitalist states through cross-border flows of trade and investment.

The Bretton Woods regime was also integral to the remaking of capitalist finance at home. Capital controls were an important foundation for maintaining Regulation Q restrictions on interest rates. This was because, at least theoretically, capital could not be withdrawn from the banking system to benefit from more competitive interest rates elsewhere. Bretton Woods restrictions removed any incentive for states or banks to attract investment by raising interest rates—thus reinforcing the low interest rate environment encouraged by New Deal regulations. Fixed exchange rates and capital controls also softened concerns over inflation resulting from low interest rates or high growth. Meanwhile, exchange rate pegs and stable interest rates protected the financial system from the volatility that otherwise may have attended currency markets. All this served to further support the postwar industrial boom and entrench the new global American empire.

In these ways, Bretton Woods incubated a global financial and monetary order in a framework of state controls. Indeed, Bretton Woods was always seen by the imperial architects in the American state as a step toward global liberalization. Throughout the postwar era, the American state worked within the Bretton Woods system to maintain a global consensus around the benefits of trade, while deepening the economic interconnections between capitalist states. This was reflected especially in the Marshall Plan for European Reconstruction. By undertaking the unprecedented act of rebuilding its major industrial rivals, the American reconstruction of the capitalist states of Europe aimed to create a world united by liberal trade and investment relations, albeit within certain pragmatic limits. The inter-imperial rivalries of the prewar years were thereby replaced by a new alliance among a "condominium of states" organized under the auspices of the American empire.[13]

However, the imposition of capital and exchange controls faced profound contradictions as European financial markets recovered from the war. Although the development of offshore and relatively unregulated "Eurodollar" and "Eurobond" markets exerted pressures on Bretton Woods controls, they simultaneously supported the internationalization of American capital. American banks themselves trafficked in these markets, and even quickly became the leading firms in them. The subsidiaries these banks established across Europe, forming a hub-and-spoke relationship between US and European financial markets, constituted the infrastructure that allowed industrial MNCs to invest abroad. As a result, the rigid distinction between trade and investment in the Bretton Woods framework proved impossible to sustain, since there was no way to account for which international flows were "trade" and which were "capital."[14]

Despite the repression of finance, it remained central to the growth, dynamism, and expansion of capitalism. Critical for this was the infrastructural connection between the US financial system and state power. The state-finance nexus served as the pivotal foundation for both industrial hegemony and the formation of a new American informal empire dominated by the marriage between multinational corporations and increasingly internationalized US banks. Meanwhile, the deepening entanglement of state and finance provided the basis for the Fed to conduct macroeconomic policy and supported fiscal expansion. The state economic apparatus, financial system, and corporation developed through a co-constitutive and mutually reinforcing process that was now substantially shaped by the imperial role of the American state.

New Deal regulations and the Bretton Woods regime sought to strengthen finance while simultaneously limiting its power and containing it within certain bounds. Even as it served to incubate finance and restore its health after the catastrophe of the crash of 1929, one of the primary effects of this regulatory order was to reduce the interest rates that banks could receive. This helped sustain massive industrial expansion after the war, but it also had a profound impact on the distribution of surplus between financial and industrial capital in favor of the latter. Indeed, along with the separation of commercial and investment banking, and the unique international role of the dollar, low interest rates were one of the three financial pillars of the postwar managerial era. Over time, finance would increasingly strain against the limits of the New Deal framework, cracking the foundations of industrial hegemony.

The New Industrial Order

The extent to which industry had stepped out from behind the shadow of bank power was discernible when, in 1933, Roosevelt formed the Business Advisory Council (BAC) to build support among capital for the New Deal reforms he saw as necessary to save the capitalist system. The BAC served to consolidate the political centrality of a vanguard group of "corporate liberals" who led the industrial corporations at the commanding heights of the economy. The War Production Board, which was responsible for coordinating industrial mobilization for World War II, largely consisted of managers from this group, as did the Office of Defense Mobilization, which succeeded it and worked to consolidate a permanent military-industrial complex after the war. This same corporate inner circle collaborated with officials in the Treasury and State departments to ensure passage of the Marshall Plan for reconstructing the capitalist states of Europe, as well as the Bretton Woods trade and monetary regime.[15]

The managerial period was defined above all by the hegemony of centralized industrial corporations controlled by professional managers, and the substantial autonomy of these firms from the banking system. This was supported by the fragmentation of equity holdings, preventing the emergence of an investor challenge to management power. Also important was the ability for industrial corporations to finance investment through retained earnings, as well as the significant state investment in these firms through the military-industrial complex that emerged from World War II. Industrial corporations were now also able to raise capital by issuing stocks and bonds autonomously from the banks.[16] All this greatly diminished the role of industrial credit as a source of bank leverage over corporations. Commercial banking came to serve more as a "reserve fund" for industry.

As we have seen, an important thrust of New Deal regulations was to prevent banks from gaining control of industrial corporations. This determination to block the reemergence of finance capital was clear from the 1956 Bank Holding Company Act, which limited banks' ability to own non-bank businesses. Severing these major financial institutions from equity ownership, other than acting as agents for family trusts, reinforced the fragmentation of shareholdings among a larger number of small holders.[17] Hiving off equity from the "common capital of the class" amassed in the banking system in this way supported the autonomy for industrial corporations from financiers, sharply limiting the ability of finance to discipline industrial firms.[18]

As Marx put it, interest is the name for that part of the profit that the industrial capitalist must pay to the financier "instead of pocketing it himself."[19] The distribution of surplus reflects relations of power between capitalist fractions. The low interest rates and dividend payments that characterized the managerial period served to shift the distribution of surplus sharply toward industrial firms. Thus, while commercial banks dwarfed investment banks, even the largest of the former were smaller than the largest industrial firms by orders of magnitude. In 1960, Bank of America, the biggest commercial bank, earned $93.3 million in profits—three times more than the most important investment bank, Merrill Lynch ($31.2 million). But this was only a fraction of the profit captured by General Motors ($873 million), Exxon ($630 million), Ford ($450 million), or DuPont ($418 million). Even after Morgan joined forces with Guaranty Trust, its profit was a mere $52 million.[20]

The limited ability of finance to extract value from industry through dividend payments to shareholders also demonstrated its relative weakness. Dividend payments made up 5.6 percent of GDP in 1929, at the

Chart 3.1: Dividends and retained earnings (% of GDP), 1935–2019

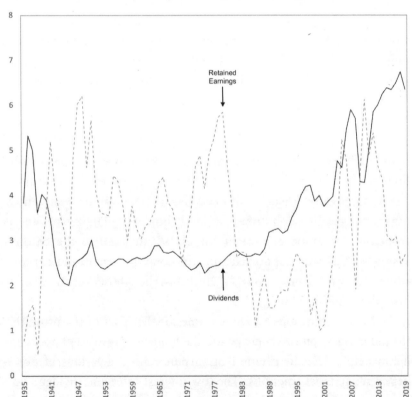

Source: Global Financial Data, WRDS, authors' calculations

height of the pre–New Deal financial frenzy. By the end of the Second World War, with the new financial constraints in full effect, dividend payments as a percent of GDP fell by *more than half*, to a mere 2.4 percent. They remained at roughly the same level through each full decade of the managerial "golden age." Chart 3.1 illustrates this dynamic, depicting the relationship between retained earnings and dividends as a percent of GDP. As it shows, dividends consistently remained below retained earnings throughout the managerial period, before this was reversed in 1979—precisely marking the beginning of neoliberalism.

The declining significance of boards of directors was further evidence of the waning power of investors and the consolidation of control over industrial firms by internal managers. As we saw, boards had been the most important venues for organizing and expressing corporate control during the finance capital period through the establishment of "interlocking directorates" by investment bankers. In the managerial period, however, they became institutional backwaters, mere rubber stamps for management.[21] Not only did insiders play the major role in determining the composition of boards, but the growing complexity and diversity of corporate operations also afforded these executives extensive power. Their inside knowledge and ability to control access to information by outside directors were important sources of their overwhelming dominance over boards.[22]

It was the very independence of industrial firms from banks that led them to begin to become "financialized." Since they retained the lion's share of the surplus, industrial firms were responsible for managing large pools of money-capital alongside and independently of the banks. This included circulating it among their internal operations, making new investments, and lending to banks and other corporations. Such financialization was encouraged by Regulation Q restrictions on interest rates, which limited the returns corporations could receive from depositing their stockpiles of money-capital in the banks. Instead, they sought out larger returns by lending on capital markets. Money markets were no longer strictly the remit of banks: in fact, industrial corporations now became the *most important* players not only in borrowing but also in *lending* to finance economic expansion and consumer credit.

73

The importance of non-financial corporations' retained earnings in the financial system was especially apparent in commercial paper markets, which grew to become a major source of short-term financing for corporations and financial institutions. By the end of the 1960s, corporations had replaced banks as the main borrowers on these markets, holding about 60 percent of the outstanding issues of commercial paper. But in addition to borrowing to cover their own costs, industrial corporations also became the primary source of *financing* on these markets.[23] Corporations thereby minimized idle funds by investing in relatively safe commercial paper markets, while receiving higher returns than they would have from relatively low interest short-term Treasury bonds or bank deposits. By circulating retained earnings as interest-bearing capital, industrial firms redistributed surplus funds across the economy, supporting industrial profits and reinforcing corporate financialization.

Non-financial corporations had started to become, in an important sense, financial institutions. Not only were they able to raise capital independently by issuing bonds and other debt securities, but they also came to invest in these markets themselves, lending to other firms through bond purchases. All this relied on the development of capacities for financial management in these corporations, leading to the substantial expansion of corporate treasurer's offices. While they still had to coordinate with investment banks in issuing securities, industrial corporations increasingly drew on their own financial capacities to independently undertake financial transactions. Insofar as they did so, this contributed to the emergence in industrial firms of a distinct M-M' logic.[24]

Corporate financialization was therefore in many respects a direct outcome of the success and profitability of the postwar golden age of capitalism. It is especially important to emphasize this point in relation to the influential arguments by William Lazonick, Greta Krippner, and others who argue that this occurred only during the neoliberal era—and even represented a sharp reversal of the prior period of industrial capitalism.[25] In fact, it was the very *weakness* of the banks, and the contradictions of the regulations that sought to constrain them, that initiated the financialization of the non-financial corporation as it sought to find profitable outlets for the large pools of money-capital it had accumulated. As we will see, the financialization of the non-financial corporation, in turn, helped to develop the very financial markets that would later lord over industrial firms in the neoliberal period.

The military-industrial complex that emerged from World War II was also a major support for managerial hegemony. Massive state investment through this system was an essential foundation for the postwar development, technological dynamism, and market competitiveness of American industrial corporations. The Big Science wartime apparatus, including the Manhattan Project, conducted scientific research on an historically unprecedented scale and generated a range of new advanced technologies. This system took the form of an extensive, state-organized network of national laboratories, universities, and private corporations. This wartime institutional complex laid the foundations for a permanent industrial policy system.[26]

If the administrative organization, technological capacities, and financial management functions of the state and corporation were essential conditions for the emergence of the industrial policy system, these institutions were also profoundly transformed by its development. Business and government became more tightly interconnected than ever before, as the most technologically intensive firms were seamlessly integrated into the state-corporate innovation system. The engineering departments of leading corporations underwent tremendous expansion as they received a steady stream of state financing and participated in advanced research alongside scientists working in public institutions. With the passage of the National Security Act of 1947 and the Defense Reorganization Act of 1958, control over this vast system was centralized in the new Department of Defense, which dominated a burgeoning National Security State.[27]

The Office of Defense Mobilization (ODM), headed by GE President Charles Wilson and populated by corporate executives, facilitated the systematic participation of business in this system as the Cold War got underway. In addition to having complete control over raw materials and establishing production quotas during the Korean War, the ODM had extensive power over military procurements, and organized longer-term corporate involvement in military-industrial planning as the innovation system was consolidated and made permanent after the war. It was also closely linked with the Committee for Economic Development (CED), the major corporate lobbying group in this period, which advocated strongly against rolling back the wartime production system after the war, and worked to consolidate it as a permanent component of the state economic apparatus.[28]

The centrality of the industrial policy system in American capitalism puts the lie to ideologies that depict the magic of the "free market" as the source of technological development. From 1953 to 1979, state investment made up nearly 60 percent of all R and D expenditure (chart 3.2). This hit a peak as the "space race" and the Vietnam War

Chart 3.2: R and D spending by funder (as a share of total), 1953–1979

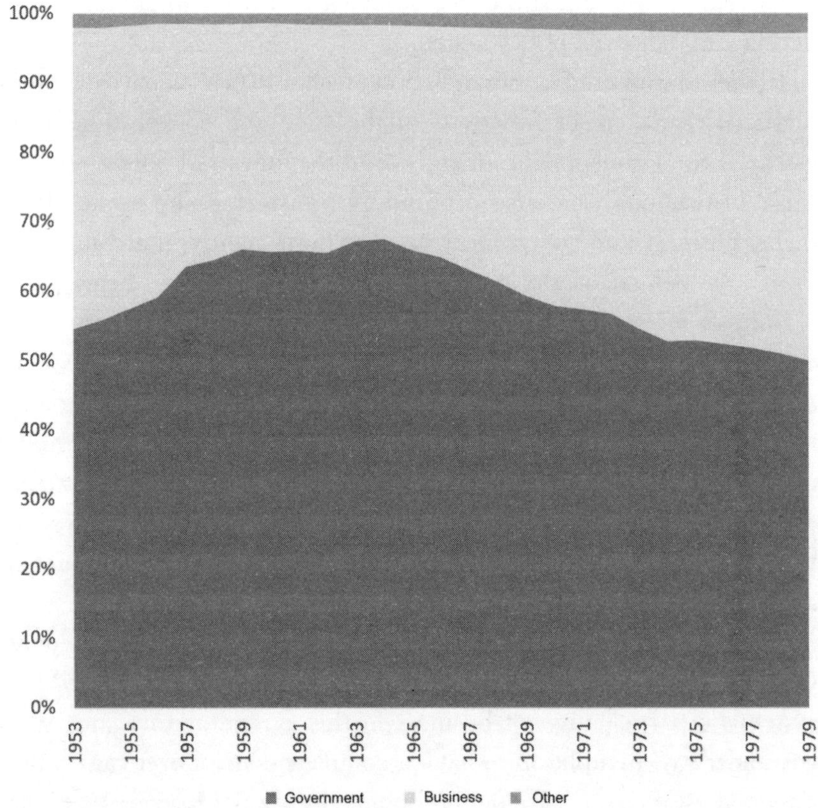

Source: *National Science Foundation, authors' calculations*

got underway during the 1960s, when the proportion of total R and D accounted for by state investment jumped to a staggering 68 percent. Moreover, that 53 percent of all state-funded R and D from 1953 to 1979 was carried out by corporations (rather than public agencies) pointed to the extent to which private corporations were integrated within this state-led system. This steady influx of state investment further reduced the dependence of industrial corporations on outside private investors, while padding profits and boosting retained earnings.

Perhaps even more important than the *level* of state R and D spending is the *form* this spending took. Indeed, business had little incentive to conduct the kinds of basic research, far removed from market applications (and therefore profits), that composed the core activity of the industrial policy system.[29] As chart 3.3 indicates, from 1964 to 1979, state expenditure made up an average of about 71 percent of total investment in basic research and development, while business spending made up only 15 percent. Such basic research was essential for innovation, generating the breakthrough technologies that corporations then "spun off" as consumer and industrial product lines. Doing so required extensive engineering capacities, but these were focused on later-stage development. The radios, x-ray, alloys, plastics, electronics, and refrigeration technologies that emerged in the postwar period were all essentially by-products of state-supported research carried out during World War II.

Despite the fundamental importance of the state economic apparatus for supporting the market power of US industrial corporations, it would be wrong to characterize this system as simply a "planned economy" centered on the military.[30] In fact, competition disciplined corporations to invest tremendous amounts of money in developing the technologies that resulted from state-supported R and D into marketable products. Such investments still involved significant risk, since the market success of products developed through "downstream" corporate R and D was by no means assured. During the 1950s and 1960s—the height of the so-called monopoly capital era, in which competition had supposedly been mostly suppressed—applied and developmental corporate R and D increased by more than 350 percent. By the end of the managerial period, this expenditure had increased by 1,000 percent.[31]

Chart 3.3: Spending on basic R and D, 1964–1979

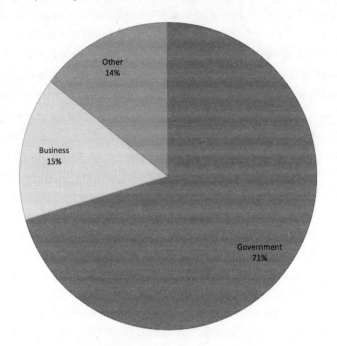

Source: National Science Foundation, authors' calculations

Given the scale and capital intensity of the projects it undertook, only the largest and most concentrated corporations could take part in this interlocking system of state-corporate investment—and they got even larger and more concentrated as a result. Rather than growing around a single line of business, these firms steadily *diversified* by spinning off technologies as new product lines. Whereas expansion within a single line of business only involved increasing the scale of existing operations and practices, diversifying into entirely new product lines was a qualitatively different form of growth—entailing an entirely new range of relationships with suppliers and markets, new business and management practices, and different strategic and tactical challenges. As the internal complexity of these multi-process firms exploded, centralized management became vastly more difficult.[32]

Corporate diversification also took place through the wave of mergers and acquisitions that occurred in the 1960s. Large corporations' easy access to credit allowed them to undertake leveraged buyouts

(LBOs), taking over other firms with borrowed funds. The state also played a substantial role in this, with antitrust regulations limiting the extent of any market that an individual firm could control—thereby encouraging corporations to grow through acquisitions in unrelated sectors.[33] While the new conglomerates pointed to supposed "synergies" between their businesses, more often than not these were chimerical. However, diversified firms' investments across a wide range of sectors did allow them to "smooth out" the business cycle, limiting risk while offering investors stable returns. As a result, stockholders could expect steady dividends, if not the constantly appreciating asset values that would later mark the return of investor power.

In this context, corporate decentralization emerged as an "adaptive response" to the challenges of diversification.[34] While firms that were primarily involved in a single line of business were *functionally* divided into the units necessary to carry out operations in one sector (legal, accounting, sales, engineering, and so on), diversified firms were restructured as *multidivisional conglomerates*. In some firms, such as General Electric, individual product lines formed the basis for various business divisions, each of which would now have its own range of functional units—thereby allowing them to operate to some extent autonomously. In others, such as the auto companies, divisions specialized around stages of production (e.g., assembly, powertrain, parts) or segments of a market (e.g., Cadillac and Pontiac are both divisions of GM, and each functioned as a relatively decentralized unit).

Operational decentralization was accompanied by the centralization of control over investment. Rather than managing specific businesses, top executives were now defined as *general* managers. While operational functions were devolved to divisional managers, general managers were increasingly concerned with entrepreneurial or investment functions. As the complexity, international scope, and diversity of industrial firms increased, top management had neither the time nor the industry-specific expertise to be involved in direct oversight and decision-making in relation to each of the firm's business operations. These tasks were entrusted to the managers of individual business units, while general managers relied on quantitative measures of performance—especially, of course, profits. These metrics became the basis upon which they allocated investment across the firm's divisions.

This amounted to the gradual and uneven transformation of the industrial corporation from a *system of production* to a *system of investment*.[35] Central to this was the growth of the firm's financial operations. New metrics for comparing, in abstract quantitative terms, the performance of qualitatively distinct business operations had to be devised and applied. These demands for new kinds of quantitative data had to be matched by the development of the institutional capacities to generate it, which was largely the remit of the corporate financial unit. Since the most direct means for drawing equivalencies between different circuits of capital is the universal equivalent form (money), it was this that increasingly powerful corporate financial units relied on to assess the performance of business divisions. Regardless of the specific use-values they produced, *every* division made money.

What was in fact occurring was the formation of capital markets inside of industrial firms. As Marx had seen, money markets "obliterated" the differences between "all particular forms of capital."[36] The development of financialized management meant that this was now taking place *inside* corporations. If the birth of the corporation had seen the "transformation of the actually functioning capitalist into a mere manager," managers were themselves now being transformed into money-capitalists. General managers increasingly managed nothing other than *money*: they were becoming investors allocating abstract money-capital across a range of concrete industrial capitals in search of the highest monetary returns. The "operation of industry by money-capital" now went well beyond the control of industrial capital by shareowners. The relationships between the internal components of the industrial corporation itself were now mediated by the circulation of financial capital.

This conception of the postwar managerial firm differs markedly from that advanced in the *Monthly Review* school, beginning with Paul Baran and Paul Sweezy in their seminal work *Monopoly Capital*.[37] In fact, Baran and Sweezy fundamentally misread the dynamics at work in the development and restructuring of these firms. For them, the emergence of the giant corporation constituted a new stage of "monopoly capital," as these firms were able to gain monopoly control of specific product markets and therefore reap profits above what would have been possible under conditions of price competition. Baran and Sweezy thus deployed a *quantity theory of competition.*[38] In this view, competition declines with the process of capitalist development as the concentration and centralization of capital over time reduces the number of sellers in a market. Perfect competition thus gives way to increasingly imperfect competition.

According to this theory, in the monopoly capital era, oligopolistic companies effectively banned price cutting by engaging in "co-respective behavior," whereby the leading firm set prices and subordinate ones took them. Meanwhile, competition revolved around the "sales effort," as companies sought to stimulate demand for their products through advertising without cutting prices. Monopolies did seek to increase profit margins by cutting production costs, but primarily because this allowed them to block new entrants and protect the monopoly structure of the market. The result was a "tendency for the rate of surplus to rise"—and a new contradiction rooted in the need to find outlets for monopoly profits. In this context, the military-industrial complex amounted to "military Keynesianism," whose primary functions were to soak up surplus profits, maximize employment, and sustain effective demand despite inflated prices while securing US domination of the global periphery.

Baran and Sweezy thus saw the corporation as mainly oriented toward protecting market shares; profits remained a concern, but primarily as a means to that end. In fact, as we have seen, corporations always compete primarily not over sales or markets, but *profits.* The competition among capitals takes place as each tries to maximize their share of the total social surplus. This means that firms compete not merely with other companies in a particular sector but also with suppliers and customers: the higher the prices charged by suppliers, or the lower the prices forced by customers, the greater share of the total surplus these rivals are able to capture. In any case, the tendency toward financialization means that it makes little sense to identify corporations with single product markets. As corporations *diversified,* they circulated investment across a range of profit-making centers. The identity of these firms became less that of any particular use-values, and more that of *money-capital*.

An analysis of competition and the corporation must begin not from *exchange*, but rather from *production*. Competition takes place as capitalists direct investment toward opportunities with high returns, and withdraw it from those with low returns. Insofar as diversified firms enhance the mobility of capital and reduce the costs of circulating investment across a wider range of opportunities, they are more competitive. The concentration and centralization of capital thus does not lead to the reduction of competitive pressures, nor to a form of "imperfect competition" that replaces an imagined previous era of "perfect competition." Rather, larger-scale capitalist organization reduces transaction costs, facilitates capital mobility across space as well as between sectors, and intensifies competitive discipline on all investments to maximize returns. The tendency of capitalist organization is not toward stagnation and monopoly, but rather toward greater competitiveness.

The development of financialized management truly came into its own in the 1970s, as top executives in conglomerates came to see business divisions as a portfolio of financial assets. Divisions increasingly competed with one another, as well as with outside subcontractors, for a finite pool of investment funds distributed by senior executives. Divisional managers developed business plans autonomously, which they presented to top managers as if they were external investors. Such managers began to act like owners, formulating strategies to secure investment for self-contained business units. In this way, rigid bureaucracies were replaced by flexible financial discipline. Meanwhile, competitive pressures incentivized divisions to cut costs, boost margins, and maximize efficiency.[39] The increasing prominence of abstract money-capital in the firm was thus the result of competitive discipline, just as it served to further enhance corporate competitiveness.

In an important sense, industrial corporations had become financial institutions. This had much to do with the accumulation of pools of money in these firms in the form of retained earnings—leaving managers increasingly in the position of being money-capitalists, looking for the most profitable outlet for these surpluses. One such outlet was lending. But the conversion of these managers into investors was also rooted in the deeper restructuring of the corporation, whose increasingly diverse operations came to be mediated by internal capital markets. This facilitated the management of a growing range of internationalized operations, which were reduced to quantitative determinations expressed in the money-form. Financialization was not a neoliberal corruption of a prior "prosperous economy" dominated by managerial firms; rather, it emerged from the very *success* of the golden age.

There was another dimension to the mediation of the industrial corporation by money-capital. In addition to the formation of circuits of financial capital, the internal organizational integrity of the multidivisional conglomerate depended on the financial system in which it was embedded. Finance constituted the essential infrastructure for corporate managers to circulate capital around the globe. Industrial corporations seeking to expand internationally partnered with banks, which were themselves establishing operations abroad. As we have seen, this had contributed to the growth of unregulated offshore lending markets, which exerted mounting pressures on the financial regulations institutionalized in the New Deal and Bretton Woods architecture.[40]

The interdependence of financial and industrial capital revealed the contradictions of a regulatory system that sought to simultaneously strengthen and contain finance, while maintaining rigid distinctions between finance and industry, trade and investment, and production and speculation. If the trajectory of corporate capitalist development in the postwar golden age pointed to the gradual ascent of money-capital both within the firm and outside it, this occurred *within* the structure of industrial hegemony. These firms were still very much tied to the M-C-M' circuit, however much an alternative M-M' logic was emerging in them. The military-industrial complex, the continued orientation of corporations toward an industrial conception of control, and regulatory restraints on finance continued to anchor the dominance of industrial capital. Yet despite the stability these foundations afforded, the fundamental contradictions of capitalism had hardly disappeared— least of all class struggle.

83

Class Struggle and the Crisis of Managerialism

In addition to restraining finance and supporting the competitiveness of industrial capital, the New Deal state also served to integrate the working class into the structure of managerial hegemony. Indeed, a cornerstone of that state form was the legalization of unions, and the development of a labor-relations bureaucracy that regularized class conflict—both by subjecting it to the institutional discipline of state regulation and by fragmenting industrial conflict within the structure of firm-level contract bargaining. While the labor movement had hardly always been docile, as was reflected in the postwar strike wave led especially by the radical Congress of Industrial Organizations (CIO) unions, the defeat of radical trade unionism after the war had paved the way for the ascent of the "responsible" business unionism of the American Federation of Labor (AFL).

The integration of labor with the managerial order and the hegemony of the business unionism model were consecrated with the merger of the AFL and CIO in 1955. While the radical CIO unions had relied on mass mobilization of workers, often led by communists or socialists, business unions accepted capitalist social relations and managerial control over industrial firms. Rather than seeking to challenge capitalist control over investment or expand worker control over the labor process, or even to promote class-wide solidarity, business unions focused narrowly on winning annual wage and benefit gains for their own members. They thus limited industrial conflict to bargaining within the framework of a restrictive state labor-relations regulatory order, relying not on direct worker mobilization, education, and engagement, but rather on highly paid experts and lawyers.

As a result, business unions became increasingly entangled in the state apparatus. In addition to sustaining the bargaining power of labor, unions served as mechanisms for disciplining workers— minimizing disruptions in the production process by enforcing bargains negotiated at the top between union officials and corporate executives on rank-and-file members. They were cornerstones of the class compromise between labor and capital made possible by the strong economic growth through the heady years of the postwar boom. The capacity for

84

such business unions to mobilize their members was steadily eroded, since their power increasingly derived not from mass mobilization, but rather from legal and bureaucratic maneuvering. The result was to reinforce the centralization of union power in the hands of technocratic professionals.

This institutional architecture sustained the class compromise at the heart of the New Deal order known as "productivism," whereby gains from the implementation of new technologies that increased productivity (that is, allowed each worker to produce more value per hour) would accrue equally to capital and labor. The productivist bargain was institutionalized in the 1950 Treaty of Detroit between the most prominent union in the country, the United Auto Workers, and the largest manufacturer in the world, General Motors. The deal was a watershed in the history of labor relations in the United States, as it established the principle that annual wage gains would be tied to productivity growth—thereby accepting that collective bargaining would not seek to challenge the distribution of income.[41] Moreover, the agreement specifically accounted for inflation by linking wages to the consumer price index, thus tying workers' wages to real changes in the cost of living.

In effect, productivism meant that what Marx called the "rate of exploitation," or the proportion of the product of labor appropriated by capital in the form of surplus value and that which flows to labor in the form of wages, would remain constant. With increasing productivity, the absolute magnitudes of both profits and wages could grow, even as the proportion of the total national income represented by each remained fixed. Productivity growth in the Kennedy and Johnson years was sustained in part by the expansion of military spending, which supported global imperialism but also provided corporations with advanced technologies at very little cost. Meanwhile, rising wages supported the formation of a substantial "middle class," characterized by steady increases in consumption and standards of living. Chart 3.4 illustrates the close relationship between wage and productivity growth throughout these years.

However, when productivity growth slowed as the postwar boom began to wind down by the end of the decade, continued union wage

Chart 3.4: Net productivity and hourly compensation (% increase), 1948–2000

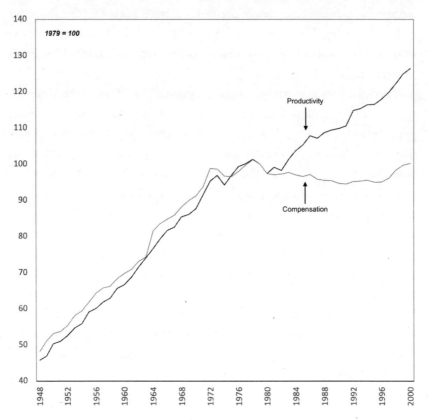

Source: *Economic Policy Institute, authors' calculations*

militancy increasingly squeezed corporate profits. At the same time, European and Japanese firms with relatively low labor costs, now recovered from the war, posed a growing competitive challenge to American firms, limiting the ability for the latter to pass costs onto consumers by raising prices. While capital initially attempted to restore profits and address the competitive challenge by ramping up investment to increase the rate of exploitation, these efforts failed. Relatively strong unions were able to prevent capital from reducing wages, while limiting the introduction of new labor-saving technologies and blocking the restructuring of the labor process to increase the intensity of work. Chart 3.5 shows capital's declining rate of profit in this period, as returns on these new investments failed to materialize.

Chart 3.5: Average rate of profit (%), 1947–2010

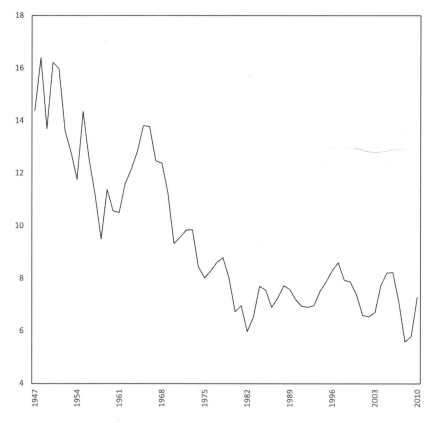

Source: *Authors' calculations based on data from Anwar Shaikh, www.RealEcon.org.*

With capital failing to reap adequate returns, investment slowed, leading to declining economic growth. By the 1970s, the slowdown had collapsed into a decade-long crisis. Unable to recover profitability by increasing investment, capital turned to raising prices, leading to a wage-price inflationary spiral. As rising prices eroded the real value of wages, workers pushed for further wage increases to keep pace—which, in turn, led to further price increases, as capital sought to escape the squeeze on profits imposed by rising labor costs. To make matters worse, inflationary pressures were reinforced by the skyrocketing energy costs that resulted from the 1973 oil crisis. This inflationary spiral combined with the economic stagnation that resulted from collapsing investment to produce the decade-long "stagflation" crisis.

Chart 3.6: State spending and GDP growth (% increase), 1947–1980

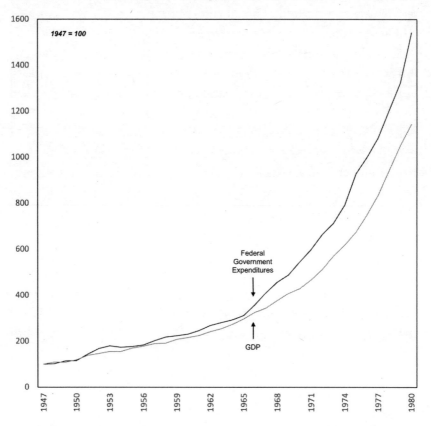

Source: *Authors' calculations based on data from FRED.* Note: *Index of billions of dollars.*

Profits were further hampered by New Left victories, as the environmental and consumer protection movements succeeded in winning an
unprecedented range of social regulations over the 1960s and 1970s.
These regulations only added to the occupational health and safety
protections won through a working-class shop-floor rebellion that
burst through the confines of productivism in the late 1960s. Compli-
ance with these regulations imposed new costs on capital and led to the
expansion of an extensive (and expensive) regulatory bureaucracy—
contributing to inflationary pressures as capital sought to pass these
new costs on to consumers as well. With profits squeezed between a
militant labor movement, growing social movements, and renewed

international competition, "red tape" increasingly became a concern for industrial firms and political elites alike.

Thus on top of the profit squeeze generated by declining productivity, wage militancy, international competition, and rising energy costs came also the increasing fiscal burden of supporting the New Deal state. As economic growth slowed, the "fiscal crisis of the state," whereby state spending grew faster than the economy as a whole, became more acute (chart 3.6).[42] That a continuously increasing share of GDP was consumed by government expenditure meant that either capital would have to pay an ever-increasing share of its profits as taxes or else the state would have to take on ever-increasing quantities of debt. Either would intensify inflationary pressures. Faced with this dilemma, pressure mounted for cuts to taxes and spending—and the fundamental restructuring of the New Deal state.

The fiscal crisis of the state and inflation crisis also constituted a crisis of imperialism. Budget deficits and rising spending generated an international dollar glut, exerting downward pressure on the value of the dollar. This added to the impact of inflation, making it more difficult to sustain the peg to gold that anchored the dollar's central position in the international monetary system. Pressures for devaluation led Nixon to suspend the dollar's convertibility to gold in 1971—temporarily adopting a free-floating market exchange rate system. While this was initially seen as a short-term solution, it became clear to policymakers that "muddling through" monetary crises by bending the rules was not an adequate basis for a stable international monetary order.[43] An entirely new architecture was necessary, which could more flexibly allow for movements in currency values.

The need to secure class discipline in order to restore accumulation and resolve the crisis of imperialism led to the eruption of a contradiction between accumulation and legitimation. For a time, the ongoing strength of trade union resistance, and especially the civil rights movement, served as a check on restructuring. Yet the crisis made clear that capitalism was unable to support the welfare state or full employment, which would have been necessary to address the socioeconomic roots of racial inequality. Unable to advance an alternative path out of the crisis, civil rights leaders ultimately confined the movement to anti-discrimination and voting rights struggles.[44] At the same time, AFL-CIO unions failed to move beyond wage militancy to fight for the more fundamental changes that would have been necessary to preserve existing gains by challenging capitalism itself.[45] The tragic outcome was to lend very real credence to the neoliberal slogan "there is no alternative."

State officials, for their part, stumbled in the dark to restore accumulation as the crisis persisted through the 1970s. Efforts to restore corporate profits at home initially revolved around the implementation of wage and price controls. Nixon, Ford, and Carter all fumbled with various mandatory and voluntary control regimes, with targets negotiated by tripartite institutions consisting of business and labor representatives. While the legitimation of the regime hinged on its ostensibly controlling not just wages but also prices, the overall objective was always to limit real wage growth. For this reason, controls met with the begrudging support of big business through most of the 1970s. This was expressed most prominently by the Business Roundtable, an organization of CEOs from the largest industrial firms, formed in 1971 at the urging of Treasury Secretary John Connally and Fed Chair Arthur Burns to build support for inflation-fighting efforts.[46]

The overriding concern among both policymakers and businesses alike, from the very start, was to terminate controls and return to market pricing as soon as possible. Yet a strategy for doing so was forthcoming from neither business nor the state. Figuring out how to do so was largely the remit of the Treasury, which saw its policy-planning capacities considerably enlarged in this period.[47] Any moves toward greater liberalization met with immediate price spikes as business sought to recoup lost profits—which only increased demands from the public for new controls. On the other hand, such new controls led to shortages of basic necessities, as diminished returns led business to stop investing. Just as workers could not be forced to accept wage restraint, the relative autonomy of the state also meant that it was unable to compel capital to invest at a rate of profit it saw as too low.

A further difficulty was that the extensive state capacities required to monitor and approve all wage and price increases went well beyond what existed or even appeared feasible, especially in the context of growing pressure for cutbacks. Almost immediately after the establishment of Nixon's initial controls regime, officials tasked with implementing the controls were insisting that carrying out their basic tasks, and therefore preserving the credibility of the program, would require substantially more resources than they had been allocated.[48] Nor was it easy to reduce wages through these arrangements, which not only depended on the voluntary cooperation of trade unions, but had to be implemented by elected officials who ultimately needed to win votes—and were also subject to congressional meddling. The ever-present threat was that popular pressures would emerge for the continuation of controls, or, even worse, their expansion into wider areas of the economy.

Reducing the living standards of the majority of the population in order to restore corporate profits was naturally a difficult task for officials who had to stand for elections. Even in a capitalist state characterized by limited forms of democratic participation, in which both major parties are closely allied with business, elected leaders were by no means eager to face the wrath of voters. This placed hard limits on the ability of the state to restore class discipline. So, too, was this dilemma at the root of the aversion by such officials to the primary alternative to wage and price controls: engineering a recession by tightening monetary policy. Caused by sharply raising unemployment, such a recession would have the effect of disciplining labor to accept lower wages. But it would hardly be popular.

During the Ford and Carter years, anti-inflation efforts came to include a substantial focus on "deregulation"—rolling back the victories of the labor, consumer protection, and environmental movements. When Congress proved unable to enact sweeping regulatory reform, Ford simply implemented the agenda by executive order, mandating that all new regulations include an "inflation impact statement" to be evaluated by the director of the Office of Management and Budget. Carter followed in Ford's footsteps.[49] Those proposing new regulations would now have to demonstrate that they would not excessively hamper corporate profits. In effect, if the social regulations won by New Left social movements had been about prioritizing a conception of the "public good" as a counter to the logic of profit maximization, these changes institutionalized the protection of profits as an overriding concern in the state regulatory regime.

The limited democracy allowed through the institutions of the American state was a problem in other ways as well, which were exacerbated by the crisis. Just as wage and price controls came to be the target of unwanted public interference, so did the crisis help protectionist forces, both among business and the broader public, to gain steam in Congress—seeking to extend protections for domestic industry and limit international competition. This was in direct contradiction to both the overwhelming thrust of American policy since World War II, as well as the objectives of Nixon, Ford, and Carter, who sought to continue full speed ahead with international liberalization. These administrations worked continuously to craft a new international trade and monetary regime to replace Bretton Woods that would not constrain but radically *increase* the global mobility of capital. As time passed, this was increasingly understood as key to resolving the crisis.

These dimensions of the 1970s crisis were ultimately addressed through the dramatic concentration of political power within executive branch agencies that were insulated from Congress. The power of the Office of the US Trade Representative (USTR), created in 1963, was continuously enhanced over the 1970s, as international negotiations on a post–Bretton Woods system got underway. Crucially, the USTR was highly autonomous from congressional input and unwanted business meddling. An extensive business trade advisory system in the Department of Commerce allowed for the interests of large corporations to be expressed, and a consensus organized, outside of parliamentary institutions and away from public view. This also allowed the trade representative to remain significantly insulated from pressures exerted by particular firms.[50]

Growing state authoritarianism reflected the prioritization of the needs of accumulation over legitimation in the face of the crisis. Ending the crisis demanded that the legitimation of capitalism through elections and welfare state programs be sacrificed to the impulses, rhythms, and demands of capital accumulation. This occurred most dramatically in relation to the Federal Reserve, whose independence from Congress, and even the president, insulated it from "political" pressures and afforded it tremendous latitude in implementing policies that could be highly unpopular with voters. While the 1977 Federal Reserve Reform Act had formally enhanced its accountability to Congress, this was more than offset by the power and autonomy the Fed gained through its role in managing inflation and the demands imposed on it for rapid, flexible intervention.

The concentration of power in the state economic apparatus, which Nicos Poulantzas appropriately dubbed "authoritarian statism," had a deep structural basis that could not be countered by simply increasing the Fed's reporting requirements to Congress.[51] Congress neither desired that the Fed's autonomy be reduced nor did it have the capacity to more directly undertake the economic functions for which the central bank was responsible. Preserving the stability of the dollar meant that Congress *had* to be separated from the Fed's management of the money supply. Such functions could not be entrusted to the whims of elected officials, who may be tempted to try to circumvent economic discipline; instead, these functions needed to be safely delegated to "apolitical" technocrats. In neoliberal ideology, this was not seen as undemocratic—on the contrary, market stability was understood as the necessary condition upon which freedom and democracy rest.[52]

Maintaining the global role of the dollar in the context of the 1970s inflation crisis hinged on the state's ability to carry out a politically painful attack on workers. The insulation of the Federal Reserve from democratic institutions afforded it the essential space to do so. In a fiat monetary system freed from a gold base, the state became even more central to maintaining confidence in the currency, and therefore the stability of financial markets. As Bretton Woods controls and pegs gave way to a new floating exchange rate system, central banks now had to continuously intervene on foreign exchange markets to ensure the stability and exchangeability of their currencies in response to market pressures. In this context, the Fed's commitment to managing inflation became especially important for sustaining the centrality of the dollar within the global financial system. The stability of the imperial order depended more than ever upon securing class discipline at home.

Paradoxically, it was the very *dependence* of the state economic apparatus on capital accumulation—the result of its organic integration with the economy—that most directly contributed to its ascent in the structure of state power. The economic apparatus was a vector for the expression of the structural constraints of capitalism in the state complex, and thus "most clearly demonstrate[d] the continuity of the state," as Poulantzas observed. Thus, the expansion of the economic apparatus did not mean that the state simply became "more powerful," nor did the deepening infrastructural link between state and capital mean that the state had greater "control" over the economy. Rather, it was the very inability of the state to master the economy that had propelled the expansion of the economic apparatus. Precisely to the same extent that capitalism came to rely on the state, so did the state become captive to capitalism's need for it to continually intervene.

The Fed's leading position in the state was dramatically asserted in 1979, when Fed Chair Paul Volcker raised interest rates to unprecedented heights through the so-called Volcker Shock (chart 3.7). By the time of his appointment, Volcker had already emerged as one of the most vocal advocates in the administration for severe monetary tightening, and consequent economic recession, as the only path out of the crisis—which Carter had previously decried as "too extreme." By choosing Volcker, Carter accepted that the only route available for resolving the crisis without challenging private control of investment was what would later be known as neoliberal restructuring. This entailed the deep reorganization of the New Deal state—which would, of course, be taken to new heights through the naked attack on the working class unleashed by the subsequent Reagan administration.

What happened over the 1970s was not simply an inflation crisis. Rather, these years saw the crumbling of the basic institutional foundations of the managerial order: the class compromise between large industrial corporations and "responsible" business unions, the contradictory repression and empowerment of finance through Bretton Woods and New Deal regulations, and the autonomy of industry from the banks underpinned by the substantial profits of the postwar boom.

Chart 3.7: Interest rates and inflation, 1960–1983

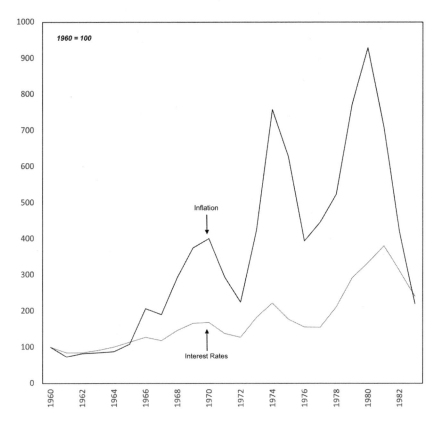

Source: *Authors' calculations based on data from FRED.* Note: *Index of percent and percent per annum; interest rates measured as discount rate, annual average; inflation measured as consumer prices.*

As we saw, the hegemony of industrial corporations was also supported by industrial policy organized through the military-industrial complex. Yet in the context of the inflationary pressures that accumulated through the fiscal crisis of the state, and the push for tax cuts on capital that resulted, even the military-industrial complex came under pressure, as military spending declined as a percent of GDP from the 1970s onward.[53]

The fissures in the institutional foundations of industrial hegemony were complemented by the renewed prominence of finance in the structure of accumulation. As corporate profitability declined, financiers increasingly exerted leverage on these firms to cut costs, enhance margins, offshore production, and restructure their operations to restore competitiveness. At the same time, the fragmentation of stock holdings that had underpinned managerial autonomy was reversed, as equity ownership was increasingly concentrated in the hands of new institutional investors, further intensifying financial discipline. All this reinforced a new pattern of global economic integration, for which global finance also provided the critical infrastructure—facilitating the free movement of investment all over the planet that was at the heart of the post–Bretton Woods trade and monetary order.

Industrial managers ultimately came to accept the empowerment of finance as necessary to end the crisis. While the Business Roundtable at first resisted new regulations that would empower investors and strengthen boards of directors, these efforts failed.[54] Whereas they had been dominated by insiders during the managerial period, stronger corporate boards now increasingly consisted of "independent" outside directors. Investor power ultimately came to be seen by industrial firms as a worthwhile trade-off: greater competitive discipline and financial power were an intrinsic consequence of the liberalization that also allowed them to globalize production, discipline labor, and dramatically restore profits over the ensuing decades. Global liberalization and low inflation would come to serve as the basis for a new unstable equilibrium of compromise between finance and industry: the neoliberal era had begun.

4

Neoliberalism and Financial Hegemony

The neoliberal capitalism that emerged from the Volcker Shock was characterized above all by a new form of financial hegemony. The rise of finance was registered not just in the growing power of the financial sector, but also in the increasing significance of financial logics and operations in the industrial corporation itself. The latter came increasingly to resemble a financial institution as top corporate executives allocated pools of investment among not only internal corporate operations but also external subcontractors offering cheaper labor, especially in the global periphery. In this way, the ongoing financialization of the non-financial firm faciliated the globalization of production.

Yet the emergence of a seamless world of capital accumulation also relied on the integration of global finance, as the capital controls and barriers of the Bretton Woods–New Deal order were restructured and cast aside. These processes of financialization and globalization restored industrial profitability and finally ended the long crisis of the 1970s. That finance provided the essential infrastructure for deepening globalization over the subsequent decades served to entangle the interests of financial and industrial capital even more closely. Both within the industrial corporation as well as outside of it, the rise of finance enhanced the mobility and competitiveness of capital and made possible a brave new world of streamlined capital accumulation.

The emergence of a more authoritarian state, characterized especially by the concentration of power in the Federal Reserve, was integral to globalization and financialization. The insulation (or "independence") of the Fed from democratic institutions was necessary to ensure its capacity for rapid, flexible, and internationally coordinated intervention to meet the demands imposed by a rigid global trade and monetary order. At the same time, the state's growing reliance on debt, as opposed to taxes, to finance its expenditures constrained fiscal policy and further reinforced the Fed's power. State institutions associated with legitimation, including representative democratic structures, political parties, welfare state programs, and trade union rights, were rolled back or hollowed out. The emergence of an authoritarian neoliberal state tightly organized around its accumulation functions meant a more nakedly coercive form of state power.

The fraction of financial capital that became hegemonic over the neoliberal period consisted of not just banks but a relatively diffuse amalgamation of different institutions. Unlike the direct control of corporations by banks that defined finance capital, what now crystallized was a polyarchic form of financial hegemony in which constellations of competing financial institutions established ephemeral alliances on corporate boards to exert broad influence and discipline. Most important were commercial and investment banks, but this fraction also included mutual fund companies, pension funds, insurance companies, hedge funds, and broker-dealers. As we will see, these firms were interconnected into the distinct system of market-based finance that evolved during the neoliberal period, whereby non-bank financial institutions became more significant in credit and money creation. It was this system that would form the epicenter of the 2008 crisis.

The Financialization of the Non-Financial Corporation

The emergence of financial hegemony was reflected in the shifting distribution of surplus value between finance and industry. As we saw, the weakness of finance relative to industry during the managerial era was indicated by its limited ability to extract surplus from industrial corporations through interest and dividend payments. Consequently, industrial firms were able to hold on to a larger portion of the surplus value generated in production in the form of retained earnings. Subsequently, the growing power of finance was reflected in its ability to capture a growing share of the surplus. As chart 3.1 shows, throughout the managerial period, retained earnings consistently represented a larger portion of GDP than dividend payments. Strikingly, this relationship was sharply reversed in 1980, after which dividend payments consistently made up a larger portion of GDP than retained earnings.

Similarly, whereas in the managerial era industrial firms dwarfed even the largest financial institutions in terms of revenue and profits, this, too, was reversed in the neoliberal period. In 1960, only one bank (Bank of America) was included among the twenty most profitable companies in the United States; by 2000, two of the top five were banks, and five of the top twenty were financial institutions. Yet even these figures tend to understate the significance financial institutions attained. More revealing than the *number* of profitable financial firms was the *share of total corporate profits* these firms captured. The share of total corporate profits accounted for by this relatively small number of financial firms went from 8 percent in the early postwar period to a high of over 40 percent in 2001 (chart 4.1). Finance thereby comprised an increasing proportion of a growing whole.

The hostile takeovers of industrial corporations carried out in the 1980s by so-called corporate raiders like T. Boone Pickens and Carl Icahn were among the first indications of the deep shift in the relations of power between shareholders and managers. Such "raids" entailed buying up controlling shares in a corporation with borrowed money, firing the CEO, and then selling off the firm's assets to pay the debt. Raiders accessed financing through "junk bonds" arranged by once-reputable investment banks such as Drexel Burnham Lambert—employer of junk bond king Michael Milken, known for his annual "Predators' Ball," which was populated by this crude new Wall Street crowd. Such investment banks were willing to underwrite high-risk, high-yield bonds based on the expectation that they would be repaid with the assets of the targeted firm once it was taken over.

Leveraged buyouts were particularly worrying for industrial corporate managers, since they allowed raiders, who lacked creditworthy status, to purchase controlling interests in targeted firms almost entirely with borrowed funds. This effectively meant that anyone could be a threat. Corporate managers responded by seeking to protect their firms through erecting defenses such as "poison pills" and "golden

Chart 4.1: Financial profits as a share of the total (%), 1948–2021

Source: *Bureau of Economic Analysis, authors' calculations.* Note: *"Neoliberal period average" spans from 1980–2008. Other financial profits as a share of domestic industries.*

parachutes."[1] In the former, existing shareholders were given the option to purchase additional shares at a discount in the event of a hostile-takeover attempt. This served to block an oppositional activist investor from consolidating shareholdings substantial enough to effect a change in management. In the latter, executives ensured exorbitant compensation packages for themselves in the event they were fired because of a takeover.

Maintaining a high share price served to prevent such takeover attempts. Indeed, firms whose share price was "undervalued" in the eyes of raiders were prime targets for potential takeovers as they could be acquired relatively cheaply and easily. Keeping the share price high raised the costs of acquiring a firm—reducing or even eliminating the profit to be made from chopping up and reselling its assets. Managers thus sought to prevent such threats by executing so-called share buybacks, whereby a company inflated share prices by repurchasing its own stock, a practice legalized by the SEC in 1982. Along with dividend payments, the increase in share buybacks in this period was reflected in the decline of retained earnings as a percent of GDP—and was an important mechanism through which finance captured a larger share of the surplus (chart 4.1).

Buybacks, as well as increased dividend payments, were thus strategic responses by industrial firms to the emerging hegemony of finance. They formed a core part of the doctrine of "shareholder value," according to which corporate strategy should focus more significantly on improving the share price. Embraced by corporate raiders, this ideology became the calling card for a new era of financial power as supposedly complacent industrial managers faced new discipline. Jack Welch, the CEO of General Electric, emerged as the foremost guru of the new doctrine. Others were slower to adapt. But as increasingly assertive boards of directors started firing management that failed to deliver improvements in stock prices, most prominently at IBM in 1992 and General Motors in 1993, it became clear that, even for the largest and most powerful companies, there was no choice but to submit to investor power.

The emergence of polyarchic financial hegemony was underpinned by the concentration and centralization of equity in the hands of large financial institutions. This was fueled by the pools of money-capital controlled by institutional asset owners, especially pension funds. Ironically, the proliferation of such funds reflected the strength of unions in collective bargaining in the 1960s. By the mid-1970s, pension funds had become the largest single holders of corporate stock.[2] While this led some to speculate about the arrival of "pension fund socialism," these funds ended up contributing to shifting the balance of class forces toward capital and intensifying financial pressure to restructure non-financial corporations. The state encouraged the growth of such funds, as tax incentives for both corporations and workers played a significant role in the extension of pension plan coverage from a fifth of the private sector workforce in 1950 to almost half by 1970.[3]

As a result, large financial institutions came to either directly own or indirectly manage a significant proportion of available equity. In 1940, stock holdings and stock trading by financial institutions accounted for less than 5 percent of the market value of all US stocks. By the mid-1970s, they accounted for about 25 percent, and they jumped to 70 percent by 2008.[4] However, even these numbers tend to downplay the extent of the concentration and centralization underway in this period. While the concentration of *ownership* of equities by large institutional investors was clearly very significant, the vast pools of equity accumulated by these institutions were then *themselves* amalgamated by other investment firms that *managed* them—creating even larger blocks of ownership power.

The size of the concentrations of equity amassed by large institutional investors meant that it was difficult for them to discipline underperforming firms by simply dumping shares, as this could depress the value of their remaining holdings. Investors thus sought other means to exert influence, including establishing more direct contacts with management. They also pushed for more powerful and independent boards of directors, which had largely been controlled by insiders during the managerial period. Similarly, shareholders could exercise voting rights to replace management, nominate outside directors, or otherwise influence corporate strategy through "proxy fights." By the 1990s, proxy fights were more common than hostile-takeover attempts, a stark reversal of the pattern in the 1980s. By the 2000s, they were the near-exclusive means for exerting investor pressure, reflecting the regularization and consolidation of the new hierarchy.[5]

Those who had been the rulers of industry, at the top of the pyramid of corporate power, increasingly found themselves answering to investors—whom they, and their allies in the business press, often accused of being excessively concerned with short-term profitability while lacking the requisite knowledge of specific sectors or firms. But if it was clear that the ascent of finance had little to do with the supposed "perfect efficiency" of capital markets in allocating the social surplus, finance was also not simply a rentier interest. Rather, it was emerging as a powerful disciplinary force on industrial production, relentlessly pushing to squeeze the maximum profit out of its investments. The enhanced margins and greater mobility of capital that resulted from financialization was not a matter of "hollowing out" or weakening industry; rather, finance intensified the pressure on firms to restructure their operations to cut costs and maximize efficiency, competitiveness, and profitability.

At the same time, shifts in the strategies, regulations, and structures of the state apparatus supported the reorganization of the power bloc around the ascendent position of financial capital, thereby crystallizing a new political hierarchy. The New Deal regulatory architecture had been based on the Fed, OCC, FDIC, and SEC acting to maintain the fragmentation of the banking system and to limit its involvement in corporate governance—that is, preventing the reemergence of finance capital. Yet powerful institutional investors were now finding these practices "arduous, confusing, expensive and generally disappointing." In the 1990s, the SEC enacted a series of regulatory changes that expanded "shareholder rights" and empowered boards of directors. Particularly significant were reforms that made it easier for large shareholders to coordinate with one another regarding firms in which they held stakes, facilitating the formation of coalitions of investors that could challenge insiders.[6]

These regulatory shifts significantly reduced the costs of undertaking proxy fights and directly contributed to their growing frequency in relation to hostile takeovers. Importantly, these changes were implemented in response to the defenses against investor discipline corporations had established during the 1980s. In addition to adopting poison pills and golden parachutes, industrial managers had sought to gain the protection of federal anti-takeover laws. When an unsympathetic Reagan administration rebuffed these efforts, industrial executives turned to the state level, where they were often the largest employers. Unsurprisingly, these efforts were more successful: by 1990, 42 states included such protections.[7] With the regulatory restructuring of the 1990s, the SEC acted to counteract these defenses and limit their impact, institutionalizing the power of investors by offering them more orderly means to exercise their influence.

The SEC had thus intervened in a conflict between finance and industry and contributed to establishing financial hegemony. But this did not mean it had been "captured" by finance. More than the influence of specific firms over the state, the restructuring of the economic apparatus reflected the importance of finance in the structure of accumulation. Stabilizing financial power required establishing "accountability" and "good governance" in industrial corporations. This was also reflected in a host of other new regulations rolled out by the SEC: while the Sarbanes-Oxley Act increased the power and independence of boards of directors, Regulation FD blocked the privileged disclosure of inside information to large institutional investors. The latter, in particular, seemed aimed at preventing the emergence of clientalist relationships between internal managers and shareholders.[8]

But the financialization of the non-financial corporation was hardly just a matter of external financiers forcing restructuring on industrial firms. As we saw, the roots of financialization reached back to the very heart of the postwar golden age, as firms responded to the complexities of diversification and internationalization. As a result, non-financial corporations had decentralized their operations, even as centralized control over investment was reinforced. This led to the growing power of the corporate financial unit in the organization, as it was charged with devising and imposing the quantitative metrics that established the basis for drawing equivalences between qualitatively distinct production processes. Insofar as these quantities were measured in the universal equivalent, money-capital came to mediate relations between the firm's different operations.

This amounted to the gradual development of a fusion of financial and industrial capital. Whereas in the nineteenth century such a fusion had been established through the interconnection between investment banks and industrial firms, now, a century later, this took the form of a convergence between M-C-M' and M-M' circuits of capital *inside* the industrial corporation. This emerged despite New Deal regulations that aimed to rigidly separate these two forms of capital. Indeed, the immediate result of these regulations had been industrial firms' internalization of a range of financial practices for which they had previously relied on investment banks. These regulatory barriers actually *incentivized* industrial corporations to offer financial services, as they were able to escape the regulations faced by formally designated financial institutions.

This emerging fusion between financial and industrial capital inside the corporation, and its reorganization as a system of investment, was especially highlighted by the rise of the chief financial officer (CFO). While no major corporation had a CFO in 1963, beginning in the 1970s corporations across the business world began to create such positions, which became all but ubiquitous by the 1990s. The rise of the CFO reflected a fundamental change in the logic of corporate management, which now afforded much greater prominence to distinctly "financial" considerations. The corporate treasurer had been a relatively sleepy and mundane position, largely concerned with bookkeeping, taxes, and the like; now, the CFO was second-in-command, the powerful right hand of the CEO in formulating all aspects of corporate strategy.[11]

CFOs were tasked with evaluating the performance of business units, devising strategies to use financial leverage in support of the firm's overall competitiveness, managing acquisitions and divestitures, and fending off hostile-takeover attempts. They were also the primary links to investors and financial analysts, especially through their management of "investor relations" functions. In addition to supplying the data and making the forecasts that determined "investor expectations," CFOs also pushed forward the discipline in the firm necessary to *meet* these expectations. Just as the influence of the CFO reflected the expansion of the firm's financial operations following its decentralization, so, too, was this power essential for pushing forward further financialized restructuring to satisfy outside investors. The CFO was thus a major pillar of shareholder value, embodying the new power of outside investors within the firm itself.

The fusion of finance and industry within the industrial corporation meant that it developed a range of financial functions that were not strictly subordinated to the circuits of industrial capital it controlled. Not only were industrial corporations increasingly organized around the circulation of interest-bearing capital *within* the firm, but they also profited from circulating it *outside* the firm. Industrial firms initially engaged in lending on a large scale as a result of the accumulation of

retained earnings during the managerial period—which would otherwise have sat idle or been relatively unprofitably deposited in banks.
Indeed, by the end of the golden age, industrial corporations had already
become the primary lenders on commercial paper markets, just as they
borrowed substantially on these markets from other corporations.[12]

The integration of non-financial corporations with financial markets
dramatically accelerated during the neoliberal period. Chart 4.2 shows
the sharp increase in the total number of bonds issued by non-financial
corporations circulating on the market during the neoliberal period.
These markets were transformed by the elimination of restrictions on the
foreign sales of such bonds in 1984—effectively globalizing US corporate

Chart 4.2: Total non-financial corporate bonds (USD billions), 1946–2008

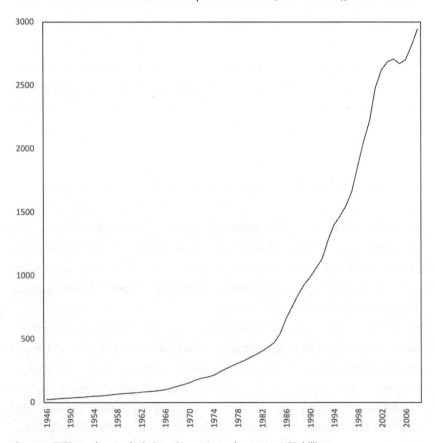

Source: *FRED, authors' calculations.* Note: *Annual average, USD billions.*

debt markets, and dramatically expanding the financing available to non-financial corporations.[13] The greater reliance of corporations on bonds also meant they were subjected to the discipline of these markets in new ways: as firms came to rely on them as an indispensable source of financing, so too did they become more focused on assessments of their creditworthiness, especially as reflected in their bond prices.

The importance of derivatives for the global mobility of capital was another factor that contributed to the fusion of industrial and financial capital within the corporation. In the Bretton Woods period of capital controls and fixed exchange rates, corporations invested abroad by "jumping over" tariff walls to establish subsidiaries, which manufactured products for sale within particular economic zones. The elimination of tariff protections in the neoliberal period, however, allowed for the streamlining of global production. Redundant facilities were dismantled, and stages of production located wherever labor, regulatory, and tax costs were lowest. The result was the creation of seamless, globally integrated networks of production. Indeed, a significant percent of world "trade" consisted of the movement of products and capital through cross-border corporate production chains.[14]

Circulating capital across national borders brought the risk that unexpected exchange and interest rate fluctuations could wipe out the value of a finished commodity before it even reached the market. Corporations managed these risks by entering into derivatives contracts: between the early 1980s and 2007, daily turnover of derivatives grew fifty-fold, from practically nothing to nearly $2 trillion.[15] Derivatives secure the right to purchase an asset at a future time for a set price—effectively "locking in" a given price. They thereby transfer risks to speculators, who are willing to assume them in exchange for the possibility of gaining substantial profit. In so doing, they establish some of the consistency that had been present with fixed exchange rates, albeit in a world of volatile floating currency markets. Derivatives thus mediate the continuity of industrial capital during the production and realization of surplus value.

In a derivative contract, one party pays a fee, called a premium, in exchange for protection against a destabilizing event (e.g., a sudden shift in exchange rates). If that event occurs, an agreed sum of money is transferred to the holder of the contract to cover some or all the losses incurred. To be trustworthy, derivatives contracts must be administered by a reputable third party who can oversee the flow of money between the parties to the contract. This role was played by large banks, which transmitted fees and premium payments, and settled the final payments when the contract was closed. Banks thereby generated new revenues by translating their centrality in the global financial system into a unique role in expanding derivatives markets. In addition to making profits by charging fees for their services, banks also entered into derivatives contracts themselves in order to hedge their own risks.

As we have seen, competition is a function of capital mobility. Insofar as it facilitated the movement of investment into and out of sectors, facilities, and geographical zones, corporate financialization intensified competitive discipline on industrial capitals (to maximize profits) and workers (exerting downward pressure on wages and working conditions). Rather than endlessly increasing in size, as had been the norm in the managerial period, *divestment* from less profitable operations became a regular practice of corporations employing the new "portfolio management." Financialized firms gained competitive advantages from this ability to divest from relatively unprofitable sectors, while quickly evaluating and investing in more profitable ones.[16]

By the end of the 1990s, these tendencies culminated in the replacement of the multidivisional conglomerate form of corporate organization that had taken shape in the decades following World War II with a new multilayered subsidiary form. Increasingly, industrial firms not only organized production in their own business divisions but also entered into subcontracts with outside firms offering cheaper labor, often on the global periphery. MNCs thus integrated external subcontractors and their own internal divisions into global networks of production and investment. The flexibility of these subcontracts further intensified competitive pressure on workers and the countries they lived in for investment and jobs, holding down wages and restraining troublesome environmental and labor regulations, while offering MNCs the ability to relocate relatively easily.

The multilayered subsidiary form, was the organizational structure through which capitalist globalization took place. The position of these MNCs at the apex of the global political economy was grounded in their possession of two unique kinds of financial assets: branding and intellectual property. Both constituted forms of monopoly power granted by the state, since ownership of these assets conferred exclusive control over the right to manufacture certain products or use particular brands. The control of MNCs over production was then secured through licensing agreements with subcontractors. In this way, the power of the multilayered subsidiary form over production was structured in accordance with the further reorganization of the corporation around the management of financial assets.[17]

More important than the changing distribution of surplus between financial and industrial capital for the rise of finance, therefore, was its changing *systemic function* in the organization of capital accumulation. The process of neoliberal globalization that unfolded over the 1980s and 1990s led to the deepening entanglement of finance and industry. Both within the corporation and outside it, finance was critical for the mobility of investment that allowed industrial firms to create a new world of globally integrated accumulation. Far from being a symptom of decline, financialization made possible a new era of prosperity for industrial corporations and financial institutions alike. The growing power of finance in the US social formation reflected its position as the nerve center of global capitalism.

Asset-Based Accumulation and Market-Based Finance

The financialized restructuring of the non-financial corporation and the rise of big institutional investors were predicated on the development of a new form of accumulation based in the ownership and control of financial assets. This model of *asset-based accumulation* was defined by the growing importance of non-cash financial assets as forms of money-capital for both financial and non-financial firms. Asset-based accumulation was part and parcel of the system of *market-based finance* that took shape during the neoliberal period, whereby the financial system and its credit-generating functions were reorganized around the possession and exchange of assets. Market-based finance integrated pension funds with investment banks, commercial banks, and other financial institutions.

A fundamental precondition for asset-based accumulation was that a wider range of tangible and intangible objects and processes be defined, constructed, and regulated as abstract financial assets. As the top managers of non-financial corporations increasingly became money-capitalists, for instance, the corporation itself was simultaneously structured around objectifying its various concrete business operations— processes of industrial capital accumulation existing across time—as abstract financial assets. This facilitated the integration of these industrial circuits in the logics of money-capital that were ever more dominant with the firm. At the same time, the operation of the financial system itself was increasingly premised on breaking down economic processes and recombining them into different kinds of tradable financial assets.

Financial assets are specific forms of money-capital. Their key feature is their ability to secure property claims on future revenues, either through sale or some other contractual arrangement (for instance, licensing agreements for the use of intellectual property). Everything from baseball cards to da Vinci masterpieces, from loans to intellectual property, can become a financial asset insofar as it is integrated into an M-M' circuit of money-capital. Seen as assets, the only use-value these things possess is their ability to be converted into a larger quantity of money through exchange. Indeed, as we saw in chapter 2, the monetary character of financial assets depends on their ability to store value, and thus to be transferred into the universal equivalent form (that is, currency). It is through being exchanged for money that gains in the value of an asset are *realized*, and the M-M' circuit completed.

Different classes and forms of assets constantly compete over their valuations as expressed in the universal equivalent form. As assets (that is, stocks), corporations are immediately placed in a competitive relationship not only with all other corporations but also with all other financial assets, from works of art to homes. Asset-based accumulation thus deepens the penetration of the money-form both within industrial corporations and across the economy. This exerts enormous discipline on corporations, with profound effects on their strategies and even on the very structure of industrial capital itself. One cannot conceive of assets as merely fictitious capital, existing in a separate financial sphere divorced from the "real" economy. On the contrary, assetification brought finance and its competitive pressures more deeply into production than ever before.

Asset-based accumulation supported the reemergence of financial hegemony through the concentration of equity within non-bank financial institutions. In Marx's model of financial accumulation, banks advance a sum of money-capital to the functioning capitalist, who assumes control of the capital until the loan is repaid with interest out of the surplus generated in production. The capital the financier advances to the industrialist then flows back to its owner, plus interest, by virtue of her property rights over this capital. However, since the non-bank financial institutions that underpinned financial hegemony during the neoliberal period did not issue bank loans, they were not able to extract surplus value from corporations in the form of interest payments in this way. As a result, they had to "get their cut" of the value created by industrial firms through other means.

One way they did so was through dividend payments. Indeed, as we saw, the growth of dividend payments reflected the rising power of finance. However, dividends were decided by boards of directors on a year-to-year basis, rather than established through a contractual arrangement in advance of receiving a loan. Therefore, dividends tended to fluctuate in ways that other interest payments did not. As a result, even more important for institutional investors were asset valuations—that is, stock *prices* themselves. While capitalizing on these valuations did not amount to a direct transfer of surplus value, it did entitle the bearer of the stock to a larger share of the total social product. Institutional investors thus accumulated wealth both through divided payments and through the increasing value of their stocks.

Once again, it is clear that the distribution of profit between finance and industry is insufficient for understanding the extent of financial power in the neoliberal period. In addition to the revenues financial firms took in, their money-power was also reflected in the value of the assets they held. Chart 4.3 illustrates the dynamic of asset-based accumulation by showing the relationship between share prices and corporate profits. As it indicates, the market price of shares increased far more quickly than corporate profits per share during the neoliberal era. This divergence points to the fact that share prices themselves had become the basis for financial accumulation. Moreover, it illustrates the extent to which neoliberalism was a break with earlier phases of capitalist development as this ratio exceeded that for any other period in the twentieth century—including classical finance capital.

Critically, the success of asset-based accumulation is fundamentally based on corporations' ability to produce profits. Holding the stock of firms that are unable to do so cannot serve as the basis for investors to accumulate money-power over the longer term. An inflated share price, without a profitable underlying firm, is the definition of a classic stock "bubble." To be sure, the stock of even profitable firms may be caught up in bubbles. Theoretically, the result in either case is an eventual market "correction," which reduces the share price to its "equilibrium" level. We have seen this happen frequently, as for instance in the "dot-com" bubble of the 1990s. The important point is that there must ultimately be some correspondence between investor expectations for future accumulation, as reflected in the stock price, and the actual capacity of the underlying firm to generate surplus value.

Accordingly, while chart 4.3 shows that the price-to-earnings ratio in general grew during the neoliberal period, and thus that the difference between stock prices and corporate profits increased, this in no way implies the suspension of the correspondence between the two. Rather, it shows that equity assets had come to serve as the basis for the accumulation of money-power in a new way—that is, through rising share prices. But this could occur only on the expectation that these firms would remain profitable. Similarly, the share prices of unprofitable firms could increase on the expectation that these firms would *become* profitable at some time in the future.

Stock prices therefore reflected speculation on the future prospects of sections of capital—which can be measured only in terms of profits. Of course, there was no guarantee that these speculations would be correct: some investors would always bet wrong, while others would be rewarded. Whichever way things turned out, it cannot be assumed

Chart 4.3: Price-to-earnings ratio, S&P 500 companies, 1880–2008

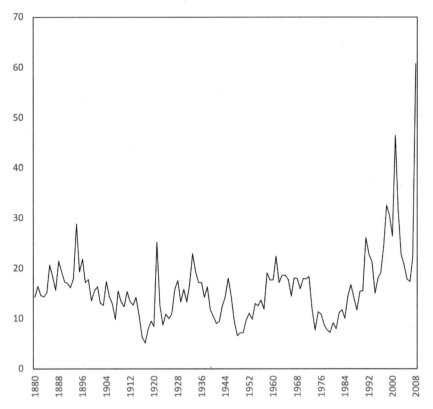

Source: *Global Financial Data, WRDS, authors' calculations*

that investment in the stock market was simply a diversion from "real" investment. The abstract nature of money-capital meant that stock market gains could be redistributed into any concrete circuit of capital, and thus find their way into new physical investment and new products. Moreover, investment in the stock market and investment in fixed capital were in no way mutually exclusive: throughout the neoliberal period, corporate investment remained within the historical average (chart 4.7), while corporate profits exploded (chart 4.8) and R and D spending increased (chart 4.6).

Financial hegemony was grounded not just in the increasing value of corporate shares, but also the specific powers afforded by share ownership. The growing importance of equity produced a new form of separation of ownership and control. Of course, the capital circulating within the firm remained under the control of its managers. However, unlike loans, which cease to exist when they are repaid, stocks entitle their owner to a share of the surplus in perpetuity. Instead of being based in ownership claims on money-capital advanced to an industrial capitalist, they establish ownership over the firm itself. This also bestows upon stock owners a certain measure of control over the corporation. The concentration of equity, and the long-termism that came with the illiquidity of these large holdings, thus tended to bring financiers *more directly* into production.

However, the concentration of asset ownership was accompanied by the *fragmentation* of the financial system. The dispersal of power across a range of financial institutions took place through the emergence of "market-based finance." Traditionally, lending was centralized under the control of banks, which served as the "general managers of money-capital." For this reason, Marx saw money-capitalists and bankers as essentially interchangeable. Market-based finance was an entirely new model of financial intermediation—that is, the way funds are channeled from lenders to borrowers. In the market-based system, borrowers could access credit directly from financial markets, without going through banks. Similarly, savers could invest in a range of financial instruments, such as stocks and bonds, through non-bank financial institutions as an alternative to making bank deposits.

With the development of market-based finance, therefore, a growing number of financial transactions bypassed banks in a process known as "disintermediation." Increasing disintermediation posed a major competitive challenge to banks in the 1970s and 1980s. First, the emergence of money-market mutual funds—pools of money-capital managed by a mutual fund company and invested in safe, short-term debt securities—drew savings away from checking accounts. As Regulation Q limits on interest payments did not apply to these funds, they were able to offer investors higher rates of return than banks could. This fueled the growth of non-bank financial institutions, especially as inflation drove market interest rates upward during the 1970s. The Volcker Shock further intensified these pressures, pushing interest rates a full 10 percent above Regulation Q levels.

In addition to these pressures on bank deposits, the formation of new pools of money-capital controlled by institutional investors, such as insurance companies, pension funds, and mutual funds, posed a further competitive threat to banks. While these institutions amassed huge concentrations of money-capital in the form of stocks and bonds, they also managed large stockpiles of cash. Since institutional investors must continuously pay out cash on demand (for instance, to pay out insurance claims or pension benefits), they must hold a certain portion of their portfolios in short-term and highly liquid investments which can be withdrawn and converted into cash on short notice. As such, the pools of money managed by institutional investors were lent to those seeking short-term capital, such as investment banks, hedge funds, and industrial corporations.

The financialization of the non-financial corporation also contributed to disintermediation and brought industrial firms further into competition with banks. As we saw, banks' industrial loan business had already become less significant by the 1960s, as large corporations primarily financed new investment with retained earnings. At the same time, the growing financial capacities of these industrial firms allowed them to issue their own debt securities—which, like money-market funds, were not subject to Regulation Q. By the 1980s, medium-sized companies began to do this as well.[18] This was registered in the growth of the US corporate bond market, as well as the development of the short-term commercial paper market used by corporations to raise funds and lend excess capital to other firms.

The growing range of financial practices undertaken by industrial corporations posed a challenge to the bank-based financial model, and was a major component of the development of the system of market-based finance. Since market-based finance took the form of a range of non-bank institutions setting their cash pools in motion as money-capital, it was in fact *predicated* on industrial corporations functioning as financial institutions. At the same time, market-based finance also reinforced the financialization of the non-financial corporation. The deepening embeddedness of industrial firms in financial markets augmented financial discipline, as these firms became more dependent on the market pricing of the corporate securities that they relied on to finance their operations. This further enhanced the power of the corporate financial unit, which mediated and managed these operations.

Banks responded to the challenge of disintermediation by internalizing a range of traditionally non-bank operations. They did so by acquiring non-bank financial institutions and folding them into their own diversified structure (forming "financial holding companies"), as well as by developing new capacities. Banks became complex, multifaceted institutions undertaking a range of financial activities on different markets. This included derivatives trading as well as expanding their role as "broker-dealers," or institutions that *make markets* through the constant purchase and sale of assets. Broker-dealers supplied liquidity by acting on both sides of asset markets—both buying and selling at set prices. That dealers were always willing to buy meant that assets could always be transformed into the universal equivalent form. At the same time, by selling assets at a set price, they helped to establish a stable market. As intermediaries in the trading of all types of financial assets, dealers were thus fundamental supports for asset-based accumulation.[19]

As a result of these changes in the banking system, the loan-making process was fundamentally restructured. In the traditional model of banking, banks issued loans and held them on their balance sheets until they were repaid. In the neoliberal period, however, banks originated loans and then sold them to other financial firms. These firms then repackaged these loans into pools of tradable assets, often categorized by risk, such as mortgage bonds and collateralized debt obligations (CDOs). Each step in the loan-making process was made a separate market activity, carried out by distinct profit-making financial institutions and disciplined by market competition.[20] This process of combining revenue streams into bonds and selling them on financial markets was dubbed "securitization." Unlike traditional banking, where loans were illiquid and thus non-transferrable, securitization created a tradable asset.

Securitization fundamentally depended on the assetification of mortgages, which were the primary form of consumer credit extended by banks.[21] Mortgages are loans issued by financial institutions secured by the market value of a house or other real estate. This means that the loan is backed by the fact that, in the event the borrower does not repay, the financial institution is entitled to seize ownership of the home. Like stock dividends, mortgages entitle their owner to a revenue stream in the form of regular mortgage payments. Also like stocks, mortgages are assets in that they are tradable and can be transferred into the universal equivalent form. Regulatory changes in the neoliberal period, such as the Secondary Mortgage Market Enhancement Act of 1984, made it easier for financial institutions to buy and sell mortgages—thereby paving the way for them to function as financial assets.[22]

While mortgages and other loans were still originated by commercial banks in the neoliberal financial system, the capacity of these banks to generate credit was now tied to a broader process whereby investment banks, hedge funds, and other financial institutions packaged and resold these loans as assets. Banks thereby became to some extent pass-throughs, originating loans and selling them to generate revenue. Meanwhile, the financial institutions purchasing the loans depended on the banks' issuance of loans to raise capital and generate profits by carrying out their stage in the process of packaging, administering, and selling these loans as assets—for which they collected fees. The result was a daisy-chain of transactions linking the original debt, and the revenue stream that accompanied it, with the final bond that was sold as a financial asset.

Securitization involved a wide range of financial institutions in the credit system, each performing different functions, even if banks remained pivotal to the coherence and organization of the system. The loans issued by commercial banks (above all mortgages) were the building blocks for the process of securitization undertaken by investment banks and non-bank financial institutions. Other financial institutions purchased these loans, then repackaged and sold them as new financial assets—generating cash, which was then used to purchase more loans and begin the process again. In fact, the securitized assets that resulted from this process also served as the collateral that allowed investment firms to obtain the cash on money-markets necessary to undertake the process of purchasing and packaging loans in the first place.

The neoliberal reorganization of the credit system also included the creation of structured investment vehicles by banks. Structured investment vehicles were financial institutions set up and administered by banks, but which did not appear on bank balance sheets. The special status of these institutions kept bank leveraging ratios formally lower, while still allowing banks to profit from higher-risk activities undertaken through these non-bank conduits. Structured investment vehicles issued short-term debt, which they used to fund purchases of mortgage-backed securities. These securities were then held on their balance sheets, allowing structured investment vehicles (and banks) to profit from the differential between the interest paid for the short-term credit they used to finance their securities (mortgage) purchases on the one hand, and the interest they received from mortgage holders on the other.

Structured investment vehicles were key to the credit transmission cycle. By maintaining a continuous source of demand for consumer mortgages, structured investment vehicles dramatically extended the capacity of banks to issue such mortgages. This demand also allowed investment banks to continually create the mortgage-backed securities and CDOs (assets formed by combining other assets) that were the key collateral on short-term money markets. Critically, the creation of structured investment vehicles allowed banks to stay at the center of a changing financial system. Banks not only issued the mortgages that underpinned mortgage-backed securities, but they were also deeply involved in creating and purchasing these securities: banks lent to consumers, and then, through structured investment vehicles, ensured that those mortgages could be securitized and transferred off their balance sheets.

With the rise of securitization, the credit creation process came to rely on short-term debt. This is because the institutions that created, bought, and sold securities did not have access to pools of money sufficient to finance their operations. Nor could they simply issue debt by creating deposits. Therefore, they had to borrow cash on short-term markets to acquire the assets that they repackaged, administered, or sold. After their stage in the securitization process was complete, the borrowed funds were repaid—only to be replaced by funds borrowed on the same short-term markets to begin the process anew. One consequence of this was that the more these institutions borrowed, the more profits they could make. This resulted in their being highly leveraged and completely dependent on the short-term markets that were their primary source of cash.

The most important source of such short-term credit was repurchase agreements, or so-called "repos." Repos involved the sale of an asset with the stipulation that it would be repurchased by the seller at a given future date. A repo was, in effect, a loan: one party temporarily transferred money to another in exchange for collateral (an asset), which was returned once the cash was repaid (with interest). Instead of a simple promise to repay, as in a traditional bank loan, funding was secured by the temporary transfer of a collateral asset. The lender held the asset until the funds were returned, and the asset "repurchased." Cash was thereby transferred from institutions that held it to those that required it. Institutions holding large amounts of assets, but lacking cash, could now quickly and easily convert their assets into the universal equivalent form.

With repo markets, the process of borrowing funds was reorganized around asset ownership. Credit was generated on these markets through the monetization of non-cash assets: the "duplicating" of money occurred by enabling key assets to function as money. For credit creation (and thus lending) to occur, parties on these markets had to accept assets as cash, holding them as an equivalent until the hard currency they lent out was repaid. In fact, money was also "triplicated," as the party holding the collateral during the repo could reuse it to acquire further credit. Repo markets were thus critical for the liquidity, and money-ness, of key assets. But these markets also required a supply of assets that were "good as gold" in that they could reliably be exchanged for the universal equivalent at a stable rate. Therefore, the system depended on an ever-growing pool of secure collateral assets to function— especially mortgages and Treasury bonds.[23]

Repo markets thus allowed institutional investors and money-market funds to lend out their massive cash holdings, and to use the interest they received to acquire new assets. In turn, the institutions that borrowed this cash sought to purchase new assets, mainly bonds, which could be either held as revenue streams or used as the basis for new credit on repo markets. The credit system was now organized around asset-based accumulation: producing more and more assets, while generating more and more demand for these assets.[24]

The restructuring of the financial system around market-based finance, repo markets, and securitization—all of which were grounded in and supported asset-based accumulation—marked the formation of a *shadow banking system*. Shadow banking can be defined as "money-market funding of capital-market lending."[25] The shadow banking system linked securities markets and money markets in a new way. Shadow banking institutions borrowed on money markets to purchase securities on capital markets, which they posted as collateral for the money borrowed to purchase these securities. The collateral posted in repo contracts by shadow banks was often then posted again by its temporary holder as collateral to obtain further financing. This process was also closely linked to derivatives markets, as derivatives were used to reduce the risk of assets purchased with repo credit.

Like traditional banks, shadow banks created money. As we saw in chapter 2, traditional banks did so by purchasing bills of exchange and creating deposits. Through this process, they expanded both the asset and liability side of their balance sheets: they discounted bills of exchange (aquiring an asset) by generating deposits (liabilities) as an equivalent for these assets. Shadow banks functioned in much the same way. By borrowing short-term cash to purchase assets, they created a liability that they had to repay. Through the same transaction, they also acquired a new asset (the security), thus expanding both sides of their balance sheet simultaneously. New credit-money, which served as an equivalent for the asset purchased, had therefore been generated as a means of payment.[26]

The money-ness of this new "shadow money" was supported by the fact that it was convertible into state money or bank money.[27] Just as bank deposits could be converted into state money on demand, shadow money could be converted into bank money or state money as it was supported by collateral of greater or equal value in comparison to the credit generated. In other words, because the liability created by the shadow bank was collateralized by a security (Treasury bonds and mortgage-backed securities), there was a high degree of certainty that it could be transformed back into cash. The collateral that backed the new credit (that is, shadow money) acted as insurance for the institutional investor that lent the cash to the shadow bank, ensuring that the liability was always (at least theoretically) convertible into bank money or state money.

Far from being a parallel system of financing, shadow banking was fully integrated with the traditional banking system. Shadow banking did not involve the creation of new deposits or new currency. Rather, it generated a new form of credit-money that had to be settled through the transfer of bank deposits and state money, which were themselves the liabilities of traditional banks and the central bank (that is, they were generated through the creation of deposits by those institutions). Therefore, the shadow banking system was interconnected with the credit-generating capacities of the central bank, and thus with the modern system of public-private hybrid money that had taken shape with the creation of the Federal Reserve in the early twentieth century. Alongside bank money and state money, shadow money became a core component of the neoliberal financial system.

The centrality of short-term money markets in the neoliberal financial system in no way implies that finance as a whole had become more "short-termist." Indeed, credit generated on short-term markets need not necessarily be used for more short-term purposes. Nor was the explosion of short-term repo markets and securities markets, or even derivatives markets, strictly an indication that the financial system had become more "speculative" or "fictitious." The credit system was now organized around the integration of derivatives markets, money markets, and securities markets. Consequently, these markets naturally expanded alongside the expansion of credit-money.

Shadow banking fulfilled the function banks had always performed in transforming short-term financing into long-term credit—"borrowing short and lending long." Instead of a sudden withdrawal of deposits, shadow banks faced risks stemming from their ability to roll over debt in money markets. The new shadow banking system simply allowed financial institutions to flexibly meet their funding needs as required on a short-term basis. This implies nothing inherent about the nature of the activities from which such funding needs arose. In fact, the market-based system facilitated the more efficient use of capital insofar as it threw into circulation idle pools of money that could in turn be allocated to the most profitable activities.

Investment banks played an especially important part in the shadow banking system. Whereas in the pre-neoliberal period commercial banks could create credit relatively independently, this process was now more dependent on the role of investment banks. It was investment banks that underwrote the bonds that industrial corporations increasingly relied on to finance their operations. Moreover, as the most significant broker-dealers, they also traded and made markets in the assets that were the basis for commercial banks to create credit through securitization.[28] Investment banks also created many of the

Chart 4.4: Growth of investment bank, commercial bank, and non-financial corporate assets, 1980–2021

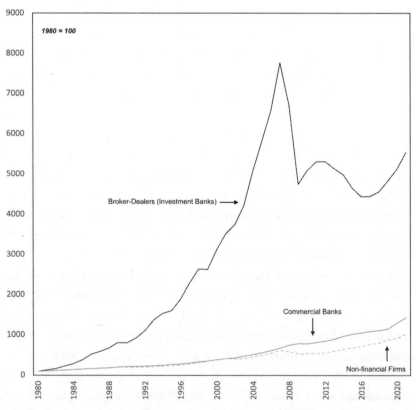

Source: *FRED, authors' calculations.* Note: *Index of billions; Security Brokers and Dealers total assets, Commercial Banks total assets, Non-Financial Corporate Business total assets.*

securities that were used in repo contracts to transfer cash between institutional investors, hedge funds, commercial banks, and other institutions. Furthermore, by purchasing securitized debt, they helped to create demand for the assets they created. They were also major players in increasingly important derivatives markets.

Chart 4.4 illustrates the dramatic growth of investment bank assets in comparison with commercial banks and non-financial corporations during the neoliberal era. Importantly, since the chart is indexed to 1980, it tends to conceal the fact that commercial banks started off much larger than investment banks and remained so throughout the neoliberal period. However, it clearly highlights the relatively rapid nature of the growth of investment banks, and thus points to their growing importance with the emergence of market-based finance. If commercial bank assets grew faster than those of non-financial corporations in the neoliberal period, those of the investment banks simply *exploded.*

To take advantage of this, commercial banks sought to expand into these markets by acquiring investment banks. While regulators initially resisted these moves, the state ultimately came around to embracing such mergers, culminating in the 1999 repeal of Glass-Steagall, which had separated commercial and investment banking and brought an end to finance capital. This regulatory change reflected an effort by state officials to construct more resilient financial institutions, as was also indicated by the Basel Accords, which set a floor on the amount of capital international banks had to have on hand. Repealing Glass-Steagall fit in with this project, as it would allow the formation of "mega-banks" capable of withstanding financial shocks, and which could more easily access liquidity provided by the Fed in the event of a crisis.

The repeal of Glass-Steagall, and the merger of commercial and investment banks, did not result in the return of the classical system of finance capital, however. In that period, investment banks represented the primary concentrations of money-capital in the economy, which they used to gain control of industrial assets. Such banks had held the securities they underwrote. In the neoliberal period, much more active equity markets encouraged very different investment banks to immediately sell the assets they created. Meanwhile, large commercial banks were far more involved in consumer debt markets, especially through the process of securitization. Although these practices were highly profitable, they oriented banks away from the corporate boardroom. As a result, the new mega-banks did not play anything like the direct role in corporate organization or management that investment banks had during the finance capital period.

Financialization and Authoritarian Statism

The importance of the investment banks in the polyarchic structure of financial power that accompanied market-based finance was further reflected in their political prominence. Goldman Sachs, perhaps the most important investment bank, acquired such an eminent place in the state, across administrations from both parties, that it acquired the nickname "Government Sachs." It maintained especially close ties to the Treasury Department. Robert Rubin, Secretary of the Treasury during the Clinton administration, had been a co-chair of the firm, while former CEO Hank Paulson occupied that post in the Bush administration. Similarly, Bush's chief economic advisor and his chief of staff, Stephen Friedman and Joshua Bolten, respectively, were both Goldman co-chairs. The firm contributed equally to Democratic and Republican candidates, and was the second-largest donor to Barack Obama.

More significant than the revolving door between leading financial institutions and state agencies, however, was the reorganization of the economic apparatus around the system of market-based finance. A range of new economic functions was internalized in the state, reconfiguring the boundary between the "political" and "economic." While the military-industrial complex continued to support the competitiveness of the most dynamic MNCs, a different set of institutions and practices now assumed the preeminent role in the state economic apparatus. The economic apparatus would now be dominated by its financial branch, led especially by the Federal Reserve, which also constituted the central hub of the financial system. Its ascent in the state reflected and reinforced the rise of finance, becoming the seat of power of that now-hegemonic fraction of capital.

All this pointed to just how wrong was the widespread idea that the state had retreated during neoliberal period. Indeed, in the late twentieth century, as in the early nineteenth, "laissez faire was planned."[29] That the OCC (the top banking regulator in the Treasury department) grew significantly faster than the financial system as a whole throughout the period of supposed "deregulation" indicated that what was at stake was not the elimination of regulations, but rather the construction of more flexible and extensive forms of regulation.[30] The SEC similarly acquired new powers to promote transparency and enforce leverage ratios on investment banks. Meanwhile, far from operating in a stateless world, the expansion of derivatives markets was supported and pushed forward by the Commodities Futures Trading Commission (CFTC), which helped to stabilize exchange rates and support market-based finance.[31] Of course, most important of all was the Fed, which coordinated the flow of finance across the economy.[32]

As we saw, the insulation of the Fed from democratic pressures allowed it to play the primary role in resolving the 1970s stagflation crisis by disciplining labor, which had proven so difficult for elected officials. The centralization of state power in such agencies was a clear illustration of the "regulatory independence" that would become a staple of neoliberal "good governance." Such independence protected these agencies from presidential or congressional intervention. This was secured by imposing legal limits on the ability for the president to remove officers, as well as placing them under the control of boards of directors or commissioners that were not appointed simultaneously and were often required to be bipartisan. As a result, the leadership and strategic direction of such agencies was insulated from "political" interference, whether in the form of pressures from the public or the capitalist firms.

Concentrating state power in such independent agencies thus effectively hollowed out democratic institutions. It removed a range of the most important decisions around macroeconomic management from the sphere of elections and politics and entrusted them instead to "neutral" technocratic administrators without any partisan or factional loyalty. This consolidation of "authoritarian statism" in the liberal democratic state diminished the role of parties, elected leaders, and representative assemblies, while empowering the state administration as not merely the "principal site" but also the "principal *actor* in the elaboration of state policy" regardless of electoral outcomes.[33] However, prioritizing accumulation over legitimation, and indeed entrenching a commitment to the former by disempowering and marginalizing the institutions responsible for the latter, generated the conditions for a legitimation crisis.

The independence of the major financial agencies in the economic apparatus originated in the 1930s. In the wake of the 1929 Wall Street crash, the independence of the SEC and FDIC was seen as essential to the construction of a new strong regulatory state. Such independence would limit popular input into policymaking and, equally importantly, would protect these fledgling agencies from being "captured" by capitalists. As we have seen, these same years also marked the origins of the Fed's independence, as the Treasury secretary and Comptroller of the Currency were removed from the Federal Reserve Board, shielding it from presidential pressure. Subsequently, the 1951 Fed-Treasury Accord fortified this autonomy, "liberating" monetary policy from the control of Congress and introducing significant new market discipline on state spending.[34]

In the structure of the New Deal state, central bank independence had served as a constraint on the expansion of social welfare programs, making spending decisions more accountable to market forces and the authoritarian institutions that embodied them. This served to internalize a contradiction in the state between, on the one hand, its *legitimation* functions, whereby regular elections, parties, representative democratic institutions, and social programs legitimated the state and social order, and, on the other, its *accumulation* functions, oriented toward creating the conditions for profitable investment. During the crisis of the 1970s, this contradiction had burst to the fore: capitalism could no longer support the largesse of the New Deal state, however popular these programs remained. This contradiction was resolved through the decisive centralization of state power in the economic apparatus, and the reorganization of the state complex more tightly around its accumulation functions.

The growing autonomy of the Fed over the managerial period had not prevented state spending from rising as a proportion of GDP—in fact, it had actually accommodated this by absorbing a large portion of government debt.[35] Despite the concern to restrain state spending, to a significant degree monetary policy in the New Deal state remained subordinate to fiscal policy decided by Congress. It was this failure to halt spending growth that generated the fiscal crisis of the state. This crisis was resolved in the neoliberal period through a shift from the "tax state" to the "debt state," whereby government expenditures were increasingly financed by borrowing rather than taxation.[36] Reliance on debt constrained fiscal policy, and thus reinforced the power of monetary authorities—that is, the Fed. As Bill Clinton famously exclaimed, "You mean to tell me that the success of the economic program and my

Chart 4.5: Federal government debt as a proportion of federal spending (%) (excluding debt held by Federal Reserve banks)

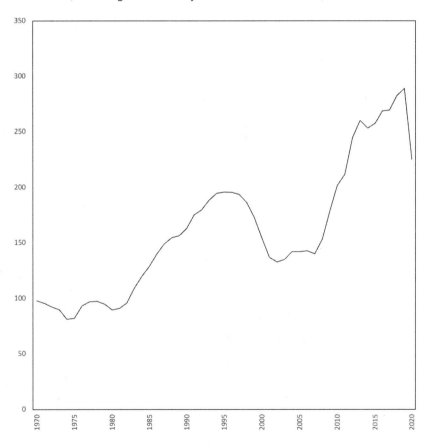

Source: *FRED, authors' calculations*

reelection hinges on the Federal Reserve and a bunch of fucking bond traders?"[37]

Chart 4.5 illustrates the transition from the tax state to the debt state. As it shows, a growing proportion of federal spending was financed through debt, beginning especially in the 1980s. One major effect of this was a dramatic increase in income inequality. Instead of paying taxes to support programs that, at least to some extent, redistributed income downward, the wealthiest now *loaned* the state money to be repaid *with interest*. These interest payments, in turn, were funded through either increasingly regressive taxation or further debt issues. The neoliberal state was thus a mechanism for the upward redistribution of wealth. At the same time, budgetary decisions came to be more dependent on the willingness of private investors to buy government bonds, reflected in market interest rates. This contributed to the pressure toward deregulation, tax cuts, and the rolling back of the New Deal state, all of which helped cut costs and restore profits.[38]

Neoliberal macroeconomic policy revolved around the low-inflation monetary regime implemented by the Fed. The objective of this policy framework was not only to reduce inflation, but also to preemptively combat *potential* inflationary pressures that could lead to the kind of wage-price spiral that had been at the root of the 1970s crisis. To do so, the Fed used its control over short-term interest rates to manage growth. Preventing the economy from "overheating" was necessary to maintain an industrial reserve army of the unemployed, disciplining labor and holding wages down by intensifying competition among workers for jobs. In this way, the Fed *actively* counteracted fiscal policy, as spending that stimulated "excessive" growth was counterbalanced by a policy of high interest rates, raising the cost of borrowing and thus dampening both investment and consumer demand.

The power of the Fed, and the imperative for it to impose discipline at home, was reinforced by the demands of its global role. The separation of the value of the currency from its link to gold meant that international confidence in the dollar relied more than ever on the Fed's commitment to fighting inflation, even at the expense of full employment. Meanwhile, stabilizing a volatile, globally integrated floating-rate monetary system required regular close coordination among central banks. This, along with the need to intervene rapidly and flexibly, also required central banks to be insulated from meddlesome parliamentary bodies. The rise of finance and the globalization of capital thus led not to the emergence of a laissez faire state, as held by neoliberal mythology, but rather relied upon the continuous intervention of an ever-more authoritarian state.

While the Fed had always provided liquidity to the financial system, the highly leveraged nature of market-based finance also made its interventions more important. Because these markets were based around short-term loans and razor-thin spreads, small fluctuations in interest rates or inflation could wipe out entire portfolios. The Fed's capacity to set short-term interest rates, and to support them through the targeted provision of liquidity, established a benchmark for all short-term lending among financial institutions. This limited the volatility that might otherwise have attended these short-term markets and created the consistency necessary for them to operate as a major source of credit. Repo markets simply could not exist without the Fed's inflation-targeting regime, and the liquidity it provided to keep these markets well-oiled.[39]

State power provided the foundation for the functioning of repo markets in other ways as well. If mortgages were one of the primary assets underpinning the provision of credit by serving as collateral on repo markets, government bonds were even more important. Recall that credit in a market-based system is generated through the exchange of collateral for cash. The expansion of credit-money in this system thus depends on the continuous production of stable collateral. As a result, US government bonds became the bedrock of the entire market-based credit system, since the backing of the state meant they were seen as an effectively risk-free and stable store of value—almost as good as cash. This allowed them to serve as the key collateral supporting the generation of credit and the production of new securities through being exchanged for the universal equivalent on repo markets.

The state, therefore, was essential to the basic integrity and routine functioning of the short-term markets that were at the center of market-based finance. Much like the bank-based credit system, whereby bank deposits could serve as money only through their integration with central bank reserves, the market-based financial system was fundamentally a hybrid of state power and private finance. The generation of repo credit (shadow money) was inseparably integrated with the production of state-backed assets. The debt state thus provided necessary fuel for the market-based financial system. The financing of state expenditure through the sale of state bonds also supplied the collateral that underpinned the purchase and sale of all securities—from corporate bonds and equity to mortgage-backed securities and derivatives. There was a direct correlation between the expansion of government debt and the expansion of private securities markets.

Meanwhile, the growing involvement of the state in the provision of mortgage debt meant that there was increasingly little difference between mortgage debt and government debt. Indeed, a major function of the economic apparatus in the neoliberal period was the conversion of private mortgage debt into quasi-government debt. This was the role of Fannie Mae and Freddie Mac. Though they were created during the New Deal to support the provision of housing for workers, in the neoliberal era they came to play an indispensable role in securitization. By this time, Fannie and Freddie were both publicly traded corporations, but were nevertheless still officially "government sponsored entities"—suggesting the state would step in to back them in the event of financial trouble. Fannie Mae even maintained an open line of credit with the Treasury Department.[40]

The integration of Fannie and Freddie with the state economic apparatus allowed them to produce a continuous supply of secure assets that could be used as collateral on repo markets. They did so through their role in securitization—purchasing mortgages from commercial banks and other mortgage originators and packaging them into bonds that they sold to other investors. These assets were formally new bond issues by Fannie and Freddie and were thus guaranteed by these institutions in that they assumed responsibility for paying both the interest and principal on the debt. They also held mortgages directly in their portfolios. Since these institutions were government sponsored, both the mortgage-backed securities they sold and the mortgages they held were effectively backed by the full faith and credit of the US Treasury

Department. By 2007, Freddie and Fannie held approximately half of all mortgages.[41]

Yet the infrastructural connection between state power and the market-based financial system went even deeper than directly and indirectly providing the collateral that supported credit creation, and limiting volatility by fighting inflation. In fact, the Fed also played a leading role in the construction of repo markets as the primary conduit of the neoliberal credit system. In the 1980s, the Fed crafted the new legal-regulatory framework that defined the complicated regime of property rights that allowed the system to function.[42] As the neoliberal period proceeded, the growing centrality of repo markets led the Fed to develop new policy strategies and modalities of intervention—which, in turn, were calibrated to further entrench the pivotal role of these markets in the financial system. The development of the economic apparatus and financial system were inextricably linked.

The Fed typically managed interest rates through the exchange of government bonds with large commercial banks, thereby affecting the supply of cash on interbank markets and influencing interest rates. Over the neoliberal period, the Fed increasingly conducted monetary policy through repo markets. It did so by temporarily selling or buying assets to increase or decrease the supply of cash, and therefore set interest rates, on these markets as well. In 1999, the Fed pushed these markets to accept mortgage-backed securities as safe collateral by accepting these assets in its own repo transactions. Critically, both means of managing interest rates required the Fed to continuously intervene in markets, adding and subtracting cash to meet its policy objectives. As much as any private institution, the trading desk at the New York Fed, through which these transactions occurred, was a mainstay in repo and interbank funding markets.

The evolution of the financial system, itself structured by the state, demanded new kinds of intervention, and the internalization of new functions in the economic apparatus. The redrawing of the boundary between the political and the economic in the neoliberal period through the expansion of the economic apparatus amounted to the growing statization of the financial system. Financial hegemony was supported by the state economic apparatus, even as the increasing importance of finance reciprocally propelled the ascent of the latter in the state. At the same time, the practices institutionalized in the economic apparatus increasingly shaped conditions on private financial markets and linked the fundamental pillars of the system more closely with state power. This process could in no sense be reduced to the "capture" of the state by parasitic financial institutions, nor did it mean that the state had simply mastered capital—quite the contrary. Indeed, the Fed's policy rates would become market rates only insofar as financial markets were functioning properly. And of course, the limits of the state's control over the capitalist economy would be revealed in dramatic fashion with the 2008 financial meltdown. The economic apparatus remained thoroughly dependent on the rhythms and dynamics of accumulation, the contradictions of which impelled still further forms of intervention.

In this way, the *decentralization* of the credit system through the development of market-based finance was supported by the simultaneous *centralization* of state power. Indeed, the fragmentation of credit creation across discrete financial institutions meant that the financial hegemony that defined the neoliberal era was distinctly polyarchic. Market-based finance integrated the new concentrations of equity ownership that had begun to take shape from the 1970s onward, especially in pension funds, into the credit system. The concentration of ownership of industrial firms and the allocation of credit were once again emerging as co-constituted and mutually interdependent processes. Credit and equity had been separated through the New Deal period; with market-based finance, these two components of the financial system began to become reunited.

Crucially, neoliberal financialization was neither dysfunctional to the health and dynamism of capital accumulation nor divorced from production and the exploitation of labor. All the "speculative" markets at the center of the neoliberal credit system—from derivatives markets to short-term repo markets and bond markets—served to competitively circulate capital across the economy. The process of loan-making was now entirely bound up with these markets and the various financial instruments that defined them. Furthermore, the development of shadow banking meant that securities were no longer sources of credit merely in the sense that investors purchased them, and thereby transferred cash to the seller in exchange for credit-money. Now, even after being issued, these assets *themselves* became foundations for further credit creation by serving as collateral on repo markets.

As such, all of these markets became critical means through which capitalist firms today acquire credit, which flows into both M-M' and M-C-M' circuits, as well as (in the case of derivatives) ensure the integrity of the financial and industrial capital they circulate globally. Moreover, insofar as non-financial corporations have themselves become major lenders on these money-markets, the interest they collect by circulating money-capital is amalgamated with the earnings generated by their industrial capitals, and can be reinvested in "productive" or financial circuits. By the same token, of course, these non-financial corporations also borrow on these markets, and direct these funds to both industrial and financial capitals that they control. Meanwhile, stock buybacks release surplus cash from highly profitable corporations into financial markets for use elsewhere.

For thirty years, the neoliberal authoritarian state presided over this financialized global capitalism, remaining fixed on its anti-inflation orientation as corporations constructed internationally integrated production networks. This configuration of power contained discontent even as working-class life became ever more precarious as plants closed and production was offshored. Both political parties embraced the neoliberal consensus, forcefully insisting that "there is no alternative." The power of the Fed to manage the economy was considered just as sacred as, and even less partisan than, the Supreme Court's authority to interpret the law. With the crucial questions of economic policy decided in venues that were largely outside of public view and beyond the reach of elections—and which thereby embodied "the continuity of the state" regardless of electoral outcomes—politics increasingly focused on cultural and civil rights issues *within* the structure of corporate capitalism.[43]

The 2008 Crisis and the Question of Decline

Through the neoliberal period, finance became increasingly prominent in the structure of accumulation, establishing the critical infrastructure that enabled the global restructuring of production, restoring industrial corporate profits and unleashing competitive pressures on a vast scale. Yet because this was accompanied by rising economic inequality and the loss of manufacturing jobs through "deindustrialization," and because finance was capturing a larger share of profits, many concluded that finance was *antagonistic* to the health and dynamism of industry. Moreover, that industrial firms were increasingly investing in financial services seemed to suggest that industry was being "hollowed out," as "real" production was replaced by financial activities. The notion that financialization amounts to a cancerous new "short-termism" has today all but become common sense.[44]

The point of departure for this perspective is often the work of William Lazonick, who has been the leading scholar making the case that restraining the power of finance can restore the "prosperous economy" of the pre-neoliberal—and supposedly pre-financialized—golden age of capitalism. Lazonick sees financialization as essentially consisting of the looting of firms by managers and Wall Street investors, who seek to divert corporate funds from productive investment into their own pockets through share buybacks and dividend payments. Since top managers are compensated in equity, they stand to make windfall gains from temporarily boosting share prices and cashing in stock options, at the expense of production and R and D. Therefore, he concludes, banning buybacks will increase industrial firms' retained earnings, which can then be invested in creating the lifelong "good jobs" that supposedly characterized the managerial period.

However, as we have seen, it was precisely the retained earnings accumulated during the postwar managerial period that contributed so strongly to the financialization of the firm in the first place. The lending of these surpluses on capital markets—an important foundation for market-based finance—contributed to the rise of an M-M' logic in the corporation. Thus, even if banning buybacks were to succeed in increasing industrial firms' retained earnings, there is no reason to believe these would necessarily be invested in non-financial activities. Moreover, the global mobility of capital means that corporate investment would be directed to wherever labor, regulatory, and tax costs were the lowest. Yet Lazonick does not call for capital controls, or any limit on the capital mobility that has driven globalization and the intensification of competitiveness. The idea that "good jobs" will return to the Rust Belt absent such barriers is pure fancy.

To be sure, the restructuring of corporate governance in the neo-liberal period does reflect the empowerment of finance, as we have seen, including a central role for the stock market in distributing surplus value to financial institutions. Corporations contribute to the valorization of the money-capital owned by these financial institutions through dividend payments as well as by undertaking buybacks and otherwise seeking to boost share values. The stock market thus serves as a nexus whereby surplus flows from the non-financial firm to investors, just as surplus generated through production undertaken in corporate divisions is distributed in the firm back to management. The primary difference is that, unlike the relationship in the industrial firm between industry and finance, insofar as top managers are themselves money-capitalists, the distribution of surplus between outside investors and insider managers occurs *within finance itself.*

In neither case can the distribution of a portion of the surplus back to money-capitalists be understood simply as cancerous or parasitic. On the contrary, as these surpluses flow to financiers, the latter invest these funds however they may be most profitably deployed. Stock buy-backs and dividends release excess funds to outside financiers, who then redistribute them to other financial activities (including speculation) as well as across the various branches of production. There is no intrinsic reason why the allocation of investment should be the sole purview of corporate executives in industrial firms that have themselves become financialized. If anything, external financial institutions and capital markets are even more mobile and competitive than even the most financialized of industrial firms.

The implication of Lazonick's analysis is that workers should form an alliance with industrial firms, which have allegedly been victimized by financialization, to rein in the power of finance. Yet it was not finance *per se* that was responsible for the loss of manufacturing jobs and the devastation of working-class communities; rather, these processes were rooted in the increasing global mobility of capital. Finance was not parasitic on industry, but actually *enabled* industrial firms to undertake new strategies for competitively restructuring their operations so as to intensify exploitation and labor discipline, restoring profits. High wages may have been part of the "prosperous economy" of the postwar decades, but this had come with its own contradictions, ultimately leading to a crisis, which finance was key to *resolving*.

If this social democratic framing avoids confronting the fundamental problems of capitalism, many Marxists have also interpreted the rise of finance as a symptom of capitalist stagnation and decline. This is seen as being an outcome either of a general capitalist tendency for the rate of profit to fall or of overaccumulation in a monopoly capitalist stage.[45] Especially influential in this regard have been Robert Brenner and the *Monthly Review* school, and more recently Cédric Durand, who have argued that low rates of profit in industry led investors and corporations to divert capital toward financial activities—driving the growth of the

Chart 4.6: R and D spending as a percent of GDP, 1980–2019

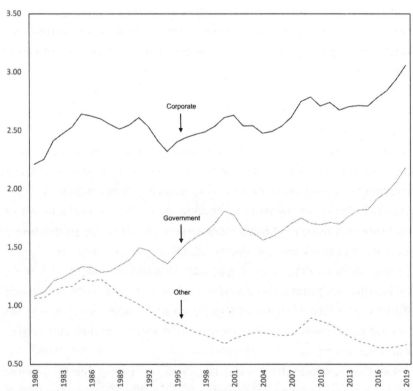

Source: *National Science Foundation, authors' calculations*

latter and creating a self-perpetuating cycle of financialization and industrial dysfunction. While declinist Marxist accounts accept that investment in fictitious capital has yielded significant profits, they argue that the underlying stagnation in the "real economy" means that this has merely postponed the inevitable reckoning by generating a series of speculative bubbles.[46]

The idea that the neoliberal period was marked by a decline in corporate profits, investment, or R and D spending is simply a myth. Far from American industry having been weakened through financialization, it was during the 1980s and 1990s that the group of cutting-edge high-tech firms that still dominate the global marketplace today, such as Apple and Microsoft, first emerged. In fact, as chart 4.6 illustrates, R and D spending as a percent of GDP grew throughout the neoliberal era. Even more remarkably, corporate R and D spending grew *faster* than state spending on R and D—more than compensating for the decline in the latter as a percentage of GDP (though still rising in absolute terms). Clearly, this is wildly inconsistent with the claim that industrial corporations have been diverting investment toward short-term speculation that jeopardizes their dynamism and competitiveness.

There was also no collapse in corporate investment during the neoliberal period. On the contrary, as chart 4.7 illustrates, corporate investment in these years sharply increased relative to GDP growth, significantly diverging from the postwar norm. Like R and D spending, investment only *appears* to have declined when seen as a percentage of corporate profits, which is the measure that William Lazonick and other theorists of "hollowing out" have typically relied on. Since corporate profits have been relatively high, this misleadingly suggests that investment is declining, as corporations divert a larger share of their income to buybacks and dividend payments. In reality, the fact that corporations are making higher profits—partly as a result of financial restructuring—means that they are able to pay out investors *without* reducing investment or jeopardizing their long-term economic health.

The sharp increase in investment in new fixed capital in this period yielded a tremendous increase in the mass of non-financial corporate profits. It is ironic that the case that investment has been low—and

Chart 4.7: Private non-residential fixed investment and GDP, 1950–2022

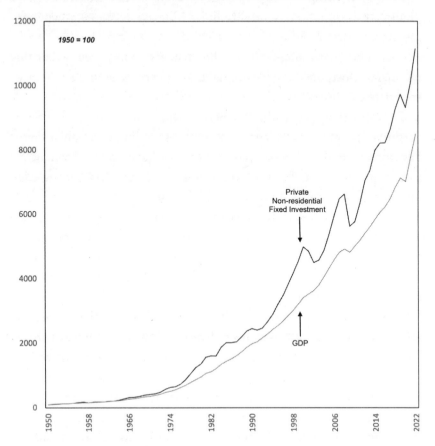

Source: *FRED, authors' calculations*

thus that industry is declining at the hands of a parasitic financial sector—is often predicated on the fact that profits were historically *high* throughout the neoliberal period. Although financial profits have grown faster than industrial profits and have therefore come to make up a larger share of the total (chart 4.1), this by no means implies that industrial profits have been shrinking in absolute terms. As chart 4.8 shows, the opposite is true: the profits of non-financial corporations exploded during the neoliberal era. Financialization and asset-based accumulation in no way came at the expense of corporate profitability; rather, they were founded on, and enabled, the *success* of corporate America.

Marxist assessments of neoliberalism as characterized by industrial decline are often based on the supposed general capitalist tendency of the rate of profit to fall. Yet far too little attention is paid to the *mass* of profits. The rate of profit refers to the mass of profit produced per unit of investment. As we saw in chapter 3, a sharp drop in the rate of profit in the face of worker resistance was at the root of the 1970s crisis, leading capitalists to refrain from investing for fear that they would not receive adequate returns. However, with the profit rate stabilized over the neoliberal period (at around 7.5 percent) through the reduction of the wage share of national income, slashing of taxes, and low interest rates, capital could again feel confident that investment would yield comfortable returns—which were more than adequate to cover new investment, executive salaries, and "shareholder value."

Central to the stabilization of the profit rate was the intensification of the exploitation of labor. The divergence between labor productivity and wages in the neoliberal period (as shown in chart 3.4) meant that a larger share of the value produced by workers was captured by capitalists. This rising rate of exploitation reflected the disciplining of labor, technological development, and the globalization of production to lower-wage zones. These gains for capital offset increasing investment in fixed capital, such as machinery and technology, thereby stabilizing the rate of profit (as illustrated in chart 3.5). Additionally, not only did these new technologies make labor more productive, but the productivity of capital increased as well: they were both labor-saving and capital-saving. On this basis, increased investment generated a significant increase in the mass of profit by the 1990s (chart 4.8).

There is no mythic "normal" rate of profit. Nor is there any reason the rate of profit should continue to rise. To be sure, the rate of profit in the neoliberal period was lower than that of the postwar managerial period. But if all eras that do not match the performance of the biggest boom in the history of capitalism are seen as being in crisis, it is no surprise that crisis is found nearly everywhere. The concept of crisis itself loses its temporal specificity. Indeed, far from representing a historical norm, the postwar boom was highly exceptional. The crucial point is that so long as capital can cover its costs and make adequate returns, there is no necessary crisis in the system. Capitalists could

Chart 4.8: Pre-tax non-financial corporate profits (USD billions), 1970–2021

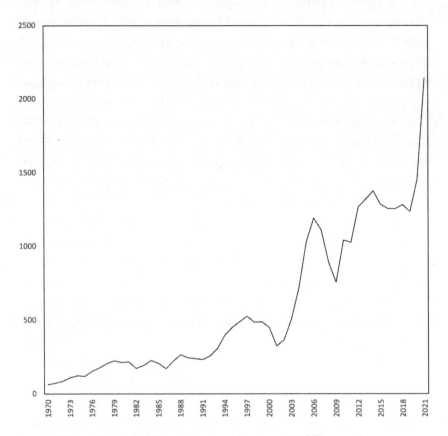

Source: *FRED, authors' calculations.* Note: *Annual average, USD billions.*

hardly have seen the tremendous mass of profits generated in the neo-liberal period as a problem.

It is simply not correct to suggest that the neoliberal era has been characterized by "secular stagnation," a "long downturn," the "hollow-ing out" of industry by finance, or American decline, as so many have claimed. Even if corporations were increasingly subject to financial dis-cipline, the most striking feature of this period is the deepening *entanglement* of financial and industrial capital. High profits allowed industrial corporations and other investors to *both* reinvest in produc-tion *and* return unneeded cash to shareholders. Nor did financialization imply that the global power of the American state was on the decline;

on the contrary, global financial integration represented the culmination of the American imperial project of "making global capitalism." The rise of finance represented a challenge neither to production nor to American hegemony, but rather the exact opposite: it was a basic component of the American imperial order that made globalization possible.[47]

Lest one conclude that all this is merely an academic exercise, it must be noted that the political consequences of these arguments are significant. If one interprets neoliberalism as a period of crisis rooted in the fundamental and eternal tendency for the rate of profit to fall—albeit mitigated by various "countertendencies"—then this implies that capitalism is bound to collapse on its own sooner or later. If, on the other hand, the rate of profit in neoliberalism is perfectly adequate for capital, and there is no inevitable reversal of this necessarily on the horizon, then it is the political agency of the working class to which we must look in seeking to create a new post-capitalist world. This implies a difficult political project of organizing workers and building class power, as opposed to simply cheering every dip in the stock market as the latest harbinger of capitalism's demise.

The crisis of 2008 was thus not a manifestation of the parasitic influence of finance or the underlying falling rate of profit. Rather, it reflected the volatility of the system of market-based finance. As the chain that supported credit creation broke down, the financial system was crippled by the most severe crisis since the 1930s. Those agencies that had come to play leading roles in the neoliberal state, especially the Fed and the Treasury, undertook a series of radical and unprecedented interventions to reconstruct the financial system and restore accumulation. These interventions greatly intensified the asset concentration that had already been a hallmark of the neoliberal period. While this ultimately led to the transition to a new phase of capitalism, as we will see, it by no means pointed to the decline of American power: on the contrary, not only did capitalism survive the deep recession, but the global role of the American state was actually *reinforced* by the crisis.

The crisis began in July 2007, when the value of the mortgage bonds supplied as collateral by two major hedge funds on repo markets suddenly dropped in value. This signaled that the mortgage assets that had been seen as unshakeable foundations for the entire system of market-based finance were tottering. As uncertainty spread, the crisis rippled through structured investment vehicles, insurance firms, derivatives markets, money-market mutual funds, pension funds, investment and commercial banks, and eventually all financial institutions that relied on the short-term funding markets that were at the center of the neoliberal credit system. The crisis struck the heart of the system when Fannie and Freddie—the state institutions that had been so critical for grounding the stability of mortgage-backed securities—collapsed in September 2008.

The problems that emerged in the financial system as the crisis spread were amplified significantly by the role of derivatives. Particularly hard hit was the market for credit default swaps (CDS), a critical cornerstone of market-based finance. Because this system is based on short-term lending among highly leveraged financial institutions rather than deposits guaranteed by the FDIC, market participants used CDS, a specific kind of derivative contract, to manage their risks. Meanwhile, the banks and insurance companies that issued these contracts collected premium payments from the purchaser. Similar to an insurance contract, since these payments exceeded likely claims, they were able to serve as a source of profit. Banks themselves also purchased CDS to mitigate their exposure to the risk that came with the CDS they issued.

Between 2004 and 2007, the CDS market grew from $6 trillion to $58 trillion.[48] The top twenty-five US banks came to hold $13 trillion in CDS obligations, with the vast majority of this market controlled by JPMorgan, Bank of America, Citibank, Morgan Stanley, and Goldman Sachs.[49] The insurance firm AIG was also a significant player in these markets. As mortgage-backed securities and other securitized debt collapsed in value and started to bring down large institutions that could not access the short-term repo markets they needed to roll over their debt, they triggered CDS and forced banks and insurance firms to make billion-dollar payments to clients. This led, in turn, to the collapse of the investment banks and insurance firms and created further blockages in short-term funding markets.

It would thus be wrong to single out *derivatives* as the cause of the crisis. Rather, it was a crisis of the system itself. In many respects, the crisis resembled that of the 1930s, in which the instability of the banks led depositors to demand their cash—in what is known as a "bank run." The 2008 crisis was also a bank run, albeit one targeted at the shadow banking system around which market-based finance was structured. As questions arose about the stability of mortgage collateral, panic ensued and investors stopped lending cash on repo markets—"a run on repo."[50] Suddenly, the institutions that depended on these markets were short of cash and had no way of rolling over their highly leveraged balance sheets. These institutions were by no means bankrupt; they had hundreds of billions of dollars in assets. The problem was a liquidity crisis: they could not transform these assets into cash. Also, as in the 1930s, the state infrastructure needed to support the system had not yet been developed.[51]

The failure of the market-based financial system demanded an unprecedented rescue by the American state. The Fed, in particular, was given extraordinary powers to manage the financial collapse. It flooded markets with liquidity and established "swap lines" of credit with central banks around the world whereby they could exchange other currencies for dollars. This helped stabilize offshore dollar markets, which were a critical source of funding for corporations and financial firms internationally. Similarly, it orchestrated the consolidation of the banking sector through the merger of commercial and investment banks, or by rechartering investment banks as commercial banks. This amounted to a radical state-led restructuring of the entire financial system, as the standalone investment banks that had existed since the end of the finance capital period, and whose broker-dealer functions were central to the market-based financial system, were once again fully merged with commercial banks.[52]

Despite massive pressure by the Treasury and the Fed to pass the Troubled Asset Relief Program (TARP) as an emergency measure, overwhelming public backlash to the "bailout" initially led to its rejection by Congress. In a glaring instance of the contradiction between legitimation and accumulation, a second vote was held just weeks later—this time succeeding, after Fed Chair Ben Bernanke warned that "the sky would collapse" if the bill was not passed.[53] Yet even the $700 billion the bill provided the Treasury to absorb "troubled assets" from banks was nowhere near sufficient. As such, just weeks later the Fed acted—on its own—to cleanse *trillions* of dollars in toxic waste from bank balance sheets through so-called quantitative easing (QE). TARP funds were instead directed to effectively nationalize the banks—albeit without gaining public control of them.

In other words, immediately after exerting massive pressure on Congress to pass TARP, the Fed essentially ignored it, undertaking a program many times its size—even though TARP was already considered too large by legislators and much of the public. Meanwhile, TARP funds were directed to purposes beyond those contained in the bill. It would be hard to find a clearer illustration of the authoritarian nature of the neoliberal state, or of the subordination of legitimation to accumulation.

Nevertheless, the lack of any real capacity to legitimate the bailout of the financial sector did come at the price of overwhelming public anger. This was especially understandable in the context of the wave of foreclosures that hit homeowners. Foreclosure filings averaged about three million per year between 2008 and 2010—equaling about one in fifty homes *each year*.[54] Even those homes that were not foreclosed upon often ended up "underwater," or with a value that was less than their total outstanding mortgage debt. This served to limit access to the home equity lines of credit that homeowners had come to rely on to sustain purchasing power in the context of stagnating or declining real wages across the neoliberal period. Yet for those managing the capitalist state, helping consumers did not constitute an emergency in the way that stabilizing the financial system did.

Especially hard-hit were holders of so-called subprime mortgages, which allowed consumers who would not traditionally be considered creditworthy to receive mortgage loans to buy houses—albeit at exorbitant rates of interest after an initially lower "teaser rate." Banks were incentivized to issue such subprime mortgages as a result of their ability to profit by selling them to other financial institutions. These financial institutions, in turn, pooled them with higher-grade mortgages and sold them as mortgage-backed securities, which, as we have seen, served as the primary source of collateral in short-term repo markets. Given the backing of the state for mortgages, it was understandable that credit-rating agencies, which assign risk categories to debt securities, classified these as highly secure investment-grade assets—equivalent to US government debt.

If the crisis revealed the extent to which the state would be dragged into the management of the contradictions of financialized capitalism, the political upheaval this produced provided a stark illustration of the significance of authoritarian statism in insulating the major power centers in the economic apparatus from public or congressional interference. The chaos and dysfunction provoked by the right-wing Tea Party in Congress, which had already engaged in hair-raising brinksmanship around raising the "debt ceiling," now took the form of efforts to derail the financial rescue and stimulus spending. However, the insulation of the Fed allowed its massive rescue effort to proceed largely without public scrutiny. Thus, when the Fed supported JPMorgan's takeover of Bear Stearns by absorbing $30 billion in toxic assets, this appeared on its balance sheet only as "Maiden Lane LLC."

But the financial crisis also created an opening for the Occupy Wall Street movement to promote a narrative of class struggle, which pointed to the failure of both parties to present meaningful alternatives to working-class indebtedness and precarity. Trillions were spent on finance, while homes were foreclosed on at record rates and police marched through one Occupy encampment after another—all under a Democratic administration. This sharply accelerated the delegitimation of neoliberal ideology, both political parties, the state, and the media system. Even as the state saved capitalism, the economic crisis was morphing into a political crisis. The crisis would reverberate out from the political parties, which were each wracked by major electoral insurgencies, throughout the state complex. The state would struggle to contain its effects, while consolidating a new regime of finance capital.

5

The New Finance Capital and the Risk State

After banks were separated from industrial firms by New Deal regulations, a new fusion of financial and industrial capital began to emerge *within* the corporation over the postwar decades. Diversification and internationalization during the "golden age" led to the characteristic pattern of corporate centralization-decentralization, in which investment functions were centralized in the hands of top management while operational control over production was decentralized to divisional managers. The result was the conversion of top executives into financiers, and the internalization in the firm of money markets. By the neoliberal period, top industrial managers were engaged in the circulation of interest-bearing capital across competing business divisions, structured as portfolios of financial assets. As a result, it became increasingly difficult to draw any clear distinction between financial and industrial firms—particularly since the latter came to engage in explicitly "financial" businesses, from lending to financial services.

The empowerment of finance within the industrial corporation was reinforced by the growing power of investors outside the firm. This power was spread across a diversity of institutions whose common interests and influence over corporations were articulated through loose coalitions, rather than the centralized financial control exercised by the investment banks of the classical finance capital period. The connection between financial institutions and corporations in this period was therefore far less direct than that which Hilferding described, and it was mediated by competitive markets for corporate control. Nevertheless, the concentration of equity into large blocs controlled by institutional investors prompted the latter to become more actively engaged in the governance of the industrial corporation—expanding "shareholder rights" and insisting on a larger number of "independent directors" on more powerful corporate boards of directors. In other words, investors were increasingly involved in the management of industrial capital: they were becoming industrialists.

Following the 2008 crisis, a new group of asset management companies—especially the Big Three, BlackRock, Vanguard, and State Street—amassed unprecedented concentrations of assets, combining the pools of money-capital accumulated in pension funds and other financial institutions. These giant asset management companies displaced the banks as the most powerful institutions in the financial system. Critical to their rise was the consolidation in the state of an extensive range of new economic practices as it was restructured in the wake of the crisis. The new "risk state" formed in this period deployed the capacity of the state to mitigate and absorb financial risk to maintain low interest rates, which also led to a prolonged period of asset price inflation and fueled the turn to "passive" investment funds managed by the Big Three. On the other hand, post-crisis financial regulations constrained the power of the mega-banks formed by the Fed after the crisis to stabilize and strengthen the financial system.

The rise of these asset management companies was part and parcel of a historic restructuring of corporate power: the formation of a new finance capital. The concentration of equity established asset managers' control over industrial capital, expressed through their interconnection with corporate governance structures. Reciprocally, surplus value generated by these circuits of industrial capital flowed back to asset managers in the form of dividend payments and stock buybacks. The holdings of these asset management companies were unprecedented not only in their extreme concentration but also in their diversification. As a result, these financial firms became the central nodes in an extensive network of corporate control that incorporated nearly every major firm from every sector in the economy. This vast new institutional superstructure established a fusion of financial and industrial capital, eliminating the old distinction between "ownership" and "control" that had been a central aspect of corporate power since the New Deal.

The new fusion of financial and industrial capital meant that these asset management firms became more actively and directly involved in governing industrial corporations. Driven by the imperative to maximize profits, these companies pushed for greater control over corporate boards that were increasingly empowered to oversee "insider" managers, alongside other reforms to increase shareholder power. The threat of exercising voting rights in shareholder meetings ensured that asset managers had the ear of corporate executives, and allowed them to exert influence through routine coordination with insiders. Indeed, asset management firms were hardly shy about voting against management when they saw this as necessary. Yet far from establishing de facto "economic planning," it was the coercive laws of competition, above all, that led these companies to transform their concentrated and diversified holdings into a system of centralized economic power unseen since the days of J. P. Morgan—and indeed surpassing it.

Crisis Management and the Risk State

Crises in capitalism are not the exception, but the rule. Because crises are rooted in the fundamental dynamics of accumulation—between production and realization, between abstract and concrete, and of course the conflict between classes—capital can never resolve its crisis tendencies. While the crises of capital can be temporarily abated through restructuring, this simultaneously establishes the conditions for the next crisis. Thus, as we have seen, the transitions between phases of capitalist development (finance capital, managerialism, neoliberalism) were marked in each case by crises. The financial meltdown of 2008 was no different. While it may appear paradoxical that finance emerged from the crisis stronger than it was beforehand, in fact the post-crisis period saw a deep and profound restructuring of the financial system—and the reorganization of the accumulation around the dominance of a new capitalist class fraction.

The new finance capital was largely institutionalized in a group of asset management firms that came to dominate the financial system in the years following the 2008 crisis as a result of the radical extension of state power over a wide range of "economic" institutions and practices. As the state economic apparatus expanded through the reconstruction of the financial system following the meltdown, asset management companies concentrated the dispersed financial power of the neoliberal period and forged deeper and closer links with industrial corporations. In place of the diffuse discipline exerted by financial institutions were concentrated, centralized, and highly diversified institutional networks. Competitive markets for corporate control were consolidated into stable networks of power, whose scope and breadth was without precedent.

The state intervened to rebuild the financial system through two interrelated phases. First was *stabilization*, characterized by the ad hoc deployment of state power to manage the immediate fallout of the crisis. In this phase, the state effectively nationalized the central organs of market-based finance. Out of these interventions came the second phase: the *consolidation* of a new "risk state" as "emergency" measures became integral to the "normal" functioning of the financial system.[1] The risk state is defined by the extension of state power to risk-proof specific asset classes and support the major institutional pillars of market-based finance. Indeed, the flip side of the consolidation of new practices in the state economic apparatus was the dramatic statization of the financial system, as state power increasingly merged with and constituted the basic architecture of the market-based financial system—which came to be dominated by giant asset management companies.[2]

The stabilization phase was characterized by the expansion of the Fed's traditional role as "lender of last resort" to *dealer* of last resort, reflecting the centrality of shadow banking in the financial system.[3] The Fed effectively became the most active agent in the market-based system, directly exchanging securities for cash, and cash for securities, to backstop the financial institutions and key assets underpinning it. In essence, the Fed extended new support for repo and money markets through temporary transfers of cash and assets, while simultaneously imposing new regulations on the banks that limited their participation in these markets. As we will see, this created space for the ascent of a group of asset management companies that were left outside of the new regulatory system.

At first, state crisis-fighting efforts relied largely on the "convening powers" of the Fed and the Treasury, whereby they could call together financial institutions and attempt to persuade them to undertake coordinated action to stabilize markets—but without the support of state funding. Such intervention was initially centered around the large commercial banks, and aimed primarily to support the structured investment vehicles that were at the epicenter of the crisis in its earliest days. The Treasury attempted to create what it called a Master Liquidity Enhancement Conduit (M-LEC), which was designed to put a floor under the mortgage-backed securities SIVs were then frantically dumping to acquire cash amid the seizure of short-term funding markets. As SIVs were the major owners of mortgage-backed securities, the Treasury's "conduit" would have effectively created a "super-SIV" that would purchase the assets of the existing SIVs.

Yet as the plan would have left the private owners of this super-SIV highly exposed, it never got off the ground. Subsequently, the Fed's actions were defined by its direct penetration of the various institutions that made up the market-based system. This started with the bailout of the large, standalone investment banks, whose functions as broker-dealers of the key forms of collateral on repo markets made them critical pillars of the neoliberal credit system. This bailout took the form of the Fed absorbing losses, and then either merging investment banks with commercial banks or re-chartering them as commercial banks. The Fed then directly took over Fannie and Freddie, thereby becoming the guarantor of the mortgage-backed securities issued by these institutions. Similarly, by taking over the insurance giant AIG, the Fed put state support behind the credit default swap market. The Fed also directly intervened to support short-term markets, including repo markets, by purchasing key securities and thereby supporting their value.

The Fed also increased the stability of the banking system by reorganizing it around a handful of mega-banks integrated more closely with state power. By either merging the largest remaining investment banks with commercial banks or converting them into commercial banks, the Fed created a smaller number of larger and more resilient banks. As a result, the Big Four banks—Bank of America, JPMorgan, Citibank, and Wells Fargo—emerged as pillars of a more robust financial order. Erasing the boundary between commercial and investment banks also extended the Fed's emergency liquidity-creating powers from commercial banks to investment banks. Critical broker-dealer functions were now more closely connected to the Fed. Orchestrating concentration in the banking sector through the merger of commercial and investment banking thereby broadened the Fed's support for market-based finance, enlarging the scope of financial practices reinforced by state power.

At the same time, the Fed also created a new monetary policy system, known as interest on excess reserves (IOER), whereby private interbank lending markets were significantly displaced by the direct interposition of state power.[4] Short-term interest rates are established by the rates at which banks lend excess capital (over and above the reserve requirements set by regulators) on inter-bank lending markets. The Fed had long managed these rates by adding and subtracting cash through the purchase and sale of Treasury bonds. Absorbing cash from, or adding cash to, bank balance sheets allowed the Fed to affect the supply of cash on interbank markets, thereby influencing interest rates. However, with the enormous expansion of the money supply through QE, it became impossible to set rates through such means. Incremental shifts in the volume of funds on this market were inconsequential in relation to the *trillions* of dollars in excess reserves now in the system.

IOER resolved this dilemma by directly paying banks interest for depositing this cash with the Fed. Since banks would never lend to each other at a lower rate than that offered by the Fed, the latter became the benchmark in these markets, and thereby across the system as a whole. This drastically reorganized inter-bank lending, which had been a crucial crisis-point in 2008. As the solvency of the big banks was thrown into question with the intensification of the crisis, banks had stopped lending to each other. Now, state power directly secured the flow of financing across the banking system. Instead of merely managing the supply of liquidity to influence interest rates, the Fed now directly provided short-term capital to financial institutions. Decentralized market exchanges between private banks were now centralized around the Fed as the primary counterparty to which banks loaned their excess reserves.

Similarly, the Dodd-Frank financial reform legislation empowered the state economic apparatus to designate systemically important financial institutions (SIFIs), which brought additional state protection by implying that such institutions were "too big to fail." Together with the state's demonstrated practice of rescuing troubled financial institutions, such a designation created a so-called "moral hazard" whereby large financial firms could not realistically expect to fail in the event of a crisis. By absorbing private financial risk through guaranteeing state support for these financial institutions, the risk state paradoxically incentivized them to accumulate larger amounts of risk than they otherwise might have. To compensate for this, such a designation came with the imposition of a more robust regulatory apparatus that integrated these firms more tightly under state supervision, and limited the risk these institutions took on.

The purpose of the SIFI designation was not to punish or weaken the banks, but rather to rebuild and strengthen the architecture of market-based finance by extending the power of the state over the core institutions that composed it. Yet this also came with additional requirements on the amount of "safe" capital that banks had to have on hand; periodic "stress tests," whereby regulators determined the ability for bank balance sheets to handle a range of extreme scenarios; and a requirement to produce "living wills" laying out emergency plans for how bank assets could be broken up and sold in the event of failure. These regulations were enforced by the Financial Services Oversight Council, created by the Dodd-Frank Act and headed by the Fed and the Treasury, which were given significant latitude in naming SIFIs and applying regulations. In addition to the expansion of its powers through Dodd-Frank, the Fed even embedded full-time staff directly in large financial firms to oversee their risk management operations.[5]

Dodd-Frank's infamous Volcker Rule prevented banks from engaging in "proprietary trading," or investing consumer deposits for their own gain rather than trading on behalf of clients for commission. The objective was to prevent banks from using FDIC-insured deposits to build their own asset portfolios—which could have resulted in the conversion of deposits into huge bank-controlled concentrations of assets, with interest paid back to depositors from asset sales or dividend payments. Meanwhile, any losses could be covered by FDIC insurance. The Volcker Rule also blocked banks from owning firms that engage in high-risk trading, such as private equity firms and hedge funds. At the same time, new leverage and liquidity rules limited the ability for banks to take advantage of the state support they were receiving to infinitely expand their balance sheets. Consequently, institutional cash pools, such as pension funds and insurance firms, were increasingly pushed into repo markets rather than bank deposits.

The stabilization phase of state intervention thus amounted to a wholesale takeover of the market-based financial system, aiming to hold its fragmenting pieces together and sustain the flow of credit. Crucial to this as well was quantitative easing. Through QE, the Fed provided cash to cash-strapped financial institutions by purchasing mortgage-backed securities and Treasury bonds. As we have seen, these assets were the primary collateral on the repo markets that were at the center of the market-based financial system, and critical for the balance sheets of shadow banks. The plunge in the value of mortgage-backed securities that would have resulted from a "fire-sale" scenario, as financial institutions panic-sold these assets, would have undermined the basic foundations of the entire credit system. By ensuring the value of these assets, the Fed was not only bailing out banks or supporting mortgage markets but stabilizing the financial system itself.

The initial round of QE thus extended the power of the state to bestow risk-free status on the large number of mortgage-backed securities issued by Fannie and Freddie, effectively making them more or less equivalent to Treasury bonds. This, in turn, supported the operation of the financial system more broadly. With the onset of the crisis, the stability of Treasury bonds was not an issue—in fact, as uncertainty spread, demand for these "safe-haven" assets, fully supported and backed by the US state, increased. By extending similar protection over the lion's share of mortgage-backed securities, the Fed further integrated the other central pivot around which the system of market-based finance revolved with state power. While the Fed could not grant these securities the status of actual currency, it could use its capacity to purchase almost unlimited quantities of them to impart equally unlimited state support—a level of backing paralleled only by government debt.

The continued expansion of QE after the immediate turmoil of 2008–2009 had subsided illustrated the extent to which the financial system had become dependent on these "emergency" measures, leading to their long-term consolidation in the state economic apparatus. What had at first seemed to be a radical and unprecedented extension of state power into the heart of the financial system now became organic to its routine functioning. It was a perfect illustration of the contradictions of state intervention, which inevitably provokes unintended consequences, demanding still further interventions. This dynamic was reflected in the fact that QE took the form of a succession of separate programs. Thus QE1 was replaced by QE2, which was replaced by QE3, until QE came to be seen as such a de facto reality of contemporary finance that it had no need to be identified as a specific program at all.[6] At each step in this process, the Fed signaled to markets that it was going to wind down asset purchases, only to announce yet another round shortly thereafter.

By purchasing these assets in tremendous quantities from private financial institutions, the Fed generated widespread asset price appreciation. This served to de-risk not only the asset classes the Fed purchased but others as well. As the Fed absorbed "safe" assets, especially government bonds, from financial institutions, it also pushed them to purchase other kinds of assets, especially corporate stocks and bonds. The resulting flood of money reduced risk and supported price inflation in these asset classes as well. In this way, the expansion of the Fed's balance sheet supported the dynamics of asset-based accumulation, continuously increasing the prices of equities, mortgages, and other assets and ensuring that the circuits of money-capital that passed through these assets would be able to realize adequate returns. Asset

Chart 5.1: Federal Reserve holdings of US federal government debt (USD billions), 1970–2022

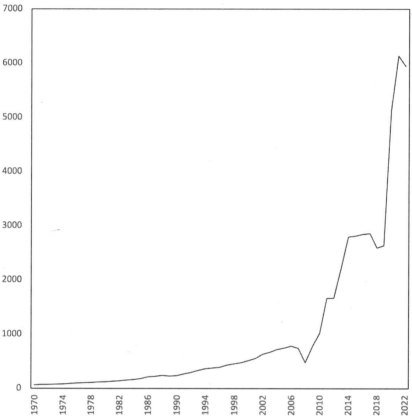

Source: *FRED, authors' calculations.* Note: *Annual, end of period; USD billions.*

inflation and the expansion of the Fed's balance sheet were two sides of the same coin.

Absorbing bonds from banks also meant that the Fed took on a new role in supporting government borrowing. A circuit was formed whereby the Treasury department issued bonds to finance government expenses, which were purchased by banks, before being purchased in turn from these banks by the Fed—thereby providing banks with cash. This dynamic is illustrated in chart 5.1, which shows the rapid expansion of the Fed's holdings of state debt after 2008. As we saw, the formation of the debt state after the crisis of the 1970s meant that state spending was increasingly financed by debt rather than taxation. While state spending continued to be debt-financed, state intervention now served to support the continuity of this flow of credit. These interventions were sharply increased during the Covid-19 pandemic, as the Fed sought to fund consumption and support business amid an unprecedented economic shutdown.

The closed circuit of government bond exchange between the Treasury and Fed amounts to what is known as the "monetization" of state debt, whereby a central bank finances fiscal policy by purchasing government debt. State debt is thereby converted by the central bank into the money needed to fund these obligations (that is, "printing money"). However, the monetization of US debt took place through the risk-proofing of government bonds on private markets. The Fed did not purchase these bonds directly from the Treasury, but rather bought them from banks, thereby shaping market interest rates. As a result of this de facto monetization, by 2020 the Fed held nearly one-third of all outstanding US federal debt. Since the Fed monetized only one portion of government bonds, it remained essential to sustain the willingness of private investors to lend to the US state. Market discipline had by no means evaporated.

Not only did the Fed facilitate government borrowing through monetization, but it also became one of the loudest voices calling for fiscal expansion to support the sluggish post-crisis recovery.[7] On the eve of the Covid crisis, the Fed formally announced its intention to loosen the strict inflation-targeting monetary policy regime that it had implemented throughout the neoliberal period.[8] The Fed now displayed a willingness to accept higher rates of inflation in order to reduce unemployment, support wage growth, and tackle racial and gender inequalities in the labor market. Perhaps most importantly, the higher levels of economic growth this afforded would support continued asset appreciation, as larger corporate profits and household savings would provide an expanded monetary base for financial investment. While in the neoliberal period the threat of rising interest rates offset fiscal stimulus, monetary policy now supported fiscal expansion.

The primary condition for all this was the defeat of the working class, which left few concerns about the kind of wage-price spiral that resulted from trade union militancy of the 1970s. This balance of forces was sustained through decades of globalization, as capital's ability to "exit" proved a powerful trump card preventing significant labor mobilization. And of course, in the event the working class began to mobilize, the Fed still possessed powerful tools to restore discipline. The functioning of the risk state, and ability for the Fed to monetize state debt, also depended on the unique international role of the dollar. The volatility of floating exchange rates requires every state in the world to hold large quantities of dollars as foreign exchange reserves, which allows them to influence the value of their own currencies by converting them into or out of dollars. The US state can tap into these global pools of dollars to finance deficits in a way that no other state could—an implicit imperial tribute paid by states around the world.[9]

At the same time, the growing political prominence of a new class fraction became increasingly apparent. No longer was "Government Sachs" the most important financial institution collaborating with the state in managing the contradictions of capitalism. As the new form of finance capital was consolidated, the "House of Fink" came into its own at the center of the new order. This was registered in the circulation of BlackRock executives back and forth to the state administration. After working with Obama, Brian Deese became Biden's top economic advisor as head of the National Economic Council. Biden also appointed Larry Fink's chief of staff and former Obama advisor Wally Adeyemo deputy Treasury secretary. Similarly, Michael Pyle, BlackRock's chief investment strategist, worked in the Obama Treasury department as well as the powerful Office of Management and Budget before serving as chief economic advisor to Kamala Harris.

This "revolving door" pointed to deeper structural links between the state and the new financial order. As the 2008 crisis unfolded, BlackRock had helped the Fed determine the value of toxic assets. Then, during the Covid-19 crisis, the Fed tasked it with administering the purchases of mortgage-backed securities and corporate bonds necessary to implement its newest "unlimited" QE program. Though neither the Fed nor the big banks had the capacity to undertake purchases of this magnitude, the Fed selected BlackRock to do so without competitive bidding. Yet this did not indicate that BlackRock had "captured" the state. Rather, the Fed's decision reflected BlackRock's unique capacities as well as its centrality in the post-2008 financial system. As one financial executive put it, any "company that takes on a project of this scale has to have significant resources available that can be repurposed instantaneously." While only "a handful of trillion-dollar asset managers" could possibly do so, in effect "the Fed was picking from a short list of one."[10]

The Rise of the Big Three

The consolidation of the risk state provided the critical foundation for the construction of a new financial architecture dominated by giant asset management companies. This took place through an interaction between state power and the "asset management" form of financial organization, which generated a self-reinforcing cycle of asset price inflation, the de-risking of equity, and increasing size and diversification of asset management companies. At the same time, new post-crisis regulations limited the ability of the banks to take part in asset management. As a result, in the years following the 2008 crisis, asset management firms were able to combine the huge pools of equity accumulated in institutional investment funds during the neoliberal period into unprecedented concentrations of assets. The centralization and diversification of these holdings led to the fundamental reorganization of corporate power: a new finance capital.

QE initiated a chain reaction throughout financial markets whereby equity became a more desirable form of money-capital for private financial firms to own. Through QE, two things happened simultaneously: first, the state purchased large quantities of assets targeted by the program, especially Treasury bonds and mortgage-backed securities; and second, the state transferred vast amounts of cash to financial institutions with which to buy other assets. In order for the money that banks and other financial institutions received through QE to become money-capital, it needed to be thrown into an M-M′ circuit. With the state absorbing a large portion of essentially risk-free bonds, financial institutions were forced to find other outlets to commence this circuit. The result was a large flood of money into corporate bond markets, reducing the cost of corporate borrowing, as well as into the stock market, resulting in continuously rising equity prices.

QE had the effect of de-risking equity while *increasing* equity prices. On the other hand, by reducing the costs of government and corporate borrowing, QE also *reduced* the returns investors could expect to receive on these bonds (that is, it reduced bond yields). With such a large quantity of capital floating around, borrowers hardly had to compete for financing by offering more attractive interest rates (returns) to bond purchasers. Both corporate borrowers and the state were effectively able to access debt financing "for free," offering investors near-zero returns. Put differently, with interest rates at or near zero, neither bond purchases nor bank account deposits seemed an attractive outlet for savings. With other forms of money-capital yielding zero or even negative returns—and therefore unable to function as money-capital—others, especially equity, became more significant.

Importantly, the growing importance of equity by no means implied that bonds became insignificant: on the contrary, the availability of "free money" led to a predictable increase in corporate indebtedness. Corporations could issue bonds at effectively no cost and then execute share buybacks, thereby serving as transmission belts for funneling value from lenders to equity owners. In this way, corporations used the low-cost capital provided by lenders to enrich stockholders. Moreover, because debt was cheap and profits were high, there was no trade-off between paying out investors and financing investment. Meanwhile, the combination of low interest rates and the de-risking of equity meant that investors could borrow money for free to finance purchases of very low-risk and high-return equity. All this contributed to the growing importance of equity as a form of money-capital.

Chart 5.2 illustrates the drop in real long-term government bond yields (on the top) alongside increasing equity prices (on the bottom) over the course of QE. Importantly, the ten-year Treasury bond establishes the so-called benchmark rate, to which many other interest rates—for mortgages, consumer loans, corporate debt, and more—are pegged. Therefore, the decline in this rate reflects a generalized reduction in the returns from these forms of interest-bearing capital. The bottom portion illustrates the simultaneous rise in market

Chart 5.2: Real ten-year Treasury bond yields (top, %) and market
capitalization, USD trillions (bottom), 2006–2021

Source: *FRED, authors' calculations; Siblis Research.* Note: *bottom, USD trillions.*

capitalization, or the total value of the shares of all publicly listed corporations. As this shows, equity prices underwent a generalized,
massive increase during the same period. From its nadir in 2008 to
2021, market capitalization increased by a historic 366 percent; by
contrast, in the same period US GDP grew by 63 percent. The increase
in market capitalization over this period was five times greater than
GDP growth.

In the context of broad asset inflation, a small number of asset management companies that specialized in "passive management" were able to
emerge as the primary vehicles for allocating savings in the financial
system. By encouraging money-capital to flow into stock, QE also

supported the continuous increase of stock prices. This created pressure on "active" mutual funds, in which professional money managers attempt to "beat the market" by strategically trading stocks. The generalized increase in equity prices made this more difficult to do, which in turn made it harder to justify the management fees these funds charge their clients. Instead, "passive" investment funds—once a niche segment of the market—became more appealing, as they could boast consistently robust returns alongside low management fees. Before 2008, three out of four equity funds were actively managed; by 2020, more than half were passive, with nearly $6 trillion in equity under management.[11]

By contrast with active funds, passive funds hold shares indefinitely, trading only to reflect the shifting weight of different firms in a market index. Like the S&P 500 or the Nasdaq, an index simply consists of a series of firms grouped together based on inclusion criteria, including size, economic sector, or growth potential. Stocks in an index are then weighted by measures such as share price or market capitalization (that is, the total value of all outstanding shares). Passive funds purchase shares of firms that are rising in an index, while selling those that are falling. Indexes therefore establish the fixed rules that govern all trades undertaken by passive investment funds, which engage in "trading by algorithm." At the same time, index funds dramatically reduce the costs of diversification, allowing investors to purchase an index of stocks representing a given segment of the market—or even the market itself—all at once rather than individually.

To be sure, passive management had been around for some time— Vanguard launched the first such fund in 1976. While State Street and Vanguard had a longer history with passive management, as the crisis unfolded, BlackRock restructured its operations to become the most important player in this market. This took place especially through its landmark $15 billion acquisition of Barclay's, along with its iShares passive funds. Meanwhile, from 2004 to 2009, State Street's assets under management increased by 41 percent, while those of Vanguard increased by 78 percent. In the same period, BlackRock's AUM grew by a staggering 879 percent—making it *by far* the largest global asset manager, with nearly $3.5 trillion in AUM, up from forty-first in 2004. Its

AUM was nearly double the second-largest firm, State Street, with $1.9 trillion.[12] By 2022, BlackRock's AUM had reached $10 trillion, while Vanguard had more than $8 trillion and State Street over $4 trillion.[13]

BlackRock, Vanguard, and State Street all continued to manage active funds, from which they derived a disproportionate share of their revenues—accounting for 26 percent of BlackRock's AUM in 2020.[14] But it was their movement into passive management that facilitated their massive concentration of asset holdings and market power. These passive funds took two different forms: exchange-traded funds (ETFs) and index mutual funds. The key difference between the two is that ETFs are traded on the stock market. Investors acquire stakes in the

Chart 5.3: Pension fund assets (USD millions), 1980–2021

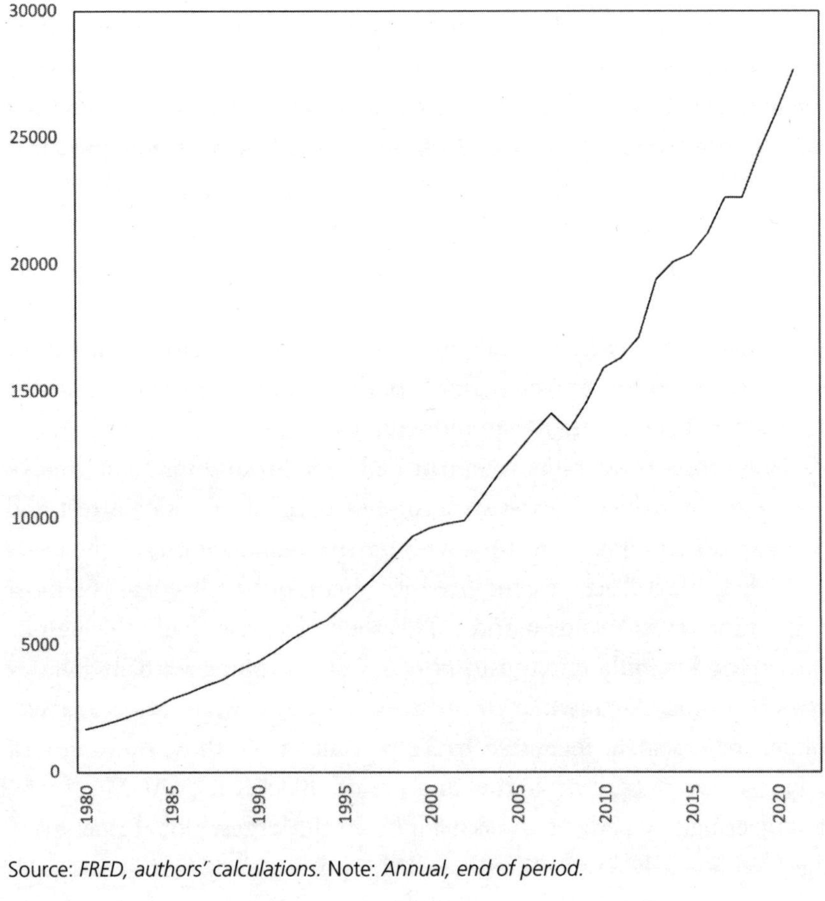

Source: *FRED, authors' calculations.* Note: *Annual, end of period.*

ETF, and therefore in the firms that it holds, by purchasing shares of the ETF on the stock exchange. The share price of the ETF is managed to reflect the values of its underlying assets. While ETFs allow investors to move money in and out of the fund more easily, both types dramatically reduce the costs of portfolio diversification—allowing investors to acquire stakes in every firm on an index with a single trade.

The growth of pension funds, illustrated in chart 5.3, was especially important for the rise of the asset management firms. This growth coincided with the growing externalization of fund management, which was entrusted to mutual funds and other professional asset managers.[15] In 2020, as chart 5.4 shows, 56 percent of BlackRock's long-term AUM was managed for institutional investors, while just 11 percent was contributed by retail investors. BlackRock does not break down its iShares ETFs, which make up roughly a third of its AUM, between retail and institutional investors, but a significant portion of these are held by institutions as well, especially pensions. Fully 66 percent of BlackRock's long-term institutional AUM is managed for pension plans on behalf of corporations, governments, and trade unions. Meanwhile, 10 percent

Chart 5.4: Sources of BlackRock's AUM

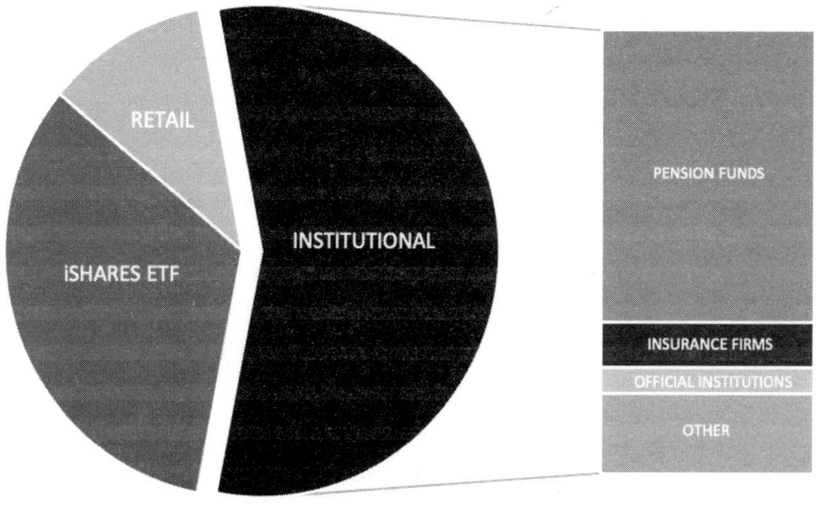

Source: *BlackRock Annual Report, 2020*

of its institutional AUM is managed for insurance companies, while 6 percent is managed for "official institutions," including central banks, sovereign wealth funds, and government ministries.[16]

The explosion of income and wealth inequality over the neoliberal period also contributed to the centralization of assets in the asset management companies in the years following the crisis. Since the wealthy can consume only so much of their income, the vast accumulation of wealth in high-income households resulted in a glut of savings that was also in search of profitable outlets. In this context, the de-risking of equity, diminished returns from other outlets, and the low-cost investment model offered by the asset management companies made investing in the stock market increasingly attractive. With interest rates near 0 percent, asset management companies constituted an institutional matrix whereby investing these savings in the stock market appeared almost as secure and accessible as a bank deposit—and almost certainly more profitable.

These dynamics were reinforced through a positive feedback loop, whereby the de-risking of equity drove the increasing size and diversification of asset management companies, which in turn supported these companies' role in allocating savings. As money flooded into the asset management companies, their growing size allowed them to further reduce management fees, since administrative costs per dollar under management declined as investment funds grew. This essentially meant that these firms' profit margins increased alongside assets under management, even as management fees declined. Moreover, as the asset management firms grew, their investment funds became even safer, since this meant they were funneling more and more savings into equity markets, thereby serving to perpetuate the inflation of stock prices; this, in turn, further encouraged the flow of still more money into the asset management companies, and so on.

As a result of the growth of these index and exchange-traded funds, index providers have also come to play a more important role in the structure of accumulation. Index providers are private, for-profit firms that (among other things) develop the indexes that passive funds track. While indexes originated as a way for journalists to gauge market performance, they now play a critical role in directing flows of capital across the economy.[17] The methodologies established by index providers for the inclusion and weighting of firms in indexes today have a tremendous impact on the movement of investment. In the context of the concentration of capital in passive funds that track these indexes, methodologies for including or excluding firms on indexes necessarily lead to substantial inflows to, or outflows from, the shares of firms. The result is to intensify the competitive pressures on corporations to comply with the metrics established by index rules.

The most prominent index providers are S&P Global, MSCI, and FTSE Russell (a subsidiary of the London Stock Exchange Group), which are responsible for indexes such as the S&P 500, the Dow Jones Industrial Average, MSCI World, and the FTSE Russell 1000. While the methodologies used by index providers to craft indexes are public— which is an important source of market confidence in the integrity of these determinations—the names of the indexes are proprietary. Asset management companies must pay these companies licensing fees in order to capitalize on the reputation and credibility associated with the brand names of these indexes, which is crucial for encouraging inflows of capital into the funds they manage. Competition for these fees has led index providers to develop a vast array of highly specialized indexes, the number of which has exploded with the rise of passive management—today reaching five thousand US stock indexes alone.[18]

The role of index providers in the current finance capital regime has led some to conclude that they may play a role in "steering capital."[19] In fact, index providers are competitively disciplined. They merely provide a *service* to asset management firms. To receive fees, index providers must develop indexes that accurately assess the relative strengths of firms across sectors or countries. Accordingly, they could hardly afford to make arbitrary choices about index methodologies, which must reflect underlying economic fundamentals. Moreover, it is the asset managers who pool money-capital and own assets, and therefore control share voting rights. More important than which specific firms are present on a given index is *how power is organized* within and above these firms. While asset management companies possess significant control over corporations on an index, index providers have no power over asset management companies.

A hallmark of finance capital today is the competitive flexibility of investment portfolios and hierarchies of corporate control. The extent of asset managers' investment in, and power over, individual firms is based on the outcome of competitive market processes at the level of corporate profits as well as equity values. The relative standing of firms in this competitive struggle is measured by index providers, whose assessments are themselves competitively disciplined. In turn, index-ation intensifies competitive pressure on corporations to get on, stay on, and increase their weight in different indexes, which enhances their ability to attract investment and strengthens their competitive position. While these competitive pressures institutionalize the dominance of asset management companies, the latter also compete with other asset management companies, banks, and all other financial institutions for control over savings—and therefore must offer competitive returns.

The special prominence of BlackRock in this finance capital regime is reflected in the competition among other financial institutions to perform ancillary support functions for the firm in exchange for fees. Thus, State Street has long derived a large share of its revenue by serv-ing as a "custodian bank" for BlackRock, holding trillions in securities managed by that firm as well as fulfilling administrative and account-ing tasks related to its accounts. In December 2021, BlackRock announced it was shifting nearly $2 trillion in assets away from State Street, and would instead employ a wider group of custodian banks, including Bank of New York Mellon, Citibank, and JPMorgan Chase— each of which BlackRock has large ownership stakes in.[20] By moving this business, BlackRock hopes to incite greater competition, thereby lowering prices while reducing its reliance on a single firm.

BlackRock's economic centrality is underscored by the role played by its cutting-edge Aladdin software platform, a sophisticated system for assessing and managing risk in stocks, bonds, derivatives, and cur-rencies. The capabilities of this software were on clear display when state officials turned to BlackRock to help price the toxic assets on bank balance sheets amid the 2008 crisis. While CEO Larry Fink reg-ularly spoke with Treasury Secretary Hank Paulson as the meltdown unfolded, BlackRock raked in tens of millions of dollars in government contracts.[21] At the same time, AIG, Lehman Brothers, and Fannie and

Freddie all hired BlackRock to assess the risk on their portfolios as well. "At a time when the credit-rating agencies like Moody's and Standard & Poor's have lost face," *Fortune* magazine declared, "Black-Rock's valuations have become a kind of de facto *Good Housekeeping* seal of approval that buyers and sellers of distressed assets trust."[22]

In the years following the crisis, Aladdin grew into what the *Financial Times* referred to as "the tech hub of modern finance"—"the central nervous system for many of the largest players in the investment management industry" as well as huge non-financial companies. Today, Aladdin manages $21.6 trillion in assets—approximately 10 percent of global stocks and bonds. In addition to BlackRock itself, the system is used by its chief competitors, State Street and Vanguard, alongside mutual funds. Half of the top ten insurance companies use the system. The Japanese government pension fund, the world's largest, also uses the system to manage its $1.5 trillion in assets. Many of the largest banks, such as Morgan Stanley, UBS, HSBC, and Credit Suisse, are Aladdin clients as well, as are the three biggest US non-financial corporations, Apple, Microsoft, and Alphabet, among untold others. Indeed, the full extent of Aladdin's reach is unknown outside of BlackRock.[23]

The widespread use of Aladdin reflects BlackRock's position as the hub around which a financial network linking asset owners, institutional investors, and industrial and financial corporations revolves. This was apparent from the fact that BlackRock was often one of the largest shareholders in both the financial and non-financial firms that used Aladdin to manage their own assets or those of their clients, as well as having representatives on the boards of directors of those firms.[24] The insurance companies, pension funds, and other institutional investors that used Aladdin were likewise among BlackRock's major clients, delegating it responsibility for managing some or all of their portfolios. The centrality of BlackRock to this network is especially clear from its links to its major competitors in the asset management industry, including both the other large asset management companies as well as mutual funds.

Asset management companies organize two circuits of money-capital. Each involves concentrating vast pools of money, setting it in

Figure 5.1: Asset management firms and the circulation and centralization of money-capital (circuit A)

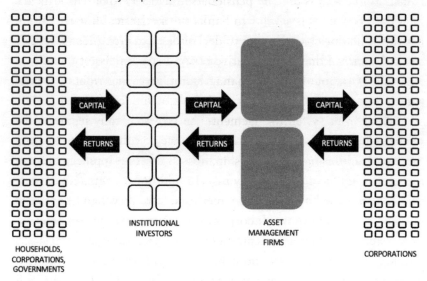

motion as interest-bearing money-capital, collecting one part of the interest generated in the form of fees, and then passing the rest on to their clients as returns. The first circuit (circuit A), shown in figure 5.1, begins with households and corporations, which contribute sums of money to institutional investors.[25] Institutional investors (along with other individual investors) then advance the amalgamated capital to asset management companies, which convert it into stocks, bonds, and other assets. These assets then yield returns: dividends in the case of stocks, debt payments in the case of bonds, and capital gains through asset sales. Asset management companies then pass these returns (minus their fee) back to institutional investors, who pay out their beneficiaries from these yields after themselves collecting fees.

The distinct structure of capitalist ownership and control on which this circuit is based leads to the continuous centralization of power in the asset management companies. Although the asset management companies are the legal owners of the assets they manage, the monetary gains derived from them belong to the original investors. The circuit of money-capital does not end with the asset management companies but is complete only once the returns flow back to the original investors. Once it has, a portion of the money falls into the sphere of consumption, as it is used by pensioners and others to purchase means of subsistence. This is similar to banks in the classical finance capital period, which paid out interest to depositors and dividends to owners of bank shares from revenue derived from loans and equity holdings. Also like these banks, asset managers retain voting rights over the shares they own.

The rise of the asset management firms thus radically separates the *powers* of ownership, which are vested in paid administrators, from the monetary *benefits* of ownership. This separation is reflected in the relatively small profits earned by asset management companies. While the profit *margins* of asset management firms are very high (surpassing the big banks and industrial corporations), their *total* profits are considerably lower. BlackRock's pre-tax profits exploded in the post-2008 period, increasing by over 500 percent from 2009 to 2021. Similarly, its profit margin was 35 percent in 2020, compared with J. P. Morgan's 27 percent, Apple's 25 percent, and Google's 23 percent. However, the total profits of the largest corporations and banks were many times greater. While BlackRock's pre-tax profits reached a near-record $8.2 billion in 2021, J. P. Morgan posted approximately $60 billion; meanwhile, Google's profits exceeded $90 billion, and Apple's reached an astonishing $117 billion.[26]

Importantly, these figures for industrial corporate profits do not include stock buybacks or dividend payments, which are especially significant forms of interest they pay out within a regime of finance capital dominated by asset owners. In 2021, Apple's buybacks equaled 69 percent of its profits ($80 billion), while Google's represented 56 percent ($50 billion).[27] Moreover, the ratio of dividend payments to retained earnings has increased substantially since 2008 (chart 3.1). That this gap is greater today than at any point since the Great Depression is a profound reflection of the power of finance, and its capacity to extract surplus value, in the context of extreme ownership concentration. However, low interest rates meant that these firms could both pay out investors *and* invest. Thus, even as industrial firms valorize the money-capital administered by asset management firms through buybacks and dividends, this has in no way diminished investment (chart

4.7) or R and D spending (chart 4.6), nor has it damaged their competitiveness or profitability (chart 4.8).

Asset management firms administer a second circuit of interest-bearing capital through their cash management and securities lending operations. Cash management refers to the management of cash portfolios for corporations, banks, foundations, insurance companies, and pensions. As we have seen, rather than letting surplus cash sit idle, corporations join financial institutions in setting it in motion as interest-bearing capital. One way they do so today is by depositing these cash reserves to be managed by a financial institution. BlackRock is one of the three largest firms in cash management, along with J. P. Morgan and Fidelity, far exceeding the operations of the other large asset management companies. This primarily takes the form of money-market mutual funds, which BlackRock and other asset management companies are leading providers of.[28]

Because cash investors often need to be able to access their capital quickly, investments made with these portfolios must be highly liquid—that is, quickly and easily transferable back into the universal equivalent form, extremely safe, and above all short-term. As we saw in chapter 4, for these reasons money-market funds emerged as the primary outlet for cash investment by the 1980s, thereby becoming central to credit provision in the system of market-based finance. Throughout the neoliberal period, these funds were important foundations for repo markets, serving as the major source of short-term cash that was lent out in exchange for non-cash assets (especially Treasuries and mortgage-backed securities). In this way, repo markets were the primary way that the non-deposit-taking financial institutions, which were increasingly powerful in the financial system, accessed cash.

Today, the money-market funds operated by asset management companies provide such financial institutions with the cash they need through what are known as "tri-party" repo markets. With tri-party repo markets, the asset being offered as collateral in exchange for cash is held by an intermediary known as a "custodian" or "clearinghouse." This allows cash to exchange hands without the actual physical transfer of the asset itself, which remains with the custodian. In these markets, money-market funds transfer cash to custodian banks. These

Figure 5.2: Asset management firms and the circulation and centralization of money-capital (circuit B)

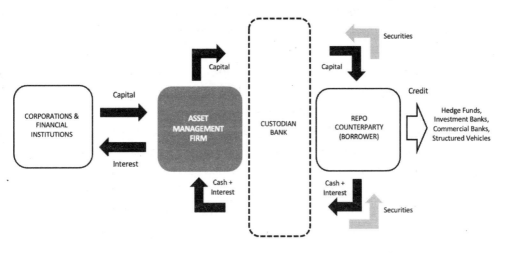

Source: *Developed from "Understanding Repo: A Cash Building Block," BlackRock*

banks then lend this cash to cash-poor (but asset-rich) institutions like investment banks and hedge funds in exchange for assets, which are transferred to the custodian. Once these borrowers return the cash to the custodian bank, the latter returns their assets. Then, the custodian bank returns the original cash back to the money-market fund, plus interest.

These lending operations constitute the second circuit of interest-bearing capital administered by asset management companies (circuit B), illustrated in figure 5.2. In this circuit, corporations and financial institutions transfer cash to asset management firms, which pool these contributions into money-market funds. Asset management companies send this cash to custodian banks, which organize repo transactions between the asset management firm and other financial institutions. The custodian bank then releases the cash to a borrowing institution and receives assets as collateral. While it retains possession of these assets for the duration of the repo, it transfers formal ownership of them from the borrowing institution to the asset management firm. Once the borrower returns the cash, plus interest, the custodian bank returns the asset to the borrower. The custodian bank then transfers cash, with interest, to the asset management firm, while retaining a fee for itself.

Asset management firms also participate in this circuit from the other side of the transaction through their "securities lending" operations. In this process, asset management companies lend stocks or bonds to other financial institutions in exchange for collateral (that is, another asset of greater value), or cash plus interest (in the form of a fee). While these are all technically short-term transactions, they can also potentially become long-term as they can be continuously "rolled over," or renewed, especially given the long-term portfolios held by the asset management companies. Engaging in this circuit allows asset management companies to further profit from the very large stocks of money-capital (in the form of assets) that they hold indefinitely. Although these assets are already involved in circuit A, by *additionally* setting them in motion through circuit B, asset management firms can further reduce management fees—and further enhance their competitiveness.

The borrowing institution can then use the loaned stock or bond to hedge against exposure to risks in another investment, or to benefit from a decline in the value of assets, through "short selling." They can also use the borrowed assets as collateral in another transaction, such as obtaining cash through repos. While hedging is essential for managing risks, short selling is important for "price discovery"—or the process whereby asset prices are competitively established. In addition to enhancing non-deposit-taking institutions' access to cash, asset management firms' securities-lending business allows dealers to hold small inventories, as they are easily able to borrow to fulfill their order flow and make markets. Asset management firms thus serve as critical backstops for the liquidity dealers provide. Given this fundamental systemic role in supporting the flow of credit, it would be highly misleading to see asset managers as merely bearers of fictitious capital.

Asset management firms also reallocate savings, increasing productivity across the economy by moving investment from relatively unproductive to relatively productive outlets. Even if investment in stock does not directly enter the circuits of industrial capital, firms receiving such investment are nevertheless strengthened, easing their access to capital markets and enhancing their competitiveness. Reciprocally, corporations contribute to valorizing the money-capital owned by asset management firms by executing buybacks and paying dividends. In a period of high corporate profits, this allows surplus cash to be released from the firm and invested elsewhere, from technologies to production facilities. Given the financialization of the corporation, buybacks and dividends effectively transfer capital from one group of finance capitalists to another, expanding investment opportunities and allowing money-capital to flow to the outlets with the highest returns.

All this points to the extent to which BlackRock and other asset management firms have become among the most important institutions in the shadow banking system. As we have seen, they are the largest owners of securities, and they also lend these securities to other firms. Furthermore, they are major *issuers* of securities: indeed, ETFs are nothing other than new securities created by combining other assets. In addition, asset management firms pool money-capital into money-market funds, which are a significant source of credit on the repo markets at the center of the modern credit system. They are thus significant players on both sides of the market-based financial system, demanding and supplying both cash and securities, and are thereby pivotal for supporting the flow of credit and investment across the economy. As we will see in chapter 6, it is this deep role in the plumbing of the financial system that led the Fed to extend greater support to these firms, especially as it sought to manage the fallout of the Covid-19 crisis.

The New Finance Capital

As Marx observed, the development of the corporation and the banking system institutionalized a separation of ownership and control of capital. Corporate managers did not necessarily own the firm's capital, but rather became mere functionaries overseeing the "capital of others." For their part, banks generated credit and assembled small quantities of money into larger pools they controlled. Financiers (bankers, in Marx's time) thereby came to represent collective ownership power, advancing money-capital to managers who oversaw industrial production. Then, by virtue of their ownership claims on this sum of money, these financiers extracted rent as money-capital flowed back to them in the form of interest (including dividends). The separation of ownership and control of capital was thereby reflected in the separation between finance and industry.

Through this process, the "private capital" of individual owners became a larger-scale "social capital" controlled by corporate managers and bankers. This socialization of capital implied enormous concentration and centralization, as investment became a social function carried out not by individual owners of means of production but by functionaries in institutional systems for amassing, allocating, managing, and valorizing capital. The managers of this social capital then paid out returns, minus their own cut, to depositors, lenders, and shareholders. Marx described this as "the abolition of capital as private property within the confines of the capitalist mode of production itself."[29] Because socialized capital was more efficient and obtained privileged access to credit, it was far more competitive, driving forward further socialization. Ultimately, the only way individual capitals could operate on a sufficient scale to be competitive (at least in major industries) was to function as part of the social capital.

As the "general managers of money capital," bankers ultimately came to play the most active part in organizing corporations, forming finance capital. The fusion of finance and industry thus also entailed the similar fusion of ownership and control, as banks became both owners and controllers of industrial corporations. Hilferding argued that these bankers preferred selling bank shares over taking deposits, as this would allow them to directly own a larger portion of the capital they managed. Nevertheless, whether paying out a portion of their returns as dividends to owners of bank shares, or interest on consumer deposits, banks functioned as financial intermediaries: money managers who invested for others as well as themselves. Thus, socialization facilitated the empowerment of investment banks over industrial corporations, while allowing small sums of idle money to function on a larger scale as money-capital in exchange for a share of the returns.

The socialization of capital was at work in the development of pension funds, which, as we saw, helped tip the balance of power between owners and managers back toward the former. Yet this concentration faced limits: only workers employed in a given sector, or country (in the case of sovereign funds), contributed to these funds. Similarly, the premiums collected by insurance companies, which they invested, were limited by their customer base. Asset management companies transcended such barriers by combining these concentrations, along with contributions from wealthy individuals, into "super pools" of money-capital. The centralization of capital that resulted from this socialization brought about the historic reversal of the separation of ownership and control that had been a feature of corporate power since the New Deal. The fusion of finance and industry was, once again, reflected in a fusion of ownership and control.

Asset management companies became "universal owners," owning not merely individual firms, or groups of firms, but *the economy itself.* Their diversification, like their concentration, is without precedent. While institutional investors had accumulated large concentrations of equity, insofar as they were diversified, their holdings were diluted across firms they held, and thus their stakes in any company were relatively small.[30] The rise of the asset management firms overcame this trade-off between diversification and strength: the new universal owners are *both* highly diversified *and* large shareholders in the firms they own. They own large stakes in the vast majority of publicly listed firms from every sector. Just as these firms socialize pools of money-capital, so too do their diversified holdings break down all concrete distinctions between capitals and sectors. Nearly every firm in the economy is united under the ownership and control of the combined social capital.

As Benjamin Braun has argued, the shareholdings of the asset management companies are distinguished by three basic characteristics.[31] First, they are extremely *concentrated.* Through their functions in socializing capital, asset management companies have been able to amass historically unprecedented concentrations of equity. This concentration of equity by asset management firms has, in turn, both resulted from and contributed to the de-risking of equity. As equity becomes less risky, asset managers gain control over a larger share of savings, which they pool into money-capital and throw into equity, which thereby becomes still less risky in a self-reinforcing cycle. By virtue of their socialization of money-capital, and continuous transformation of it into equity, asset managers become the representatives of universal ownership power.

Second, these companies are *large owners*. The centralization of social capital in the asset management companies, and their conversion of it into equity, has led these companies to amass huge holdings in particular firms. Generally speaking, the Big Three asset management companies are together (and even independently) the largest share-owner in each of their portfolio firms. This means that, at least potentially, these asset management companies have substantial clout in the governance, strategy, and organization of their portfolio firms. In addition to this intensive ownership of particular firms, the power of the asset management companies is also incredibly extensive, as indicated by their status as "universal owners."

Thus follows the third characteristic of the structure of the Big Three's ownership: the holdings of these companies are incredibly *diversified* across the economy. There are many shareholders in the economy. However, the vast majority of these are relatively insignificant, controlling small stakes in a small number of firms. The Big Three, by contrast, are substantially larger than even other large owners, such as Fidelity and JPMorgan, and they sit at the very center of ownership networks. The firms in which they have the most substantial stakes are those that have the densest connections to the biggest and most diversified shareholders. Moreover, the Big Three are the largest owners of many of the *other* largest shareowners, including the big banks. Simply put, the Big Three are thus the largest shareholders in the most important companies: they own the "commanding heights" of the economy.

Chart 5.5 clarifies the unprecedented concentration of ownership by the Big Three. As it shows, the Big Three are collectively the largest or second-largest shareholder in firms that constitute nearly 90 percent of total market capitalization across the entire economy. These firms have a total market capitalization of nearly $45 trillion dollars—

Chart 5.5: Ownership of the Big Three in publicly listed US companies by market capitalization and number of companies

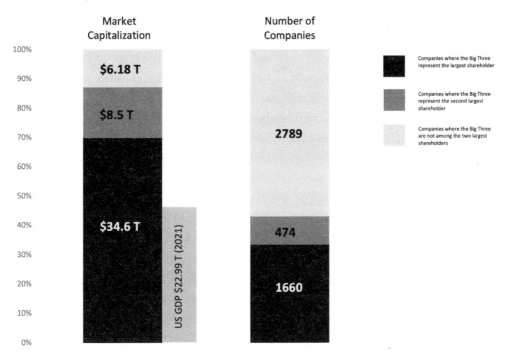

Source: *Orbis database, authors' calculations*

approximately double US GDP. Even if one focuses only on cases in which the Big Three are the largest shareholder, the market capitalization of these firms substantially outstrips US GDP. The tremendous power of the Big Three is especially clear from the ownership structure of firms listed on the S&P 500 index, which tracks the largest US companies. Stunningly, the Big Three are the largest or second-largest holders of 98 percent of S&P 500 firms and own an average of over 20 percent of any given company. This constitutes a truly staggering scale and scope of ownership concentration.

Asset management companies thus organize control over social capital by amalgamating pools of money-capital, as well as through their ownership of industrial corporations across the economy. It is this socialization of capital that serves as the basis for a new fusion of financial and industrial capital. Asset management companies embody the power of universal ownership, but they also become more directly and actively involved in controlling industrial firms. This active role of financiers in managing industrial capital is the defining feature of finance capital: in Hilferding's terms, such financiers "become industrialists," leading to the "operation of industry with money-capital."[32] In the case of the asset management companies of today, this power is primarily established through their possession of huge concentrations of corporate *stock*, that form of money-capital that Hilferding saw as a crucial nexus between financial and industrial capital.

As we saw in chapter 2, the classical form of finance capital that existed in the nineteenth and early twentieth centuries stood largely on two pillars: equity and credit. Stock is a unique form of money-capital, capable of being transformed into the universal equivalent form quickly and easily, but one that also establishes a particular relationship to production. The concentration of equity in financial institutions tends therefore to be accompanied by the centralization of corporate control. Bank control over corporations was also supported by the ability to control the flow of credit into the circuits of industrial capital organized by corporations. Through these two levers, banks maintained control of industrial firms, leading the interests of these institutions to become deeply intertwined. This was reflected in banks acquiring seats on boards of directors to monitor corporate performance and issue strategic guidance.

However, high profits and retained earnings now meant that corporations were hardly dependent on external financing, just as the development of market-based finance meant that bank loans were largely displaced by corporate bond issues as a source of industrial credit. If corporations had come to rely less on bank loans during the managerial period, this was even more the case during the neoliberal period. Indeed, the financialized industrial corporation, independent from banks and able to autonomously engage with financial markets, is one of the hallmarks of market-based finance. As a result, the ability for banks to use credit as leverage over corporations was drastically reduced. The development of market-based finance thus marked a major shift in the form that financial power could thereafter take.

If banks had lost their ability to control corporations through credit relations, the separation of investment banking from asset management also meant they could no longer do so through their possession of equity. In classical finance capital, investment banks underwrote stock issues and held on to such shares indefinitely. Underwriting thus equated to asset management. Today, investment banks immediately sell the overwhelming majority of the assets they underwrite on the stock market. This is where the asset management companies come in: they can pool the equity that is dumped on the market by investment banks by socializing the money-capital pooled by institutional investors. In this way, large asset management firms are the functional modern-day equivalent of Hilferding's investment banks.

Like classical finance capital, the new finance capital in no way resembles "organized capitalism." Indeed, despite the extreme concentration of stock ownership, this regime is intensely competitive. Asset management companies compete not only with one another, but also with all other outlets for savings, including banks, hedge funds, and private equity firms. To attract savings, these firms seek to maximize returns for clients: they must offer better returns and lower risk than their competitors. As we have seen, such competition imposes sharp limits on the fee rates these firms can charge, which led to the shift toward passively managed funds in the first place. Unable to increase fee rates, asset management firms increase profits by expanding their AUM, as the fees they receive are typically calculated as a percent of this. For the same reason, these firms also seek to boost the value of the AUM they already hold.

Such competition drives these asset management companies to maximize their direct control over firms in which they own large blocks of shares. Despite being *passive investors*, the big asset management companies are highly *active owners*. The passive funds that are the basis of the ownership power of the Big Three are contractually barred from trading other than to track the performance of firms on fixed indexes. While the size of the stock holdings of pension funds and other institutional investors made it difficult for them to trade without damaging the value of their own portfolios, the holdings of asset management companies are thus even less liquid. Unable to simply dump shares of underperforming corporations, asset management companies must turn to other, more direct means of influencing corporate managers. In the absence of the option to "exit," therefore, competition takes the form of intervention.

As the asset management companies are effectively permanent owners, equally permanent interconnections condense between these financiers and industrial corporations. These relationships are organized through the asset managers' "stewardship divisions," which centralize oversight of industrial corporations. This includes coordinating the asset management firms' share voting strategies, as well as collaborating with portfolio companies to implement governance reforms, influence board composition, approve executive compensation, and supervise strategy. This is very different from the activism of "active" investors, which have a relatively high portfolio turnover. While such active investors may exercise significant leverage over firms, this does not result in the formation of the kind of stable fusion between finance and industry characteristic of finance capital.

Asset management companies have frequently advanced and supported proposals to further institutionalize shareholder power, building on the gains of the neoliberal years. This has taken the form of demands for the elimination of "classified shares," whereby some shares (usually held by managerial insiders) have more voting power than others—pushing instead for the principle of "one share, one vote." Similarly, they have insisted upon the right to nominate independent directors and to approve them through a simple majority vote at shareholder meetings, as well as supporting independent board compensation and audits. Moreover, they have sought to expand the power of shareholders to bring proposals to meetings for a vote, and they have exercised significant oversight over executive compensation. At stake in these conflicts is nothing less than control over the corporation itself.

In this respect, the Big Three asset management firms, from Black-Rock to State Street, explicitly present themselves as units of finance capital, and publicly report on their extensive engagements with firms they own. Rakhi Kumar, the head of corporate governance at State Street, proudly declared to the *Financial Times*:

> Our size, experience and long-term outlook provide us with corporate access and allow us to establish and maintain an open and constructive dialogue with company management and boards. The option of exercising our substantial voting rights in opposition to management provides us with sufficient leverage and ensures our views and client interests are given due consideration.[33]

Asset management companies engage in routine "behind-the-scenes" coordination with management on an ongoing basis. While their power over their portfolio firms is ultimately secured by their voting power, voting against management is only a last resort—a coercive, strong-arm tactic should all else fail. It is only when normal forms of dialogue break down that asset managers "go nuclear" and publicly vote to discipline their managerial subordinates.

All the asset management companies monitor portfolio companies and reach out to discuss any concerns. In 2020, BlackRock held over 3,500 company engagements, covering nearly 65 percent of global equity under management, while Vanguard engaged with companies representing 52 percent of its US holdings.[34] For BlackRock, the Aladdin system helps to prioritize these engagements, ensuring that resources are targeted efficiently. Portfolio companies also recognize the power of the asset management firms by requesting meetings to discuss strategies and plans, or to address unforeseen events that may impact the performance of the company. Such routine coordination means that asset management firms are rarely surprised by strategic developments or operational issues regarding their portfolio firms, as well as ensuring that portfolio companies are clearly aware of the expectations and interests of the asset managers.

As BlackRock's 2021 *Investment Stewardship* report summarized this process, the company urges firms it holds to "adopt sound business practices." When it believes these "fall short," BlackRock executives meet with management, board directors, and even the company's advisors (such as legal teams and investor relations units), as well as with other shareholders "where appropriate." Throughout the process, BlackRock emphasizes that it aims "to be constructive, patient, and persistent" in working with portfolio firms. Similarly, the company states, "By keeping the details of our engagements private, we build the trust that supports continued, effective dialogue." "However," the company stresses, "our patience is not infinite—when we do not see progress despite ongoing engagement, or companies are insufficiently responsive to our efforts to protect the long-term economic interests of our clients, we will exercise our right to vote against management recommendations."[35]

This means that, as Vanguard put it in its own 2020 *Investment Stewardship* report, the "progress" the firm makes each year toward restructuring corporate governance and other matters related to shareholder rights "is not captured neatly in a voting record." Thus, in order to illustrate such "progress," like other asset management companies it presents detailed case studies in annual stewardship reports, showing qualitatively how it is working to institutionalize finance capital. Such reports also show that these large asset management companies are very willing to exercise their trump card by voting against management when necessary. In 2019–2020, BlackRock voted against one or more management recommendations at 30 percent of shareholder meetings in the United States, including 8 percent of management recommendations on governance-related issues. Similarly, in 2020, Vanguard voted against 12 percent of management proposals on governance-related issues.[36]

The argument that a new form of finance capital emerged from the 2008 crisis is distinct from accounts that see this as what Braun has called "asset manager capitalism."[37] Braun has done the most important work to date analyzing this "new regime of corporate governance." Nevertheless, he ultimately falls into the trap, which has plagued so many critical understandings of corporate power throughout the twentieth century, of seeing concentration and centralization as leading to the suppression of competition. As we have already seen, the multinational corporation is in fact *the most* mobile, and therefore *the most* competitive form of capitalist organization. Similarly, we have shown how the assetification of capitalism beginning in the neoliberal period led to the intensification of competitive pressures, extending the operation of market mechanisms and integrating ever-wider swaths of social life in circuits of money-capital.

Finally, we have shown above that the formation of finance capital is the inexorable result of the operation of competitive pressures in the context of a financial system dominated by giant asset management companies. According to Braun, however, as fee-based financial intermediaries, asset management firms have "no direct economic interest" in the performance of their portfolio companies.[38] Since all gains are passed on to their investors, Braun assumes that these companies have little reason to pressure firms to improve performance. This is especially the case since any gains reaped through such interventions are bound to be disproportionately captured by active investors who have placed bets on specific firms. Indeed, since asset management firms have substantial holdings across firms in any given sector, they supposedly have an incentive to *squelch* damaging competition among these companies in favor of monopolistic coordination.

The formation not merely of asset manager capitalism but of *finance capital* hinges on the significance of competition. While it is true that the revenues collected by asset managers take the form of fees, Braun downplays the fact that competing for savings means offering investors the highest possible returns—thus giving asset management firms a very direct interest in the performance of firms they hold. The higher the value of the assets they manage, the higher the fees they receive. These same competitive pressures lead asset management companies to offer specific products, in the form of funds, intended to serve the needs of different investors. As a result, their portfolios are hardly interchangeable, but in fact diverge significantly (chart 5.6). This, in turn, means that gains wrought from the differential performance of corporations are unevenly distributed across these companies—again incentivizing intervention.

Even if intervening in portfolio firms produces benefits for competitors, this should not lead us to expect asset managers to inherently eschew such actions. A similar logic is at work when General Motors, for example, boosts its profits by introducing a new machine that

Chart 5.6: Percent difference in BlackRock and Vanguard holdings of top 100 firms by market capitalization (firms largest to smallest, horizontal axis)

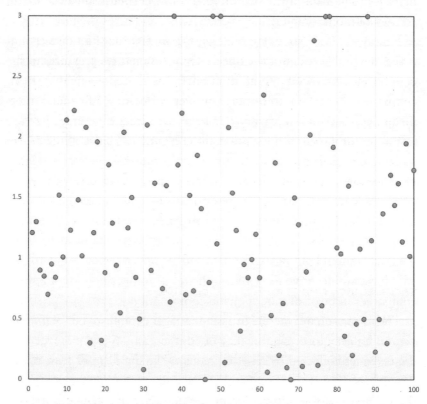

Source: *Orbis database, authors' calculation.* Note: *The vertical axis is measured as the difference in the **total** share of equity owned in each corporation by BlackRock and Vanguard.*

reduces the labor time needed to produce an automobile. Although it is virtually certain that its competitors will copy the innovation sooner or later, this does not stop GM from introducing the new machine (if it is economically feasible—i.e., it saves more labor than it costs). This is what Marx saw as the "ephemeral form" of surplus value, destined to fade away once the new breakthrough is generalized across a particular sector.[39] The fact that competitors will eventually benefit clearly does not stop corporations from undertaking such investments: in fact, this search for ephemeral surplus value is central to technological and organizational change in capitalism.

Asset management companies thus have a clear interest in maximizing the value of the money-capital they administer. This both increases their own profits in the form of larger fees, since these are fixed as a percent of the value of their AUM, and helps them to attract savings (and build AUM) by offering higher returns than competing outlets do. Strikingly, Braun himself discusses how asset management firms benefit from the asset inflation caused by QE, asserting that these companies are a "powerful easy money constituency" supporting central banks in maintaining low interest rates as a result.[40] Nevertheless, he simultaneously insists that these companies have no incentive to pressure their portfolio firms to improve shareholder value—which is nothing but another mechanism to achieve the same result. All this illustrates that the contemporary form of finance capital is directly built upon, and reproduced through, the forces of capitalist competition.

Private Equity, Hedge Funds, and Finance Capital

The asset management companies specializing in passive investment are not the only asset managers, though they are certainly the largest and most powerful. The rise of asset management has also been reflected in the tremendous growth in private equity and hedge funds. Each of these is a distinct type of financial firm, engaged in profit-making strategies at different locations in the overall financial system. Yet they are all organized around the management of financial assets, and therefore the flows of money-capital that constitute asset-based accumulation. In their own ways, these companies each extract interest through their ownership of financial assets. As such, all reinforce financial discipline and investor power, forming distinct points in the overall constellation of the new finance capital.

The growth of private equity has been an especially widely noted change in the financial system since 2008. Firms like Blackstone, KKR, Carlyle Group, and Apollo manage private equity funds, which pool contributions from institutional investors and high-net-worth individuals. Such contributions have exploded since 2008. As *Bloomberg* declared in 2019, "private equity managers won the financial crisis."[41]

As in the case of the Big Three, the largest and most important contributors to private equity have been public pensions and sovereign wealth funds, whose allocations more than tripled between 2008 and 2020. Today, seven major US pension funds each have more than $15 billion invested in private equity, led by the California Public Employees' Retirement System (Calpers), Washington State Investment Board, and the Teacher Retirement System of Texas. But even these are dwarfed by sovereign wealth funds.[42]

Private equity firms typically acquire struggling companies, restructure their assets, and resell them at a profit. Their operations are oriented around turning low-value into higher-value assets through highly interventionist strategies. They take over private (that is, not listed on public stock exchanges) or public companies by borrowing against their assets and future cash flow (that is, a leveraged buyout). In the case of publicly listed firms, they "take the company private" by purchasing all outstanding stock and delisting the company from public stock exchanges. In either case, "internal operating groups," supported by wider "external operating groups" of executives and consultants, manage the acquired companies and execute restructuring.[43] This is a particularly intimate instance of the fusion that constitutes finance capital—and even resembles the relationship between financialized management and operating divisions in the financialized industrial corporation.

Private equity firms are often derisively referred to as "vulture capital."[44] Yet these firms are certainly not simply *dysfunctional* to capitalism. For one thing, capitalism in every period develops and grows through "creative destruction."[45] The relentless innovation that characterizes capitalist production takes place through the simultaneous destruction of old investments, labor skills, institutional forms, technologies, paradigms, and even nature itself. This basic dialectic is the essence of capitalism's vitality: its dynamic ability to transcend barriers and grow through continuous restructuring. The process of creative destruction is driven forward by the force of competitive pressures, which compel firms to either compete or perish—or be swallowed by larger and more powerful firms. That private equity firms are among the agents enacting such creative destruction thus hardly amounts to the corruption of capitalism but is rather an expression of its very laws of motion.

Contrary to another common misperception, private equity firms are not particularly short-termist. Quite the opposite: their focus on restructuring acquired firms means that private equity tends to have a rather *long-term* outlook. The median length of time that these funds hold portfolio companies is approximately five years, and over 30 percent are held for seven years or more.[46] According to Blackstone, the "life cycle" of private investment is often upward of ten years, and it is only in the final three to seven years—what Blackstone calls the "harvest period"—that "most investments are realized."[47] Even when they do sell, almost half of these sales take the form of "partial exits," whereby the private equity firm retains ownership of a portion of the equity. Moreover, roughly one-third of these firms were sold to other private equity companies.[48] On the other hand, less than 20 percent were unloaded through initial public offerings (IPOs) whereby they became listed on public stock exchanges.[49]

Private equity firms manage value flows across the economy, breaking down dying firms and reselling valuable assets while building up other firms through targeted investment and restructuring. They are not simply "one thing" but manage a range of funds that employ a variety of strategies operating at different time horizons, all of which share the overall aim of turning money into more money (M-M') through increasing asset values. This includes the much-maligned "asset stripping," whereby a private equity firm breaks a company into different parts and auctions off its assets for profit. In this strategy, the assets possessed by a company, such as brands, operating divisions, equipment, intellectual property, and real estate, are seen to be more valuable than the company itself. While the underperforming firm may not survive intact, the result is to increase the value of the assets it owned by restructuring ownership.

This strategy is predicated on the conclusion that the cost of making the target company competitive exceeds the benefits to be gained from breaking it up. Accordingly, the gains are typically used to make dividend payments to investors, rather than paying down the target company's debt. Once stripped of its valuable property, the company is often forced to take on additional debt through what is known as "recapitalization." The borrowed capital is passed on to the private equity firm and other investors, while the stripped-out company, lacking collateral and facing high interest rates, in many cases simply defaults. However destructive this is for the dismembered corporation, investors can then invest these returns in more profitable and competitive firms. Similarly, the assets stripped out of failing firms can be used by stronger companies to generate profits. Private equity firms thus play a role in the reallocation of capital from non-competitive to competitive firms and sectors.

If asset-stripping generally aims for a relatively "quick turnaround," even this requires considerable time to develop strategies and identify undervalued assets, gain control of targeted companies, and find suitable buyers. Other strategies involve even longer time horizons and have nothing to do with stripping assets, but rather aim to improve company performance and boost long-term value. Such strategies are implemented by instituting management changes, streamlining operations, increasing efficiency, or expanding the company through new investment. The cycle of re-engineering companies, pushing their valuations upward, and reselling, takes considerable time to devise and implement. During this period, the fund holds increasingly valuable assets, which it therefore feels little urgency to sell. Indeed, private equity firms reap considerable gains by simply holding profitable restructured firms, and thus often choose to sell only partial stakes.

Competition incessantly drives private equity firms to increase asset values, and to realize these gains through sale: money thus begets more money through an M-M' circuit. Their business model depends entirely on their ability to unlock latent value present in underutilized assets in uncompetitive corporations. Moreover, given the scale that the biggest private equity firms operate at, their competitiveness is based on their ability to retain ownership of valuable corporations they have invested in to manage their risks. While these assets can always be sold for cash in an emergency, the ability of these firms to access the cheap credit that is essential to their operations depends on their ownership of valuable collateral. All this, too, leads private equity companies to adopt a long-term perspective. Critically, it also shows the extent to which these firms hardly engage in wanton destruction, as their interests are tied to the increased market valuation of assets that they hold as well as those they sell.

Though it exploded after 2008, private equity had been growing consistently since the 1990s. As institutional investors concentrated money-capital, they increasingly externalized investment management—and delegated a steadily growing share of their capital to private equity companies to invest.[50] However, substantially reduced risk and increased returns following the 2008 crisis dramatically accelerated the growth of private equity: from 2006 to 2018, the number of US firms owned by private equity funds at least doubled. This resulted from the de-risking of equity through QE, as well as the success of the big asset managers in attracting savings and pouring them into these markets. Meanwhile, extremely low interest rates allowed private equity firms to easily access cheap credit, which they used to fund buyouts.[51] De-risking and low interest rates thus facilitated private equity firms' ability to profit from the purchase and sale of appreciating assets.

In addition to the significant growth in the number of companies controlled by private equity firms, the value of these private companies has also grown significantly. Nevertheless, the value of public corporations has remained substantially higher—and grown substantially faster—than that of private corporations. From 2006 to 2018, the total value of private companies increased by approximately $2 trillion. During the same period, however, the total value of public companies (that is, total market capitalization) increased by more than $11 trillion (chart 5.2). Similarly, as of 2018, the Federal Reserve calculated the total value of all publicly traded firms to be $31 trillion, compared with only $5 trillion for privately held companies.[52] This means that the Big Three, which have substantial holdings in nearly all publicly traded companies—and especially the largest and most powerful firms—occupy the "commanding heights" of the economy.

In many ways, private equity firms resemble hedge funds: both are typically organized as limited partnerships (that is, they are not publicly traded) and pursue active investment strategies while paying fund managers high fees. However, hedge funds invest in both public and private firms, which they do not typically play a direct role in managing. Hedge funds seek to make profits for small groups of investors by taking "long positions" in undervalued stock, and "short positions" in overvalued stock. Each constitutes a bet that the market has misidentified the value of particular securities, and thus that their price will rise or decline over time. Hedge funds also engage in derivatives trading—purchasing risk from other market actors as well as "hedging" by selling these risks. These funds are able to take positions that go well beyond their relatively limited capitalization, and hence generate larger returns for their investors, by taking on enormous amounts of leverage (debt).

Hedge funds rely on highly activist, high-risk, and high-fee investment strategies. Consequently, they have been among the victims of the historic shift toward passive investment after 2008. For one thing, the de-risking of equity that resulted from QE and the rise of the giant asset management firms made it harder for hedge funds to compete for savings as a result of their high fees. Even more fundamentally, this dramatically reduced the market volatility that these funds rely on to make money. In the context of a generalized rise in asset prices, it became more difficult for fund managers to identify undervalued or overvalued stocks. Unsurprisingly, hedge fund managers have been outspoken opponents of "easy money," often placing them at odds with the political interests articulated by the giant asset management companies.[53]

However, a certain group of highly interventionist hedge funds that emerged from the proxy fights of the 1990s has fared differently. As we saw, these conflicts, which succeeded the more violent takeovers by the "corporate raiders," reflected the rising power of investors over internal managers. Instead of relying on leverage, derivatives, or short selling as vehicles to increase returns, these funds—such as Trian Fund Management, Elliott Management, Starboard Value, Carl Icahn, and ValueAct—seek to improve shareholder value by pressuring management and directly gaining seats on boards of directors. Between 2004 and 2019, these funds increased their AUM by roughly 650 percent, from $19.5 billion to $146 billion.[54] Though this is still only a fraction of the over $4 trillion global hedge fund industry, and truly minuscule in comparison to the giant asset management firms, they have been able to exert an outsized impact on corporate governance.

These newer hedge funds are distinguished by their use of more aggressive, public-facing tactics that aim to shape the composition of boards of directors through proxy contests, or "put a company up for sale or engage in divestitures" of a firm's non-core assets.[55] From 2013 to 2020, such activist firms led at least two thousand public campaigns in the United States, targeting companies as large as Xerox, Apple, and Morgan Stanley, and obtaining over one thousand board seats.[56] Interestingly, these campaigns are actually *less* likely to emerge in relation to firms in which the Big Three are major shareholders—reflecting the big asset managers' routine monitoring and control of these firms, which reduces the need for activist campaigns by other investors to win reforms. Nevertheless, the *threat* that the giant asset management firms could vote their huge blocks of shareholdings in support of such a campaign no doubt enhances their "voice" in corporate governance.

In fact, as the Big Three have acquired larger stakes, they have been less inclined to support manager proposals, and more willing to support shareholder proposals at shareholder meetings. Among the Big Three in general, support for investor-nominated board seats increased 94 percent from 2013 to 2018.[57] In 2020, Vanguard supported 84 percent of shareholder proposals on board composition, as well as 40 percent of such proposals related to "shareholder rights." Even in the case of environmental and social matters, Vanguard supported 7 percent of shareholder initiatives. BlackRock, meanwhile, backed 19 percent of shareholder proposals on environmental issues.[58] Of course, not all shareholder proposals are hostile to management, but these figures give some sense of the Big Three's level of support for outsider initiatives. As BlackRock CEO Larry Fink said in 2018, "the role of activists is getting larger, not smaller," adding that "in many cases their role is a good one."[59]

Ownership by the Big Three has been correlated with significant changes in corporate governance: a larger number of independent directors on corporate boards, fewer anti-takeover defenses (like poison pills and golden parachutes) that shield management from investor discipline, and more extensive "shareholder rights" provisions.[60] The latter includes moving away from the "dual class" stock structures adopted by a range of firms, including Facebook (Meta) and Google (Alphabet), and toward a one-share, one-vote model. In dual-class structures, not all shares possess equal voting rights, thus protecting control of the firm by an "insider" entrepreneurial group. In the case of Meta, for example, the class A shares held by the insider group have ten times the voting power of class B shares.[61] Given the role played by these mechanisms in reducing investor control, it is no surprise that the Big Three and other financial institutions have sought their removal.

Private equity companies and hedge funds thus form part of a constellation of power that reinforces the dominance of the giant asset management firms. In addition to supporting the provision of credit and allocating savings, the role of the asset management companies in the management and organization of industrial capital makes it even harder to understand these firms as embodying fictitious capital. As we have shown, the rise of these firms was linked with the restructuring of corporate power through the establishment of a new form of finance capital. It has entailed these financiers *becoming industrialists*. Asset management firms are directly fused with the corporate institutions in which the circuits of industrial capital are articulated. As such, they are no more "fictitious" than the "inside" managers of these firms.

Yet it bears repeating that the formation of finance capital was not merely the result of the colonization of industrial corporations by external financiers. On the contrary, the fusion of finance and industry took shape at first *within* the industrial firm, during the very heart of the postwar period often glorified as a supposedly "pre-financialization" era, to which we must supposedly aim to return to restore the "prosperous economy." This framing is grounded in a reading of history that is simply mythological. As we saw in chapter 3, the separation of banks from industrial corporations at the end of the finance capital era led the latter to internalize a range of financial functions. Subsequently, the logic of abstract money-capital gradually became dominant in these firms through their internationalization and diversification. By the neoliberal period, industrial firms had effectively become financial groups, and any clear distinction between financial and non-financial firms was blurred.

The tendency in corporate organization throughout the postwar period was the *centralization* of control over investment and *decentralization* of operational control. This tendency reached its apotheosis with the multi-layered subsidiary form, whereby centralized management and planning were undertaken by a group of investors circulating money-capital across networks of subcontractors and internal divisions. The relationship between these managers and operating divisions was markedly similar to the organization of private equity firms: top managers advanced money-capital into circuits of industrial capital organized in operating divisions, which they also played a role in overseeing. These operating divisions, of course, were not publicly traded but wholly owned by the corporation—similar to the portfolio companies owned by private equity firms. They could always be spun off or restructured and were constantly competing with other alternatives for investment.

The extent to which competitive pressures have been internalized by the (financialized) industrial corporation itself again highlights the folly of seeing this system of finance capital as restraining competition. While it is certainly true that asset management companies often hold shares across all the firms in a particular sector ("horizontal shareholdings"), competition remains an overriding disciplinary force within, as well as between, corporations. While the centralization-decentralization of corporate organization intensifies competitive discipline in the firm, the fact that the socialization of capital throws corporations from every sector into competition with one another intensifies such pressures between firms. And of course, the activism of shareholders, from asset management firms to hedge funds, is always explicitly aimed at maximizing profitability and therefore competitiveness—not the reverse.

An analysis of the current form of finance capital makes especially clear just how central competition is to the reproduction of the entire order. Competition between asset management companies (as well as between asset management companies and other financial institutions) for savings drives these firms, in order to maximize investor returns, to intervene extensively in their portfolio companies to maximize profits and shareholder value. These interventions, along with the deeper competitive dynamics within and outside the industrial corporation, drive continuous corporate restructuring to boost margins, cut costs, and increase efficiency. As a result, this process not only benefits the financial firms at the center of the new finance capital but also strengthens the industrial corporations in which they invest. As ever, while competition may weaken—or even destroy—particular firms or circuits of capital, it strengthens the capitalist class *as a whole*.

6

Crises, Contradictions, and Possibilities

The period following the 2008 crisis saw a change in the organization of corporate power in American capitalism: the rise of a new form of finance capital centered around the Big Three asset management companies. The scaffolding of this regime was constituted by a new risk state, which facilitated the valorization of the money-capital thrown into circulation by these firms through its support for continuous asset price inflation. The giant asset management companies and the risk state formed an interlocking nexus of power that enabled the continuous de-risking of corporate equity—leading savings to flow into stocks, which thereby further de-risked these assets. The power of the new class fraction of finance capitalists was exemplified by their prominent advisory positions in the Trump and Biden administrations, as well as the intimate coordination between BlackRock executives, in particular, and the Federal Reserve.[1]

The growing political clout of these finance capitalists was rooted in their structural position in the financial system, and thus the need for the state to coordinate with them in making policy. However, the extent to which the ascent of the new fraction of finance capitalists in the power bloc would require, or support, the consolidation of a new policy paradigm that would break with that which had prevailed over the post-1980 neoliberal period remained an open question. That these companies were "universal owners," with stakes not merely in a particular firm but the market as a whole led some to conclude that their rise could create space for a new politics of class compromise around fiscal expansion and "green" investment. Yet the defeat of Biden's moderate expansion of social programs amid new economic turmoil suggested this was wishful thinking, as were hopes that the "green" investment strategies associated with finance capital could lead to significant decarbonization of the economy.

At the same time, rising inflation following the unprecedented shutdown and reopening of the economy through the Covid-19 crisis raised deeper questions about the durability of this form of finance capital. As the Fed turned once again to raising interest rates and moved from quantitative easing to quantitative tightening, whereby it "tapered" new purchases of government bonds, the dependence of the new finance capital on the "easy money" policies that had been so instrumental to its rise faced a new test. In this context, new market volatilities, and the looming possibility of a liquidity crisis in the shadow banking sector, similarly appeared to threaten the new rulers of capitalist finance. Yet however much a potential economic crisis posed a risk to asset management firms, this threat was offset by other factors—not least including the continued statization of the market-based financial system through the further expansion of the Fed's powers.

Despite market volatility and rising inflation, the concentration, centralization, and diversification of ownership by the giant asset management companies were not challenged—in fact, ownership was further consolidated. Nevertheless, storm clouds gathered on the horizon. Even if the Fed could navigate the contradictions arising in the new conjuncture, the acceleration of ecological collapse, which the paltry "sustainable investment" strategies deployed by finance capital have proved utterly incapable of addressing, threatened not only capitalism, but human civilization itself. Meanwhile, a persistent legitimation crisis produced other morbid symptoms. As an emboldened hard right captured positions in state representative democratic institutions, efforts to insulate key agencies from the chaos and disorder were redoubled. The challenge of democratizing the state, and building a genuine alternative to market discipline and production for profit, was more pressing than ever.

The Statization of Market-Based Finance

The ever-closer integration of the state economic apparatus with finance over the decade following the 2008 crisis exhibited the dialectic Poulantzas had identified long before: state intervention generated contradictions, which, in turn, called forth further state intervention, resulting in new contradictions, and so on. Thus, with the deepening state involvement in the circulation and reproduction of capital, state intervention itself became a site of crisis formation, which impelled the deeper penetration of state power into the economy. If this was already clearly on display throughout the post-2008 period, it was accelerated by the Covid-19 crisis. To hold together the financial system and support non-financial corporations, the Fed unleashed all the powers it had accumulated since 2008 and then some. And, apparently having learned its lesson from the difficulties of passing TARP, this time it did so without so much as a fig leaf of democratic legitimacy.

The flip side of the consolidation of new economic practices in the state was the further statization of the financial system, which, as we have seen, had already developed substantially during the post-2008 period. Most important was the deepening infrastructural connection between state power and repo markets, the primary means whereby the state supported the shadow banking system that was by then the center of American finance. This increasingly close interrelationship between the state economic apparatus and the institutions and assets that were the foundations of the shadow banking sector was the strongest possible demonstration of the growing prominence of the latter, surpassing the traditional banking sector alongside the consolidation of the new form of finance capital over the decade following the 2008 meltdown.

Following the crisis, the largest banks and broker-dealers faced an increasingly long list of regulations limiting the size of their balance sheets and the practices they could undertake. Meanwhile, a new set of controls were being consolidated to integrate the shadow banking system into the state economic apparatus.[2] These new supports resembled those initially developed in relation to the traditional banking sector in the wake of the Great Depression. Of course, as we have seen, QE served to fix the price of collateral assets on repo markets, especially mortgage-backed securities, through extensive purchases of these assets by the Fed. This was not merely a matter of "bailing out the banks," but supporting the financial *system*, which relied on these assets to generate credit. Had the Fed not stepped in to backstop the value of these assets during the crisis, it would have been difficult—perhaps impossible—to rebuild the system of market-based finance.

QE and the Fed's other post-crisis interventions also provided liquidity to shadow banks and Treasury securities to institutional investors in need of a safe and reliable counterparty with which to invest their cash. In 2013, the Fed went even further, developing a special overnight repo facility targeted not just at the banks (which had become more deeply entangled with state power and regulated more closely than ever before) but at shadow banks as well. The Overnight Reverse Repo Program (ONRRP) established a floor on the interest rates on tri-party repo markets by standing ready to supply collateral to shadow banks in exchange for cash, thereby controlling the supply of cash relative to collateral and impacting the interest rate. This meant that the overnight interest rate could not go below the Fed's ONRRP rate.

ONRRP aimed to address the contradictions of QE for repo markets. As the Fed dumped trillions of dollars of liquidity into the financial system, money flooded into repo markets, threatening to drive interest rates below zero. As we have seen, the IOER facility controlled the interest rates at which banks deposited excess reserves with the Fed, thereby setting rates across the banking system. ONRRP effectively extended this power to repo markets and shadow banks. By putting a permanent floor on interest rates in these markets, the Fed ensured that the money-market funds that shadow banks operated would be able to make positive returns, despite the flood of liquidity from QE. Thus, at the same time that the Fed was supplying dollars to the market and buying Treasuries, it was also selling Treasuries and buying cash—acting on all sides of the market to ensure stability and providing a state backstop, as was done earlier with the FDIC and the discount window.

Following a repo crisis in September 2019, in which the overnight interest rate on repo markets spiked to more than 10 percent and made it difficult even for shadow banks with secure collateral to fund asset purchases, the Fed expanded its power to set a ceiling on repo market interest rates as well. This was subsequently made permanent with the establishment of the Standing Repo Facility (SRF) in 2021. As it had long done by lending to banks through its discount window, the Fed now stood ready to supply money on repo markets at specified interest rates. That these rates were above the market rate ensured that institutions would turn to the Fed only if there was significant stress on repo markets. This was far more than just another measure to provide liquidity to markets, but a significant institutional change in the economic apparatus: the Fed had now completely integrated its balance sheet with the shadow banking system.

By expanding its powers in these ways, the Fed significantly de-risked repo markets. Establishing both a floor and ceiling on interest rates on these markets allowed the Fed to effectively control repo spreads within a particular bound, thereby limiting possible losses for the shadow banks that operated on them. Critically, the counterparties that met the criteria to use these facilities did not include institutional investors and pension funds, encouraging these institutions to continue to channel their money-capital to giant asset management firms, such as BlackRock and Vanguard, as these firms had access to state support. In this way, the statization of the financial system supported the socialization of capital by the asset management firms that had become the preeminent financial institutions in the economy, further entrenching the power structure of finance capital.

If this amounted to the dramatic incorporation of the shadow banking infrastructure in the state economic apparatus, it was dwarfed by the interventions undertaken during the Covid-19 crisis. Before the 2008 crisis, the Fed's balance sheet was around $900 billion. On the eve of the Covid pandemic, in March 2020, its balance sheet had ballooned to $4.3 trillion. Two years later, in March 2020, following the Covid interventions, it had exploded to $9.01 trillion. By this time, the Fed held roughly 30 percent of outstanding Treasuries. Not only did the Fed purchase mortgage-backed securities and Treasury bonds, as it had done in earlier rounds of QE, it now coordinated with Black-Rock to purchase corporate bonds, including those rated junk status, without any congressional authorization. The Fed now claimed the power to lend unlimited funds to industrial corporations, regardless of their creditworthiness, all but eliminating the distinction between public and private debt.

The implications of the extension of the Fed's powers from its traditional role as lender of last resort, and subsequently dealer of last resort, for financial institutions to non-financial corporations were profound. For the first time, the Fed signaled its willingness to

Chart 6.1: Corporate debt as a percent of earnings, 1947–2020

Source: *FRED, authors' calculations*

purchase effectively unlimited quantities of corporate bonds—thereby risk-proofing the debt of major corporations. Corporations that received such support included Apple, Goldman Sachs, and Microsoft, as well as more high-risk companies. The Fed also supported corporate debt markets by putting money into ETFs with diversified holdings in a range of corporate bonds. These actions complemented the other aspects of the QE program, slashing corporate borrowing costs as well as increasing the prices of the funds (managed by the Big Three asset managers) that the state had invested in.

These interventions, in turn, generated new contradictions. De-risking corporate bonds after maintaining interest rates at near-zero for fifteen years encouraged corporations to take on large amounts of debt, as they could effectively borrow "for free." The tremendous increase in corporate indebtedness that resulted is depicted in chart 6.1. As it shows, following a dip during the 2008 crisis, corporate indebtedness grew steadily from 2011 to 2015, and then exploded from 2016 onward—reaching an all-time high of 606 percent in 2018. Such high levels of corporate debt constrained the policy space open to the Fed in addressing inflation, as a sustained spike in interest rates would impact the ability for corporations to repay this debt and potentially trigger defaults. This could cause a severe crisis of the system of market-based finance—which would be difficult to address in the context of high inflation, as it would mean adding liquidity that would undermine interest rate increases.

There were also potential contradictions in the Treasury market. Indeed, the Fed's interventions in March 2020 were motivated by the need to address an unprecedented collapse of liquidity in these markets— meaning that instead of flocking to Treasuries as "safe-haven assets," investors were selling them. This created an acute crisis, which the Fed immediately addressed by further monetizing state debt. Nevertheless, fears remained about what this might mean for the liquidity of Treasury markets more generally, which continued to remain below 2019 levels. Adam Tooze, for instance, suggested that the Fed may not have the capacity to manage a repeat of the March 2020 liquidity collapse with its credibility intact. The result would be either a major economic crisis or a severe institutional crisis.[3] Yet if these worries were not entirely unwarranted, the idea that the Fed would be unable to manage a crisis in the Treasury market still seemed far-fetched.

In fact, the Fed's de-risking of repo and bond markets through its Covid-19 interventions displayed its willingness to undertake any action necessary to support these markets. This also reinforced the structure of finance capital by drawing asset management firms into a closer relationship with the state. As the cash generated by the Fed's bond purchases found its way into money-market funds, these funds turned to the Fed's ONRRP facility to generate risk-free positive returns. In the context of this flood of money, for ONRRP to serve its function of preventing interest rates on repo markets from dropping below zero, it had to offer above-market interest rates. Naturally, this created an incentive for managers of money-market funds to sell cash back to the Fed in exchange for Treasury bonds. The Fed thereby became the central intermediary for the cash pools accumulated within these money-market funds—the most important managers of which were the large asset management firms.

Again, even as the Fed was throwing money into the financial system through QE, it was simultaneously absorbing money and selling Treasury bonds. Not surprisingly, given that it was a lynchpin of the shadow banking system, BlackRock was a major beneficiary of these new state practices, engaging extensively—and profitably—in such transactions with the Fed on a daily basis. Between August 2021 (after the Fed raised the ONRRP rate) and October 2022, the average turnover between the Fed and the two BlackRock funds most heavily invested in government securities was $133 billion *every day*. As interest rates increased, the profitability of such risk-free transactions with the Fed rose in proportion. Moreover, since these were overnight transactions, rates were set daily, and the funds engaging in them were effectively protected against inflation. In August 2021, the yield was 0.05 percent—not insignificant for an overnight rate. By the end of 2022, it had risen to 4.3 percent.

Yet the benefits that accrued to BlackRock and other firms were not the objective of these interventions, but a byproduct of the Fed's support for the market-based financial system. As such, they did not signify a new era of financial "plunder," as Robert Brenner has claimed.[4] Quite the contrary: they were undertaken by a highly autonomous, independent Fed, acting not in the narrow interests of individual capitalists, but to serve the systemic imperatives of capital accumulation. The scale of the interventions reflected the severity of the crisis, while their form registered structural changes to the financial system. The long chain of intermediation that constitutes market-based finance means that it is not sufficient to simply prevent banks from going under. This system demands the Fed act as a *dealer of last resort*, buying and selling assets to support the valuations of key collateral and provide liquidity to repo and other money markets.

The reorganization of the state economic apparatus to support the shadow banking system also meant that it increasingly relied on financial firms other than traditional banks as vectors for implementing its monetary policy. As the Fed raised ONRRP rates, money-market funds were increasingly deposited with the Fed, which meant drawing money away from the private institutions that borrowed the cash these funds provided on repo markets. In addition to coordinating with primary dealer banks, which had long been responsible for implementing the Fed's monetary policy by agreeing to buy and sell Treasuries and thereby impact rates on the federal funds market (as we saw in chapter 3), it now collaborated with shadow banking institutions to influence interest rates in the tri-party repo market. Exchanging assets and cash with money-market funds managed by these firms now became a pivotal mechanism allowing the Fed to set critical short-term interest rates.

The growing statization of shadow banking helped to make the system of finance capital more resilient amid the return of market volatility and the emergence of inflationary pressures unseen since the crisis of the 1970s. As the Covid shutdown and reopening created unprecedented disruption to global supply chains and collapsed the service sector, and as the Fed stepped in to support consumption by monetizing state debt, huge macroeconomic imbalances between supply and demand led to the return of inflation. Contrary to the assertions of conservative economists, this was not simply a repeat of the wage-push inflation of the 1970s, which had been the result of trade union militancy. Indeed, labor remained weak and disorganized, and wage increases lagged prices—thus actually amounting to *declining* real wages. Nevertheless, to policymakers at the Fed, *any* acceleration of wage growth amid tightening labor markets was a potential threat that had to be stamped out.

Although initially insisting that inflation was merely "transitory," as inflationary pressures proved more prolonged and acute than Fed Chair Jerome Powell had anticipated, and especially as nominal wages started to slowly creep upward, the Fed acted. It did so first by halting its bond-buying program (QE), followed by an even more decisive move to quantitative tightening (QT), actively shrinking its balance sheet by not rolling over expiring bonds. Thus, as existing bonds matured, the gains were not reinvested in new ones, reducing the Fed's holdings. QT also reinforced the Fed's decision to raise interest rates on both interbank and repo markets. To demonstrate its unwavering commitment to upholding its fundamental anti-inflationary mandate after such a prolonged period of easy money, the Fed aimed to shock the market through a series of aggressive interest rate hikes designed to increase unemployment, slow the economy, and bring down prices.

Far from the "escalating plunder" of state coffers by financial institutions, these moves demonstrated just how autonomous the Fed in fact was. Yet in controlling inflation, the Fed was nevertheless acting in the general interest of capital. Despite the relaxation of inflation targeting it entailed, QE was never about allowing inflation to become "unanchored." Both the initiation of QE and the turn to QT were deployed to manage the contradictions of capitalism, which were continuously in motion as the system evolved and conditions changed. While QE had been necessary to resolve a severe liquidity crisis, QT was initiated to dampen credit creation in a hyper-liquid financial system. Both were innovative means through which the Fed managed interest rates and maintained its credibility amid a changing financial order. And even as the Fed drained liquidity, the new protections it had created for shadow banking enhanced financial stability.

Given that wages were not the primary driver of inflation, the Fed's turn to QT and higher interest rates may not have been the most effective policy—in the abstract—to deal with the problem. As some on the left insisted, targeted wage and price controls, or even an emergency wealth tax, could theoretically have been more effective.[5] But the structure of the capitalist state as it had evolved up to that moment meant that interest rates were the primary tool for macro-economic management available to those agencies in which power had been continuously centralized since the 1980s. If this policy turn illustrated the extent to which the Fed was acting on *behalf*, if not necessarily at the *behest*, of capital, it also raised important questions about the relationship between QE and the new finance capital—as well as whether the ascent of this class fraction in the power bloc could constitute the basis for a break with the post-1980s policy consensus.

The Macroeconomic Policy of Finance Capital

Neoliberal policy was defined by a strict coherence between fiscal and monetary authorities, whereby restrictive monetary policy set the parameters within which fiscal policy operated: monetary policy constrained fiscal policy. The Fed's implementation of a low-inflation monetary policy regime meant that its power served as a check on sustained fiscal policy expansion that might jeopardize the credibility of its commitment to maintaining monetary discipline. Demands for spending that exceeded the limits set by these highly autonomous monetary authorities were often sacrificed at the altar of monetary stability. This structure of state power was fortified by its reliance on debt, whereby spending was significantly financed not through taxation, but rather through borrowing. State spending therefore relied on the assent of investors to finance it.

The role of the state in managing inflation was not merely a policy choice; it was built into the structure of globalization. The stream-lined world of accumulation that emerged from the 1970s crisis depended on currency and interest rate stability to support the movement of capital internationally. To some extent, the risks that attended this could be managed by derivative contracts. But these could only do so much: the entire system had to be anchored by a low-inflation monetary regime. The commitment of central banks to controlling inflation was an essential condition for the stability of the interrelationship between the complex web of currencies through which value had to circulate as it moved through global capitalism—not only in a given moment but, more importantly, in the *future*, when the profits produced through globalized production systems would be realized.

Globalization required that industrial capital accept the low-inflation regime, and therefore fiscal and monetary restraint, along with the overall dominance of financial capital. Industrial firms had to forgo the potential benefits offered by a more active state industrial policy in favor of the dramatic increase in capital mobility afforded by the integration of global finance. Rather than state subsidization for industrial competitiveness and export-led growth, industry secured the power to freely circulate investment internationally in search of lower labor costs, cheap resources, and low taxes, thereby also obtaining working-class discipline at home. That industrial corporations had themselves by this time come to be organized around the increased dominance of money-capital, as top managers evolved into investors, also supported the extremely close convergence of interests between finance and industry throughout the neoliberal period.

Moreover, inflation targeting dictates low wage growth. When economic growth accelerates too quickly, the available "reserve army of labor," as Marx called it, gets absorbed into production—what economists refer to as "tight labor markets." Companies are therefore forced to compete against one another for labor, seeking to attract workers by offering better wages and other benefits. The result is inflation, as corporations try to protect profits by offsetting rising wage rates with higher prices. Yet these price increases erode the real value of wages, potentially pushing workers to demand higher wages to protect their purchasing power and standard of living—leading to a wage-price inflationary spiral as in the 1970s. Therefore, even though inflation targeting means restraining economic growth, industrial capital still benefits insofar as low inflation is sustained through the maintenance of a reserve army of the unemployed that serves to hold wages down.

The concentration of ownership power in asset management companies reinforces the class consensus around globalization. As we have seen, asset management companies do not stifle corporate competitiveness, but intensify it. As universal owners, these firms seek the most efficient allocation of resources, and lowest prices, across all sectors of the economy. This means giant asset management firms have a direct interest in maximizing the profitability of corporations they own and control—and therefore in increasing labor exploitation and the mobility of the capital managed by these companies. Since any reduction in capital mobility could only increase costs and thereby reduce corporate profits, asset management companies have a clear interest in sustaining globalization. In this way, the formation of finance capital only further cemented the congruence of interests among financial and industrial capital.

The interests of asset management companies are therefore at least partly tethered to the prevailing post-1980s policy framework. As we have seen, the continuous increase in the value of their AUM, and thus the valorization of their money-capital, has been connected to the Fed's QE policies, and the more permissive attitude toward inflation it adopted in 2019. Yet for asset management firms to realize gains, asset prices must be increasing faster than the rate of inflation across the economy. This means that the price of the assets they own would increase relative to the universal equivalent form (dollars), and therefore that these assets represent a larger share of the total social product. And again, the competitiveness of their portfolio companies, to which their own profitability is closely linked, is predicated on the monetary stability that underpins globalization. There are thus strong reasons asset managers need the Fed to control inflation.

However, Benjamin Braun has recently suggested that asset management firms have an interest in breaking with the low-inflation monetary regime that persisted throughout the neoliberal period. Because they fear the asset devaluation that would result from a restrictive monetary policy more than they fear inflation, Braun argues they may constitute a "powerful easy money constituency."[6] This contrasts with the interests of banks, which have been among the most consistent supporters of low inflation. In addition to complicating their role in supporting globalization and the international circulation of money-capital, inflation directly reduces bank profitability. Since high inflation means that the real value of dollars declines, the dollars paid back to lenders are worth less than the dollars initially lent out. Banks were therefore central to the "hard money" consensus of the neoliberal era.

In fact, while the Fed's loose money policies were a critical foundation for the rise of the Big Three, their continued financial dominance, and the persistence of the regime of corporate governance constructed around it, does not appear to hinge on the continuation of monetary policy stimulus. To begin with, the diversification of asset management companies between a range of money-market and securities funds means that they benefit in some ways from higher interest rates—profiting from both QE and QT. Not only do asset management firms operate relatively high-fee actively managed funds, but their deep involvement in the shadow banking system through cash management and bond holdings ultimately means their interests are not entirely different from those of "normal" banks in sustaining monetary stability.

More importantly, the attractiveness of passive management itself does not fundamentally depend on low interest rates: even in the context of greater volatility, active managers' ability to "beat the market" is dubious. Moreover, the economies of scale established by the Big Three grant them considerable cost advantages, allowing them to offer extremely low-cost diversified passively managed funds—which could retain a considerable competitive edge, and thus preserve the ownership power that is the major foundation of finance capital. In fact, since passive managers offer the safest path to invest in stocks, market uncertainty may actually *increase* these companies' ability to attract savings and build AUM. In any case, the continued very strong growth of passive management funds amid rising interest rates, declining asset values, and greater volatility suggests that the new finance capital may be durable indeed, despite the end of QE.[7]

If all this suggests that the political interests and economic durability of finance capital do not simply hinge on the endless continuation of QE, the turn to QT does not signify that the macroeconomic policy of finance capital is simply identical to neoliberalism. Indeed, managing inflation will *always* be a fundamental task of the central bank under any imaginable policy paradigm. This is especially the case in a floating rate monetary system, unmoored from a metallic base in gold. Thus, the exercise of the Fed's authority to rein in spiraling inflation should not be taken to imply that "nothing has changed," even if it clearly demonstrates that not *everything* has changed. In any case, it would be a mistake to see neoliberal policy as a strictly coherent body of doctrine. "Neoliberal" policy was always developed and applied in a contradictory and evolving political-economic order, on the basis of a given structure of state power and balance of class forces.

Focusing excessively on the need for the Fed to manage inflation conceals the institutional changes in the state economic apparatus, which both reflect and reinforce a regime of accumulation that is very different from neoliberal shareholder capitalism. As we have seen, this has taken place through the Fed's increasing orientation toward supporting shadow banking and the statization of market-based finance. This means that the Fed has undergone significant institutional change since the pre-2008 period. These developments have provided it with new policy levers, most importantly including the ability to manage macroeconomic performance and structure the flow of liquidity and credit by expanding or contracting its balance sheet— and often by doing both simultaneously. As a dealer, the Fed has frequently supplied liquidity to some sections of the market, while withdrawing it from others at the very same time.

As we have seen, the de-risking of the market-based financial system during the new finance capital period involved the Fed moving from being a lender of last resort for the traditional banking system, to supporting shadow banks by becoming a *dealer* of last resort on repo markets. However, the statization of finance has reached such an extent that the Fed is less and less even merely a dealer of last resort, stepping in to provide liquidity to stabilize or adjust interest rates on repo markets. Rather than sitting idly by and allowing market prices to form, the Fed now proactively structures these markets *in the first instance*, setting rates and preventing market prices from ever actually taking hold. While the Fed has always shaped interest rates through the federal funds market, intervening to establish the short-term rates it believes are necessary for financial stability, this represents a dramatic step forward in the encasement of financial markets by state power.

At the same time, the increasing absorption of shadow banking into the state economic apparatus marks a shift in the relationship between monetary and fiscal policy that persisted throughout the neoliberal period. Neoliberalism was characterized by the rigid separation between monetary and fiscal authorities, and in particular the concentration of power in the former acted as a disciplinary brake on the latter. The expansion of the Fed's balance sheet after 2008 attenuated this separation somewhat. As it bought up Treasury bonds to support credit creation and stabilize repo markets, the Fed became more active in shaping the interest rates that the Treasury paid to borrow funds and finance government spending. Yet if this represented a break with the neoliberal state, it was also quite different from the role the Fed had played in supporting government borrowing prior to the 1951 Fed-Treasury Accord, which helped establish its "independence."

Indeed, despite its more active role in bond markets, the Fed had not simply once again become institutionally subordinated to the Treasury and made the captive of fiscal policy; nor had it suddenly become oriented, in policy terms, toward keeping borrowing rates low to support fiscal expenditure. What this in fact amounted to was the development of what Daniela Gabor has called a "shadow monetary financing regime," in which the Fed purchased government bonds to support private credit creation in the shadow banking system.[8] This regime did not negate, but actually reinforced, the independence of the Fed, as it alone determined the frequency and extent of these interventions based on its assessments of the needs of the financial system. This recombination of fiscal and monetary policy was thus predicated on the authoritarian concentration of power in the Fed, rather than the return of control over macroeconomic policy to fiscal authorities (that is, Congress).

Rather than enabling expansionary fiscal policy, as the Fed had done prior to 1951, it sought to channel funds into the institutions and markets that were the basic pillars of the market-based financial system. That the mechanism whereby it did so—the purchase of government bonds from financial institutions—reduced interest rates on government borrowing and enabled deficit spending was a byproduct, not the objective, of this regime. Theoretically, the Fed could always restore discipline by ceasing its bond-buying. Yet this was beset by contradictions. Stopping bond purchases would also mean curtailing support for the shadow banking system. Additionally, revoking monetary support for fiscal policy could produce a currency crisis if private buyers did not step in to fill the gap and absorb state bonds. To be sure, such a limit seems remote in the case of the United States—but it is "out there somewhere."

That the extension of state power deeper into the system of market-based finance has embroiled it in such contradictions points to the extent to which these interventions cannot simply be "withdrawn" at will. As state power is pulled into the economic "sphere" through the expansion of the economic apparatus, it has become not "more powerful" but more dependent on the rhythms of capital accumulation, and more profoundly afflicted by its contradictions. Sustaining any pretense of "neoliberal" policy coherence is becoming increasingly difficult in the face of the contradictions that beset state intervention in the new financial order. Whatever those occupying the leading state agencies may desire, there is no going "back to normal," defined as the pre-crisis, neoliberal status quo. Despite similarities to the neoliberal policy framework, the emerging modalities of intervention demarcate a new moment.

The False Promise of Universal Ownership

Some have argued that the rise of asset management firms provides the basis for a break with neoliberalism because of their status as "universal owners," which gives them a stake not just in the competitiveness of certain firms, but *general* economic health.[9] The implication is that this may entail limiting the profits of individual firms in order to maximize long-term system-wide performance. Universal owners are held to have a special interest in capturing the "externalities" associated with the operations of particular firms.[10] Universal ownership is therefore seen to alter the logic of the competitive market system, which normally leads firms to displace as many costs of production as possible onto other firms, the state, or society as a whole. Corporations destroying the environment, and then leaving states and the public to bear the costs, are one obvious example of this.

As a result, these arguments hold, the new finance capital opens the possibility for a renewed social democratic class compromise either around the environment or the expansion of the welfare state and income redistribution. Such speculation was supported by the fact that finance capital was closely identified with the proliferation of "green" investment vehicles, especially in the form of environmental, social, and governance (ESG) funds. So, too, were such notions bolstered by the involvement of BlackRock in crafting Joe Biden's economic strategy, which was heralded as signaling a break with the neoliberal economics of the past several decades.[11] Indeed, while BlackRock offered a range of popular ESG vehicles, touting "sustainable" ways to invest money-capital, its executives occupied leading roles in the Biden administration—in particular Brian Deese, who served as chair of the powerful Council of Economic Advisors.

While Larry Fink had urged Trump to implement fiscal stimulus, this turn initially appeared to have arrived with the election of Joe Biden.[12] That Deese, Biden's top economic advisor, strongly advocated for a "twenty-first century American industrial strategy" appeared to indicate that the distinct interests of finance capital would shape the post-neoliberal policy Biden openly called for.[13] Biden's industrial strategy aimed to channel state investment into strategic assets, especially infrastructure, thereby encouraging private capital to follow suit. Meanwhile, the mild social democratic policies he proposed led some to speculate that finance capital would not only support the subsidization of infrastructure for corporate competitiveness, but may even constitute a "liberal financial bloc" that could possibly serve as the foundation for a new social democratic class compromise.[14]

Just a year into the Biden administration, BlackRock was celebrating what it saw as a "new investment order" marked by fiscal stimulus and low interest rates. It understood what many other financial institutions seemed to miss: that "the unprecedented cooperation between fiscal and monetary policies" that resulted from the Fed's shift "had upended the policy landscape."[15] The extent of the change was starkly illustrated by Biden's proposal for $6 trillion in stimulus spending within his first hundred days in office. BlackRock quickly expressed support for these initiatives—even breaking with the Business Round-table, National Association of Manufacturers, and Chamber of Commerce in backing increased taxation on business.[16] Its orientation seemed to reflect an understanding that fiscal stimulus could serve as a successor to QE in supporting the continued growth of equity prices, while promoting more stable and balanced growth over the long term.

Even if the investments Biden proposed were oriented toward maximizing corporate competitiveness and fostering public-private partnerships, many progressives saw such stimulus as good for workers in that they could lead to tighter labor markets and therefore potentially higher wages. So, too, would this put on the agenda the question of what form state spending would take, opening the possibility for at least some expansion of social spending.[17] In this way, "Bidenomics" seemed to take up the call of post-neoliberal social democrats for a renewal of industrial strategy to support corporate competitiveness and technological development, which, it was assumed, would go some way toward recreating the "good jobs" of the golden age.[18]

Despite comparisons of Biden's program to that of Franklin D. Roosevelt, the extent to which any of this could serve as the basis for a renewed class compromise, let alone one on the order of the New Deal, was always rather dubious. There is little reason to see state support for corporate competitiveness as intrinsically pro-labor. Indeed, this represents a massive retreat from traditional social democratic demands for decommodified public services, not to mention public ownership of industry, born of decades of defeat and accommodation. In any case, Bidenomics fundamentally depends on low inflation. While fiscal expansion may tighten labor markets, and thus create an opportunity for workers to bargain for increased wages, to the extent that this results in price increases the entire strategy is undermined. Thus Biden's rhetorical support for trade union rights was not *complementary* to the supposed interests of finance capital, but directly *antagonistic* to them.

It is equally unclear how the moderate expansion of social programs Biden proposed, such as universal pre-kindergarten, affordable child-care, free community college, strengthened unemployment insurance, and enlarged Obamacare could fit with the interests of finance capital. While the monetization of debt has relaxed constraints on congressional spending, as we have seen, the congruence between an expansive state fiscal policy and the interests of asset management companies is primarily around enhancing the competitiveness of MNCs. Insofar as this competitiveness rests on globalization, the mobility of capital and the power of firms to "exit" will continue to serve as a powerful disciplinary force on workers—thus negating any class compromise. Similarly, the initial openness of BlackRock to tax increases to correct current grotesque levels of inequality has very real limits. Indeed, the growth model of asset management firms relies on inequality, and the availability of surplus savings, to grow their AUM.

Even the support of finance capital for "easy money" evaporates the moment the working class begins to mobilize, or inflation reaches beyond certain limits. Not only did Larry Fink explicitly support increasing rates, but he even challenged Powell's initial assessment that inflation was merely transitory, and he insisted before the fact that the Fed would have to change policy.[19] In the context of higher rates, BlackRock will likely turn even more intensively to pushing its portfolio firms to ruthlessly cut costs and find profits. Similarly, the firm's much-vaunted emphasis on ESG investing has already been very publicly reined in. While ESG was always primarily about marketing and risk management, a BlackRock memo now explained that the firm would endorse fewer shareholder proposals on environmental responsibility over the coming year than it did in the prior one, because, in Fink's words, these are now too "constraining" and "prescriptive."[20]

In addition to its role in legitimation, ESG is also a tool for investors to manage the financial risks associated with ecological breakdown, as well as those emanating from controversies related to gender and racial discrimination. While the threat posed by climate chaos to global supply chains is clear, in the wake of the Black Lives Matter and #MeToo movements, public outcry related to corporate practices around gender and race can also significantly impact asset values. Therefore, ESG is not merely a form of greenwashing, but is also a tool for capital to try to account financially for a range of social and environmental risks. In addition to seeking to mitigate these often hidden costs, a range of investors, including pension funds, seek out "responsible" or "sustainable" investments for ethical reasons. Offering ESG products is thus motivated by the pursuit of competitive advantage. This is especially the case since these funds often have higher fees than other index funds.[21]

ESG strategies require that firms be rated and ranked according to their performance in relation to environmental and social factors. MSCI, an index provider, has taken the lead in developing such metrics, seeking to mimic credit-rating agencies that assess the risk that a company will default on its debts based on financial data. ESG ratings, on the other hand, are determined using far less clear-cut criteria.[22] These rankings determine the placement of firms on ESG indexes, which are then tracked by passively managed funds. By getting on ESG indexes, firms aim to improve their stock price and access capital by issuing "green bonds." In theory, this strengthens the competitive position of these firms and incentivizes the adoption of ESG practices. Meanwhile, "external" costs are captured on corporate balance sheets.

ESG ratings do not actually measure the harm to the environment caused by corporations, but the precise opposite: they assess the sustainability of *a firm's profitability* in the face of social and environmental risks. Environmental harm impacts these rankings only insofar as it poses a risk to future profits. The aim is to encourage individual firms to preserve their long-term profitability by properly accounting for the risks posed by climate change, not to address climate change itself. Furthermore, ESG performance is measured in relation to a sectoral average; therefore, it is possible for a firm to *improve* its ESG rating while *increasing* its carbon output, so long as it does so less rapidly than other firms in its sector.[23] The destructive nature of the system itself is thereby neutralized. The logic that supposedly follows from universal ownership—that such owners have a stake in mitigating system-wide risks—is not reflected in any way whatsoever in the structure of ESG ratings.

ESG strategies are based on reinforcing firm-level competitiveness and market discipline. They seem to hold out the promise that we can address climate change without challenging the power of multinational corporations, or even limiting the mobility of capital. All that is needed, from this perspective, are informational improvements to more efficiently allocate investment. At best, ESG incentivizes firms to account for the risks to their own operations, and therefore asset values, that result from their environmentally destructive activities. Since positive ESG ratings are compatible with continually rising CO_2 emissions, not to mention the destruction of habitats and other threats to biodiversity, there is no reason to believe that ESG strategies will be anywhere near sufficient to slow the pace of environmental degradation, let alone reverse it, or to decarbonize the economy. And despite the significant expansion of ESG, such funds remain relatively small.

Even if asset management companies had an interest in the general health of capitalism, they lack the capacity to implement an economy-wide plan that could break with competitiveness and market allocation. Winning seats on corporate boards or casting votes at shareholder meetings hardly provides a basis for overriding market imperatives. Moreover, as long as there is profit to be made by investing in any particular business, some capitalist will do so. Even if BlackRock were able to force certain oil companies to divest from fossil fuel production, for example, others would quickly step in to fill the gap. Meanwhile, BlackRock would either lose AUM to its competitors or be pressured itself to reinvest. Likewise, forcing a firm to adopt more costly but environmentally sustainable production methods would result in its competitors doing the exact opposite—and thus offering lower prices. Should such changes somehow be imposed on every firm in a sector, other firms would quickly enter to take advantage of the situation.

In any case, as we have seen, the empirical evidence is overwhelmingly clear: the extensive interventions by asset management companies into their portfolio firms are in every way aimed at enhancing firm-level competitiveness. It is impossible to imagine *reducing* competition, and the higher costs and inefficiencies this would bring, fitting in with the principles that guide these interventions—from governance reforms and shareholder rights to board composition, cost-cutting, independent auditing, and improved risk management. Moreover, the Big Three asset management firms are extremely long-term, even permanent, shareholders. It is difficult to believe that they would see it as being in their interest to promote the development of clumsy, inefficient, and uncompetitive companies. Nor would such firms find it easy to attract financing from bond markets. All this is especially the case in the context of competitive global markets.

Competitiveness is built into the structure of the current form of finance capital. Not only have contemporary industrial firms internalized the logic of finance and the discipline that comes with it, but competition between these firms has also intensified as they fight to maintain or enhance their position on the most important indexes. Index funds do not challenge but effectively lock in the market logic of allocating capital to those assets that generate relatively high returns, while withdrawing it from those where it is low. Similarly, asset management firms compete ferociously with each other, as well as all other outlets for savings, based on their ability to offer returns. Competition in this order is therefore not simply the result of subjective decisions made by those at the top—is a structural condition within which all strategies are formulated. It could not be overridden except through a radical institutional reorganization of the system itself.

The promise of universal ownership is largely a chimera. Asset management firms have neither the desire nor the means to enact the forms of economic coordination, or negotiate the trade-offs, among their portfolio firms that such conceptions suggest. Rather than aiming to enact a general plan for the economy, asset management companies strive to maximize the competitiveness and profitability of each and every individual firm in which they hold stakes. This includes a concern with the long-term risks these companies face, which asset managers encourage them to mitigate. Properly accounting for such risks includes addressing hazards to their bottom lines that management may have dismissed as externalities. What is at stake is not a revolutionary new logic, but *accurately* accounting for future threats to profitability, and managing these costs in the most efficient way possible.

The formation of the new finance capital does not seem to have created space for a meaningful social democratic class compromise. Rather, it has served to entrench the consensus among all fractions of capital around globalization and class discipline. While the ascent of the new fraction of finance capitalists in the power bloc has come with some limited moves toward a more robust industrial policy, whereby the state would extend greater subsidies to corporations for advanced manufacturing and cutting-edge R and D, such initiatives are narrowly focused on improving corporate competitiveness in the context of free capital mobility, not reversing four decades of neoliberal devastation of working-class communities. The political paradox the left faces today is that even as the working class is arguably as weak as it has ever been, winning substantive reforms and shifting the balance of class forces requires a truly radical confrontation with capital.

This points to the continued impasse of social democratic politics, which has been clear since the crisis of the 1970s demonstrated that "Keynesian" managed capitalism was not viable. In particular, the analysis we have presented reveals the bankruptcy of two mutually exclusive strategies. First, the new finance capital does not constitute a "liberal financial bloc" with which workers can achieve a new class compromise around fiscal expansion, social programs, or the environment. On the other hand, the proposition that workers can form an alliance with industrial capital (that is, their bosses) around reining in a parasitic financial sector—as suggested by narrow critiques of financialization that hold that finance "exploits" industry, just as capital "exploits" labor—is equally hollow. It is not possible to separate a discrete group of "industrialists" who have been victimized by globalization from "financiers" who have benefited from it.

Creating a more just future requires deeper structural change, beginning with challenging the capitalist globalization of recent decades.

Through the process of globalization, the interests of finance and industry have become more deeply intertwined: while the financialization of the firm converted industrial managers into financiers, the international restructuring this enabled also made finance more essential to industrial production. Breaking with globalization by imposing capital controls, thereby obstructing capital's ability to "exit," can create space for workers to win significant gains. Yet this raises the question of what happens with the capital that stays home—and thus points to the need to democratize control over investment. Rather than aiming to restore competitiveness by "breaking up the banks," a more robust socialist strategy today begins from the objective of nationalizing finance and running it as a public utility.

Democratizing Finance

The persistence of financial volatility points to a fundamental contradiction of the new finance capital: *it is not possible to de-risk capitalism.* The risk state can deflect certain financial risks, thereby shaping market calculations of cost and benefit and influencing the flow of investment. Yet it cannot *eliminate* the risks that attend these assets. While the flood of savings into equity and other securities that resulted from state de-risking increases their prices and supports asset-based accumulation, it also creates the conditions for large-scale devaluations and even a stock market crash. As these assets are attached to the rhythms of accumulation, their prices ebb and flow with the business cycle and financial market conditions. State intervention in shaping assessments of risk, contributing to the explosion of price-to-earnings ratios, thus potentially sets the stage for dramatic corrections, as stock prices are brought into line with realistic projections of corporate performance.

As we have shown, greater market volatility does not *automatically* threaten passive investment strategies or the market dominance of asset management companies. Nevertheless, as for all investors, the risk of a stock market crash does pose real problems for these firms. The rapid decline of equity prices would translate into a similar fall in the AUM, and therefore the profits, of asset management companies. Of course, any drop in stock prices is directly reflected in AUM, since the latter is nothing other than an expression of the value of the assets owned by asset managers. Since the fees charged by asset management companies are calculated as a percentage of AUM, in such an event the revenues of asset management companies would also sharply contract. Moreover, as fewer savers would be willing to invest in stocks in such circumstances, these companies' AUM would further shrink. A market crash could be just as fatal for finance capital today as it was a century ago.

The risk state de-risks specific financial assets by declaring its willingness to exchange them for US Treasury bonds and dollars. Its functioning therefore depends on the credibility of the central bank and the value of the assets it holds. Should investors come to doubt the future worth and soundness of Treasury bonds, or the continued stability of the dollar, the Fed's capacity to engage in de-risking would evaporate. Of course, investors no longer accepting Treasury bonds, or such a severe crisis of the dollar, would signify an existential crisis of global capitalism. But even short of this, declining demand for these assets could make the Fed reluctant to flood the market. There are also other contradictions of de-risking. For instance, monetizing state debt has exacerbated already historically unprecedented levels of economic inequality. This has worsened the crisis of legitimation currently afflicting the state, which poses a threat to liberal democracy itself.

Periodic crises have been the norm throughout the history of capitalism. In this regard, it is important to distinguish between *economic* crises—which are rooted in contradictions that are immanent to the functioning of the capitalist economic system—and political, ecological, and social crises, though of course these are complexly interrelated. By all accounts, we are currently living through a severe, and worsening, multidimensional ecological crisis. Similarly, the devastation left in the wake of four decades of neoliberalism, as social services were rolled back, wages stagnated or declined, and factories closed, constitutes a significant social crisis.[24] The delegitimation of capitalism that has resulted from all of this has generated a major political crisis, particularly registered in the widespread discrediting of the media system and political parties. This crisis of legitimation has ebbed and flowed since the 2008 economic crisis, alternating between particularly acute manifestations, simmering tensions, and "morbid symptoms."

The legitimation crisis has most immediately afflicted the ideological state apparatus, reverberating out from the political parties and spreading throughout the state complex. The election of Donald Trump was a direct result of this crisis, and exacerbated it, introducing heightened chaos into state administration while further discrediting the political establishment, globalization, and even electoral institutions themselves. Conflicts and practices of power that normally take place "behind the scenes" were thrust into the open, as typically "apolitical" agencies worked to contain the damage and preserve the routine operation of the state and its global imperial role. While this, together with the insulation of state administration from "political" interference perhaps helped to limit some of the immediate damage Trump could do, it also accelerated the wider delegitimation of the political system, fueling the far-right mobilization he encouraged.[25]

Although some have argued that all this adds up to an "organic crisis"—a comprehensive crisis that engulfs the totality of the social system—such suggestions seem premature.[26] An organic crisis would mean that the ability of the ruling class to *rule* is fundamentally in doubt. Thus far, the challenges facing the American state and ruling class do not seem to approach such an existential level. Economic inequality and working-class precarity have *benefited* capital insofar as they resulted from lower wages and intensified labor discipline. To be sure, these issues have contributed to the legitimation crisis, which may create openings for a challenge to the system. Yet so far it has been the far right, which is hardly anti-capitalist, that has benefited the most from this crisis. So long as the dissatisfaction with life under capitalism does not translate into working-class organization and mass action, capitalism will remain, albeit perhaps in a more barbaric form.

The capacity of finance capital and the risk state to navigate these crises is now being put to the test. Whatever political renegotiation is entailed by the reshuffling of relations within the power bloc will be determined by *political*, not just *economic*, factors. The failure of Brian Deese's industrial strategy indicates that finance capital may have some way to go in consolidating its hegemony. Doing so will require the formulation by the state of an economic strategy, as well as an approach for dealing with the legitimacy crisis and managing the climate crisis, that can serve as the basis for a class-wide consensus under conditions of ecological collapse and deep social malaise. Whether the rise of finance capital creates sufficient space to enact hegemonic strategies that break with the delegitimated neoliberal paradigm remains unclear. If Bidenism was an attempt to deal with these challenges, the vacuum left by its defeat foretells further possible dangers from the far right.

The political contestation surrounding the rise of finance capital significantly pertains to the forms and extent of state intervention required to address these problems. Many social democrats have insisted that an approach to decarbonizing the economy led by "big finance" is destined to fail, and have called for the state to play a larger role in guiding investment to decarbonize the economy.[27] In demanding a more active fiscal policy, these progressives notably stop well short of calling for taking the productive capacities of private corporations under public control and deploying them in service of a wide-ranging green transition, as socialists have advocated—progressives even cheer the new monetary and fiscal union.[28] Meanwhile, finance capital has pointed to its ESG strategies to demonstrate that it is equipped to address the climate crisis, as well as address racism and gender-based oppression, without the need for a significant extension of state control over investment.

The challenge before us is no less than developing a more balanced metabolic relation between human society and nature. Taking even minimal steps toward addressing the ecological crisis demands going well beyond offering incentives to firms based on market signals; it demands implementing a massive state-led program of green transition.[29] Any green transition will require the state to mobilize the productive capacities currently owned and controlled by private corporations based on a public plan for allocating investment. If this is to amount to more than contracts with capitalist firms, the structure of the capitalist state, based as it is on the private control of capital, must itself be called into question. Instead of being given subsidies and contracts, firms that are critical for the "greening" of the economy should be nationalized—which, in turn, raises the question of how to democratically organize these economic activities.

What this calls for, in other words, is a theorization of a green socialist transition—which entails a fundamental transformation of the state by developing its capacities to manage a democratic economy. The severity and rapid acceleration of the climate emergency means that this is no longer merely a matter of utopian theorizing. It is an urgent and pragmatic necessity to ensure human survival. The preeminent agencies in the current authoritarian structure of state power— especially the Fed and the Treasury—will constitute major sites of resistance to even minimal reforms. Developing a plan for how these institutions can be reorganized to support the needed economic trans- formation is therefore critically important. Pivotal for such a plan would be extending public control over the financial system, which is the mechanism through which investment is distributed across the various branches of production.

Despite ownership concentration, the economy remains disorgan- ized at the macro level, structured around the allocation of capital based strictly on its ability to generate profit. Unplanned markets offer a choice between Coke or Pepsi, but not between highways or an effi- cient high-speed rail system. Similarly, there is no market choice that results in a system that is not based on the consumption of fossil fuels— which, however harmful for the planet they may be, are quite profitable. Getting past the limited "democracy of the market" is therefore funda- mentally about reversing the capitalist prioritization of *exchange* over *use*, such that production comes to be organized around meeting social needs rather than serving the endless accumulation of money.

For Hilferding, the formation of finance capital immensely eased the difficulties of socialist transition. Capitalism, he believed, was auto- matically evolving the basis for socialism. The emergence of "organized capitalism" was replacing anarchic market competition with a coordi- nated system of economic planning—albeit one planned not to meet social needs, but to maximize capitalist profits. As a result, he rather hyperbolically claimed that "taking possession of six large Berlin banks would mean taking possession of the most important spheres of large-scale industry."[30] Yet the persistence of what Marx called "the coercive laws of competition" meant that this task could hardly be so straightforward. Then, as now, a socialist transition demands a much deeper transformation of political and economic institutions, so that investment decisions can escape market dependence—which is inherently antithetical to democracy—and come under conscious social control.

Despite the tremendous ownership power of the Big Three, simply nationalizing them would, on its own, amount to little. For one thing, they do not engage in anything like the kind of society-wide economic planning that would characterize socialism; instead they rely on price signals and profitability to determine the allocation of investment. Moreover, their power depends on voluntary contributions of capital. Pension funds and other investors would be unlikely to entrust the management of their capital to an institution that had been taken under public control with the explicit objective of reducing (even if not immediately eliminating) its reliance on competitiveness and monetary returns. Establishing meaningful social control over finance, therefore, requires capturing a wider range of institutions—including the institutional pools of money in the pension funds, as well as the credit-generating capacities of the traditional banking system.

Clearly, the state is the only social structure capable of carrying out such a transition. Yet the capitalist state is above all characterized by its relative autonomy from capital, and is founded upon the institutionalization of private control over investment. Moreover, as state institutions evolved over the twentieth century to deal with the crises and contradictions of capitalism, a particularly authoritarian structure of power was consolidated. The goal of democratizing finance is therefore inherently bound up with the task of transforming the state, such that it can serve as the central organ of a democratically planned economy. Democratizing the state in this sense means capturing and fundamentally remaking the centers of state power, such that in place of their current functions in sustaining the system of class rule, they come to facilitate radical new forms of popular participation in economic and social life—from national investment decisions to community involvement in running social services.

Any approach to "democratizing finance" that does not connect this to the need to transform the state is bound to end up subordinated to the discipline of market competitiveness. Democratic workers' cooperatives or community financial institutions, so long as they are not connected to a wider system of credit creation and distribution that is shielded from market competitiveness, are bound to reproduce the same limitations as the capitalist institutions they are trying to replace: allocating investment based on the need to maximize returns, enforcing wage restraint and the cheapening of commodities, and so on. Connecting democratic workplaces and community financial institutions to a financial system run as a public utility by the state is the only way to transcend such challenges, allowing investment to be allocated based on social and ecological need rather than market competitiveness and profit maximization.

The fundamental role of the Fed in the creation of money and the organization of the financial system makes it pivotal for any strategy to democratize finance. The Fed is the central institution in the modern financial system that unites its disparate components into a coherent whole, underpinning the capacity of private institutions to distribute credit and investment across the economy. Not only does the Fed stand at the top of the monetary system both domestically and internationally, but it constitutes a unique nexus of the banking and shadow banking systems: both the repo money issued by shadow banks and the hybrid money issued by traditional banks are constituted through the Fed's monetary capacities. Democratizing the economy necessarily involves reorienting the Fed's operations to provide the credit to fuel a green transition and support widespread public ownership of social productive capacities.

Given the immense challenges this entails, calling for socialist transition may today seem utopian. Yet in the face of the mounting threat to civilization posed by ecological collapse, the real utopians are not those who dare to dream of a better world but, rather, those who believe it is possible to keep things as they are. Despite the constant stream of catastrophic news across social media feeds and cable news channels, doom is not inevitable. The possibility for the fundamental social transformation that is more urgently needed now than ever before is not foreclosed. Even in this dark hour, it is up to us to maintain what Leo Panitch called "the optimism of the intellect," searching for cracks in the current order from which a better future could bloom.[31] It is time now to turn the page on our capitalist prehistory, so that a truly human history can begin. The next chapter in human development could be a socialist one. Whether this comes to pass depends on all of us.

Notes

1: The Latest Phase of American Capitalist Development

1. Rudolf Hilferding, *Finance Capital: A Study in the Latest Phase of Capitalist Development*, London: Routledge, 1981 [1910].

2. Stephen Maher, *Corporate Capitalism and the Integral State: General Electric and a Century of American Power*, London: Palgrave, 2022.

3. Of course, the structure of bank power in the United States and Germany differed, but notwithstanding particularities and nuances, Hilferding's analysis broadly applies in both cases. See J. Bradford DeLong, "Did J. P. Morgan's Men Add Value? An Economist's Perspective on Financial Capitalism," in Peter Temin, ed., *Inside the Business Enterprise: Historical Perspectives on the Use of Information*, Chicago: University of Chicago Press, 1991, 205–50; Mary A. O'Sullivan, *Dividends of Development: Securities Markets in the History of US Capitalism, 1866–1922*, Oxford, UK: Oxford University Press, 2016; Peter A. Gourevitch and James Shinn, *Political Power and Corporate Control: The New Global Politics of Corporate Governance*, Princeton, NJ: Princeton University Press, 2005.

4. Alfred Chandler Jr., *The Visible Hand: The Managerial Revolution in American Business*, Cambridge, MA: Harvard University Press, 1977; Adolf A. Berle and Gardiner C. Means, *The Modern Corporation and Private Property*, New Jersey: Transaction Publishers, 1932; John Scott, *Corporate Business and Capitalist Classes*, Oxford, UK: Oxford University Press, 1997; Miguel Cantillo Simon, "The Rise and Fall of Bank Control in the United States: 1890–1939," *American Economic Review* 88: 5, 1998.

5. Wolfgang Streeck, *Buying Time: The Delayed Crisis of Democratic Capitalism*, London: Verso, 2014.

6. Stephen Maher and Scott M. Aquanno, "From Economic to Political Crisis: Trump and the Neoliberal State," in Rob Hunter, Rafael Khachaturian, and

Eva Nanopoulos, eds., *Capitalist States and Marxist State Theory: Enduring Debates, New Perspectives*, London: Palgrave Macmillan (forthcoming).

7. Streeck, *Buying Time*.

8. Leo Panitch and Sam Gindin, *The Making of Global Capitalism: The Political Economy of American Empire*, London: Verso, 2012.

9. Michael Useem, *Investor Capitalism: How Money Managers Are Changing the Face of Corporate America*, New York: Basic Books, 1999; Stephen Maher, "Stakeholder Capitalism, Corporate Organization, and Class Power," in Simon Archer, Chris Roberts, Kevin Skerrett, and Joanna Weststar, eds., *The Contradictions of Pension Fund Capitalism*, Ithaca, NY: Cornell University Press, 2017.

10. Scott, *Corporate Business and Capitalist Classes*.

11. Neil Fligstein, *The Transformation of Corporate Control*, Cambridge, MA: Harvard University Press, 1990; David Harvey, *The Limits to Capital*, updated edition, London: Verso, 2007, chapter 5; Claude Serfati, "The New Configuration of the Capitalist Class," in Leo Panitch and Greg Albo, eds., *Socialist Register 2014: Registering Class*, London: Merlin Press, 2013; Maher, *Corporate Capitalism and the Integral State*.

12. Dirk M. Zorn, "Here a Chief, There a Chief: The Rise of the CFO in the American Firm," *American Sociological Review* 69: 3, 2004, 345–64.

13. Dick Bryan and Michael Rafferty, *Capitalism with Derivatives: A Political Economy of Financial Derivatives, Capital, and Class*, London: Palgrave, 2006.

14. Harland Prechel, "Corporate Transformation to the Multi-Layered Subsidiary Form," *Sociological Forum* 12: 3, 1997, 405–39.

15. Stephen Maher, Sam Gindin, and Leo Panitch, "Class Politics, Socialist Policies, Capitalist Constraints," in Leo Panitch and Greg Albo, eds., *Socialist Register 2020: Beyond Market Dystopia: New Ways of Living*, London: Merlin Press, 2019.

16. Giovanni Arrighi, *The Long Twentieth Century: Money, Power, and the Origins of Our Times*, London: Verso, 1994; Giovanni Arrighi and Beverley J. Silver, *Chaos and Governance in the Modern World System*, Minneapolis: University of Minnesota Press, 1999.

17. Gretta R. Krippner, *Capitalizing on Crisis: The Political Origins of the Rise of Finance*, Cambridge, MA: Harvard University Press, 2012; William Lazonick, "Profits Without Prosperity," *Harvard Business Review*, September 2014; William Lazonick, "The Financialization of the U.S. Corporation: What Has Been Lost, and How It Can Be Regained," *Seattle University Law Review* 36: 2, 2013; William Lazonick and Mary O'Sullivan, "Maximizing Shareholder Value: A New Ideology for Corporate Governance," *Economy*

and Society 29: 1, 2000, 13–35; William Lazonick and Mary O'Sullivan, eds., *Corporate Governance and Sustainable Prosperity*, London: Palgrave, 2002.

18. Seth Fiegerman, "Uber Is Losing Billions: Here's Why Investors Don't Care," *CNN*, June 1, 2017.

19. Timothy B. Lee, "Tesla Keeps Losing Money. So Why Is It Worth More Than Ford?," *CNBC*, April 5, 2017.

20. "Corporate Short-Termism Is a Frustratingly Slippery Idea," *The Economist*, February 16, 2017.

21. David Harvey, *A Brief History of Neoliberalism*, Oxford, UK: Oxford University Press, 2005; Robert Brenner, *The Boom and the Bubble: The US in the World Economy*, London: Verso, 2003; Robert Brenner, "Escalating Plunder," *New Left Review* 123, May/June 2020; Dylan Riley and Robert Brenner, "Seven Theses on American Politics," *New Left Review* 138, November/December 2022; Cédric Durand, *Fictitious Capital: How Finance Is Appropriating Our Future*, London: Verso, 2017.

22. François Chesnais, *Finance Capital Today: Corporations and Banks in the Lasting Global Slump*, Chicago: Haymarket Books, 2018.

23. Costas Lapavitsas, *Profiting Without Producing: How Finance Exploits Us All*, London: Verso, 2014.

24. Ben Fine, "Financialization From a Marxist Perspective," *International Journal of Political Economy*, 42: 4, 2013, 47–66.

25. Panitch and Gindin, *Making of Global Capitalism*.

26. Harvey, *Limits to Capital*, 321; David Harvey, *The Enigma of Capital and the Crises of Capitalism*, Oxford, UK: Oxford University Press, 2011, 55.

27. Scott, *Corporate Business and Capitalist Classes*.

28. Gerald F. Davis, "A New Finance Capitalism? Mutual Funds and Ownership Re-concentration in the United States," *European Management Review* 5:1, 2008, 11–21.

29. Ibid., 13, 20.

30. Benjamin Braun, "Asset Manager Capitalism as a Corporate Governance Regime," in Jacob Hacker, Alex Hertel-Fernandez, Paul Pierson, and Kathleen Thelen, eds., *The American Political Economy: Politics, Markets, and Power*, Cambridge, UK: Cambridge University Press, 2021, 273.

31. Benjamin Braun, "From Exit to Control: The Structural Power of Finance Under Asset Manager Capitalism," Working Paper, Max Planck Institute for the Study of Societies.

32. Jan Fichtner, Eelke M. Heemskerk, and Javier Garcia-Bernardo, "Hidden Power of the Big Three? Passive Index Funds, Re-concentration of Corporate

Ownership, and New Financial Risk," *Business and Politics* 19:2, 2017, 298–326.

33. David Harvey, *Seventeen Contradictions and the End of Capitalism*, Oxford, UK: Oxford University Press, 2014.

34. Hilferding, *Finance Capital*, 109.

35. Adolph Reed Jr., *New Labor Forum*, December 12, 2013.

2: Classical Finance Capital and the Modern State

1. Karl Marx, *Capital: Volume III*, trans. David Fernbach, London: Penguin Books, 1981 [1894], 432–3.

2. Ibid., 460.

3. Ibid., 528.

4. Charles F. Dunbar, *The Theory and History of Banking*, New York: Knickerbocker Press, 1922 [1891]; Allyn Young, "The Mystery of Money," in *The Book of Popular Science*, New York: Grolier Society, 1924; Mitchell Innes, "What is Money?," *The Banking Law Journal*, May 1913.

5. Marx, *Capital: Volume III*, 525.

6. Ibid., 572, 601, 604. Emphasis added.

7. Ibid., 490–1.

8. Ibid., 512.

9. Ibid., 567.

10. Ibid., 567, 570.

11. Ibid., 570.

12. Ibid., 570–1.

13. Ibid., 597.

14. Ibid., 595–6.

15. James O'Connor, *The Corporations and the State: Essays in the Theory of Capitalism and Imperialism*, New York: Harper Collins, 1974; James O'Connor, *The Fiscal Crisis of the State*, New York: St. Martin's Press, 1973.

16. Mariana Mazzucato, *The Entrepreneurial State: Debunking Public vs. Private Sector Myths*, London: Anthem Press, 2013; Mariana Mazzucato, *Mission Economy: The Moonshot Guide to Changing Capitalism*, New York: Harper Business, 2021; Fred Block and Matthew R. Keller, *State of Innovation: The U.S. Government's Role in Technological Development*, Oxfordshire, UK: Taylor & Francis, 2015.

17. Dunbar, The *Theory and History of Banking*; Young, "The Mystery of Money,"; Innes, "What is Money?"; Giorgio Pizzuto, *The US Financial System and Its Crises: From the 1907 Panic to the 2007 Crash*, London: Palgrave, 2019.

18. Dunbar, *Theory and History of Banking*; Young, "The Mystery of Money."

19. Chandler, *The Visible Hand*, 319; Joshua Barkan, *Corporate Sovereignty: Law and Government Under Capitalism*, Minneapolis: University of Minnesota Press, 2013, 56–7.

20. Chandler, *The Visible Hand*, 320; Martin J. Sklar, *The Corporate Reconstruction of American Capitalism 1890–1916*, Cambridge, UK: Cambridge University Press, 105–45; William G. Roy, *Socializing Capital: The Rise of Large Industrial Corporation in America*, Princeton, NJ: Princeton University Press, 197–8.

21. Marx, *Capital: Volume III*, ch. 36.

22. Hilferding, *Finance Capital*, 226.

23. Marx, *Capital: Volume III*, 495.

24. J. Bradford DeLong, "J. P. Morgan and His Money Trust," *Wilson Quarterly* 16:4, 1992.

25. Louis D. Brandeis, *Other People's Money and How the Banks Use It*, New York: Frederick A. Stokes Company, 1914; Ron Chernow, *The House of Morgan: An American Banking Dynasty and the Rise of Modern Finance*, New York: Grove Press, 1990; United States Congress House Committee on Banking and Currency, 1865–1974, Arsène Paulin Pujo, 1861–1939, and Sixty-Second Congress, 1911–1913, "Exhibit 134-C: Interlocking Directorates" in Money Trust Investigation: Investigation of Financial and Monetary Conditions in the United States Under House Resolutions nos. 429 and 504, Before a Subcommittee of the Committee on Banking and Currency, House of Representatives, 1912–1913.

26. Hilferding, *Finance Capital*, 119–20.

27. Ibid., 225.

28. Ibid., 120–21.

29. Ibid., 121, 119.

30. Brandeis, *Other People's Money*, 22.

31. Ibid., ch. 1.

32. Hilferding, *Finance Capital*, 121.

33. Ibid., 109.

34. Ibid., 109, 114.

35. Ibid., 177.

36. Ibid., 156.

37. Ibid., 154.

38. Mary O'Sullivan, "The Expansion of the U.S. Stock Market, 1885–1930: Historical Facts and Theoretical Fashions," *Enterprise & Society* 8: 3, 2007, 489–542.

39. Martijn Konings, *The Development of American Finance*, Cambridge, UK: Cambridge University Press, 2011.

40. Hilferding, *Finance Capital*, 180.
41. Ibid., 180.
42. John Weeks, *Capital and Exploitation*, Princeton, NJ: Princeton University Press, 153.
43. James A. Clifton, "Competition and the Evolution of the Capitalist Mode of Production," *Cambridge Journal of Economics* 1: 2, 1977, 137–51.
44. Marx, *Capital: Volume III*, 742.
45. Ibid., 281.
46. Rudolf Hilferding, "The Materialist Conception of History," in Tom Bottomore, ed., *Modern Interpretations of Marx*, Oxford, UK: Basil Blackwell, 1981 [1941].
47. Stephen Skowronek, *Building a New American State: The Expansion of National Administrative Capacities, 1877–1920*, Cambridge, UK: Cambridge University Press, 1982.
48. Chernow, *House of Morgan*, 125.
49. Perry Mehrling, *The New Lombard Street: How the Fed Became the Dealer of Last Resort*, Princeton, NJ: Princeton University Press, 2010; Perry Mehrling, "The Inherent Hierarchy of Money," in Lance Taylor, et al., eds., *Social Fairness in Economics: Economic Essays in the Spirit of Duncan Foley*, London: Routledge, 2012.
50. Young, "Mystery of Money."
51. Maher, *Corporate Capitalism and the Integral State*, ch. 3.
52. Ibid., ch. 3.

3: Managerialism and the New Deal State

1. Fligstein, *Transformation of Corporate Control*.
2. Harvey, *Enigma of Capital*.
3. Chernow, *House of Morgan*, ch. 18; Simon, "Rise and Fall of Bank Control."
4. Mehrling, "The Inherent Hierarchy of Money"; Zoltan Pozsar, "Shadow Banking: The Money View," Office of Financial Research, Department of the Treasury, Working Paper 14-04, July 2, 2014.
5. Panitch and Gindin, *Making of Global Capitalism*, 58–59; Allen H. Meltzer, *A History of the Federal Reserve: Volume I, 1913 to 1951*, Chicago: University of Chicago Press, 2003; Peter Conti-Brown, *The Power and Independence of the Federal Reserve*, Princeton, NJ: Princeton University Press, 2016; Mehrling, *New Lombard Street*.
6. Lester Chandler, *Benjamin Strong: Central Banker*, Washington, DC: Brookings Institution, 1958; Kenneth Garbade, "The Early Years of the Primary Dealer System," Federal Reserve Bank of New York, Staff Report no. 777, June 2016.

7. Garbade, "Early Years of the Primary Dealer System."

8. Antoine Martin and Joshua Younger, "War Finance and Bank Leverage: Lessons from History," Yale School of Management, September 8, 2020; Kenneth Garbade, "Managing the Treasury Yield Curve in the 1940s," Federal Reserve Bank of New York, Staff Report no. 913, February 2020.

9. Martin and Younger, "War Finance and Bank Leverage: Lessons from History."

10. Herbert Stein, *The Fiscal Revolution in America: Policy in Pursuit of Reality*, Chicago: University of Chicago Press, 1969.

11. Yannis Dafermos, Daniela Gabor, and Joe Michell, "FX Swaps, Shadow Banks, and the Global Dollar Footprint," *Economy and Space*, 2022.

12. Panitch and Gindin, *Making of Global Capitalism*.

13. Panitch and Gindin, *Making of Global Capitalism*.

14. Scott M. Aquanno, *The Crisis of Risk: Subprime Debt and US Financial Power 1944 to Present*, Northampton, MA: Edward Elgar, 2021; Eric Helleiner, *States and the Reemergence of Global Finance: From Bretton Woods to the 1990s*, Ithaca, NY: Cornell University Press, 1994.

15. Maher, *Corporate Capitalism and the Integral State*, chs. 3 and 4; Alan Brinkley, *The End of Reform: New Deal Liberalism in Recession and War*, New York: Random House, 1995.

16. Useem, *Investor Capitalism*; Henwood, *Wall Street*; Edward S. Herman, *Corporate Control, Corporate Power: A Twentieth-Century Fund Study*, Cambridge, UK: Cambridge University Press, 1982; Scott, *Corporate Business and Capitalist Classes*.

17. Joe Mahon, "Bank Holding Company Act of 1956," Federal Reserve Bank of Minneapolis, 2013.

18. Useem, *Investor Capitalism*; Scott, *Corporate Business and Capitalist Classes*.

19. Marx, *Capital: Volume III*, 460.

20. Fortune 500 Database, 1960.

21. Useem, *Investor Capitalism*, 208.

22. Chandler, *The Visible Hand*, 451–2.

23. Robert Johnston, "Rebirth of Commercial Paper," Federal Reserve Bank of San Francisco, Monthly Review, July 1968.

24. Maher, *Corporate Capitalism and the Integral State*, 119–28, 229–42.

25. Lazonick, "Profits Without Prosperity"; Lazonick, "Financialization of the U.S. Corporation"; Krippner, *Capitalizing on Crisis*.

26. Brian Waddell, *Toward the National Security State: Civil-Military Relations During World War II*, Westport, CT: Praeger Security International, 2008; Mazzucato, *Entrepreneurial State*.

27. Stephen A. Cambone, *A New Structure for National Security Policy Planning*, Washington, DC: Center for Strategic and International Studies, 1998; Daniel J. Kaufman, "National Security: Organizing the Armed Forces," *Armed Forces & Society* 14: 187, 1987; Waddell, *Toward the National Security State.*

28. Maher, *Corporate Capitalism and the Integral State*, ch. 4.

29. Mazzucato, *Entrepreneurial State.*

30. As was especially the case with Seymour Melman's classic study, *Pentagon Capitalism: The Political Economy of War*, New York: McGraw-Hill, 1970.

31. National Science Foundation. R and D increase is measured in relation to the 1953 benchmark.

32. Alfred Chandler Jr., *Strategy and Structure: Chapters in the History of the American Industrial Enterprise*, Cambridge, MA: MIT Press, 2000, 299–314; Maher, *Corporate Capitalism and the Integral State,* ch. 4.

33. Louis Hyman, "Rethinking the Postwar Corporation," in Kim Phillips-Fein and Julian E. Zelizer, eds., *What's Good for Business: Business and American Politics Since World War II*, Oxford, UK: Oxford University Press, 2012.

34. Joseph A. Schumpeter, "The Creative Response in Economic History," *The Journal of Economic History* 7: 2, 1947, 149–59; Chandler, *Strategy and Structure*, 284.

35. Fligstein, *Transformation of Corporate Control.*

36. Marx, *Capital: Volume III*, 490–1.

37. Paul A. Baran and Paul M. Sweezy, *Monopoly Capital: An Essay on the American Economic and Social Order*, New York: Monthly Review Press, 1966.

38. Weeks, *Capital and Exploitation.*

39. Fligstein, *Transformation of Corporate Control*; Serfati, "New Configuration of the Capitalist Class"; Maher, *Corporate Capitalism and the Integral State*, 229–42; William E. Rothschild, *The Secret to GE's Success*, New York: McGraw-Hill Professional, 2007.

40. Aquanno, *Crisis of Risk*, ch. 6; Panitch and Gindin, *Making of Global Capitalism*, ch. 5.

41. Daniel J. Clark, *Disruption in Detroit: Autoworkers and the Elusive Postwar Boom*, Champaign: University of Illinois Press, 2018, ch. 2; John Barnard, *Walter Reuther and the Rise of the Auto Workers*, Boston: Little, Brown and Company, 1983, 154.

42. O'Connor, *The Fiscal Crisis of the State.*

43. These were the words of Paul McCracken, the chair of Nixon's Council of Economic Advisers. See Maher, *Corporate Capitalism and the Integral State*, p. 292.

44. Adolph Reed Jr. and Touré F. Reed, "The Evolution of 'Race' and Racial Justice Under Neoliberalism," in Greg Albo, Leo Panitch, and Colin Leys, eds., *Socialist Register 2022: New Polarizations, Old Contradictions,* London: Merlin Press, 2021.

45. Sam Gindin, "Rethinking Unions, Registering Socialism," in Leo Panitch, Greg Albo, and Vivek Chibber, eds., *Socialist Register 2013: The Question of Strategy,* London: Merlin Press, 2012.

46. Maher, *Corporate Capitalism and the Integral State,* ch. 7; Benjamin Waterhouse, *Lobbying America: The Politics of Business from Nixon to NAFTA,* Princeton, NJ: Princeton University Press, 2013, 77.

47. Maher, *Corporate Capitalism and the Integral State,* 251.

48. Ibid., 253–4.

49. Waterhouse, *Lobbying America,* 181.

50. Nitsan Chorev, *Remaking U.S. Trade Policy: From Protectionism to Globalization,* Ithaca, NY: Cornell University Press, 2007; Jamey Essex, "Getting What You Pay For: Authoritarian Statism and the Geographies of US Trade Liberalization Strategies," *Studies in Political Economy* 80: 1, 2007, 75–103; Maher, *Corporate Capitalism and the Integral State,* ch. 8; Panitch and Gindin, *Making of Global Capitalism,* 164.

51. Nicos Poulantzas, *State, Power, Socialism,* London: Verso, 1978, part 4.

52. Andrew Gamble, "The Free Economy and the Strong State," in Ralph Miliband and John Saville, eds., *Socialist Register 1979,* London: Merlin Press, 1978.

53. Military expenditure (% of GDP)—United States, Stockholm International Peace Research Institute (SIPRI), Yearbook: Armaments, Disarmament and International Security, 2021.

54. Maher, *Corporate Capitalism and the Integral State,* 282–6.

4: Neoliberalism and Financial Hegemony

1. Michael Useem, *Executive Defense: Shareholder Power and Corporate Reorganization,* Cambridge, MA: Harvard University Press, 1993.

2. Peter Drucker, *The Unseen Revolution: How Pension Fund Socialism Came to America,* New York: Harper and Row, 1976, 1–2; Herman, *Corporate Control, Corporate Power,* 138; David Kotz, *Bank Control of Large Corporations in the United States,* Berkeley: University of California Press, 1978; Jeremy Rifkin and Randy Barber, *The North Will Rise Again,* Boston: Beacon Press, 1978, 10, 234; Scott, *Corporate Business and Capitalist Classes,* 67.

3. Marshall E. Blume, Jean Crockett, and Irwin Friend, "Stockownership in the United States: Characteristics and Trends," *Survey of Current Business,* Federal Reserve, November 1974, 24–5.

4. Ibid., 17–18.

5. Vyacheslav Fos, "The Disciplinary Effects of Proxy Contexts," *Management Science* 63: 3, 2017, 658.

6. Joseph Evan Calio and Rafael Xavier Zahralddin, "The Securities and Exchange Commission's 1992 Proxy Amendments: Questions of Accountability," *Pace Law Review* 14: 2, 1994, 465.

7. Calio and Zahralddin, "Security and Exchange Commission's 1992 Proxy Amendments," 465; Useem, *Executive Defense.*

8. Securities and Exchange Commission, "Final Rule: Selective Disclosure and the Insider Trading," 2000; Stephen Wagner and Lee Dittmar, "The Unexpected Benefits of Sarbanes-Oxley," *Harvard Business Review*, April 2006.

9. Marx, *Capital: Volume III*, 490–1.

10. Fligstein, *Transformation of Corporate Control.*

11. Zorn, "Here a Chief, There a Chief."

12. Johnston, "Rebirth of Commercial Paper."

13. Aquanno, *Crisis of Risk.*

14. Mihir A. Desai, "The Decentering of the Global Firm," *World Economy* 32: 9, 2009, 1271–90.

15. Bank for International Settlements, Monetary and Economic Department, "Triennial Central Bank Survey of Foreign Exchange and Derivatives Market Activity in April 2007," September 2007; Bryan and Rafferty, *Capitalism with Derivatives.*

16. Robert E. Hoskisson and Michael A. Hitt, *Downscoping: How to Tame the Diversified Firm*, Oxford, UK: Oxford University Press, 1994; Michelle Haynes, Steve Thompson, and Mike Wright, "The Impact of Divestment on Firm Performance: Empirical Evidence from a Panel of UK Companies," *The Journal of Industrial Economics* L: 2, 2002; Hsiu-Lang Chen and Re-Jin Guo, "On Corporate Divestiture," *Review of Quantitative Finance and Accounting* 24: 4, 388–421.

17. Prechel, "Corporate Transformation to the Multi-Layered Subsidiary Form."

18. Simon Mohun, "A Portrait of Contemporary Neoliberalism: The Rise and Economic Consequences of the One Per Cent," in Albo, Panitch, and Leys (eds.), *Socialist Register 2022.*

19. Zoltan Pozsar, Tobias Adrian, Adam Ashcraft, and Hayley Boesky, "Shadow Banking," Staff Report no. 458, Federal Reserve Bank of New York, July 2010; Samuel Knafo, "The Power of Finance in the Age of Market Based Banking," *New Political Economy* 27: 1, 2022, 33–46.

20. Mohun, "A Portrait of Contemporary Neoliberalism."

21. Tobias Adrian and Hyun Song Shin, "The Changing Nature of Financial Intermediation and the Financial Crisis of 2007–09," Federal Reserve Bank of New York, Staff Report no. 439, March 2010 (rev. April 2010).

22. Aquanno, *Crisis of Risk*, ch. 7.

23. Daniela Gabor, "The (Impossible) Repo Trinity: The Political Economy of Repo Markets," *Review of International Political Economy* 23: 6, 967–1000.

24. Adrian and Shin, "Changing Nature of Financial Intermediation."

25. Perry Mehrling, Zoltan Pozsar, James Sweeney, and Daniel H. Neilson, "Bagehot Was a Shadow Banker: Shadow Banking, Central Banking, and the Future of Global Finance," New York: Institute for New Economic Thinking, 2013.

26. Pozsar, "Shadow Banking"; Daniela Gabor and Jakob Vestergaard, "Towards a Theory of Shadow Money," INET Working Paper, London: Institute for New Economic Thinking, 2016.

27. Pozsar, "Shadow Banking"; Gabor and Vestergaard, "Towards a Theory of Shadow Money."

28. Pozsar, Adrian, Ashcraft, and Boesky, "Shadow Banking."

29. Karl Polanyi, *The Great Transformation*, Boston: Beacon Press, 2001, 141.

30. Eugene N. White, "The Comptroller and the Transformation of American Banking 1960–1990," Washington, DC: Office Comptroller of the Currency, Department of the Treasury, 1992.

31. Michael Moran, *The Politics of the Financial Services Revolution*, New York: Palgrave Macmillan, 1990.

32. Leo Panitch and Sam Gindin, "Political Economy and Political Power: The American State and Finance in the Neoliberal Era," *Government and Opposition* 49: 3, 2014, 369–99.

33. Poulantzas, *State, Power, Socialism*, 224.

34. Stein, *Fiscal Revolution in America*.

35. David Andolfatto and Andrew Spewak, "Debt Monetization: Then and Now," *On the Economy*, Federal Reserve Bank of St. Louis, April 2, 2018.

36. Streeck, *Buying Time*, ch. 2.

37. Bob Woodward, *The Agenda: Inside the Clinton White House*, New York: Simon and Schuster, 1994, 73.

38. Streeck, *Buying Time*, ch. 2.

39. Timo Walter and Leon Wansleben, "How Central Bankers Learned to Love Financialization: The Fed, the Bank, and the Enlisting of Unfettered Markets in the Conduct of Monetary Policy," *Socio-Economic Review* 18: 3, 2020, 1–29; Tobias Adrian and Hyun Song Shin, "Financial Intermediaries, Financial Stability, and Monetary Policy," Staff Report no. 346, Federal Reserve Bank of New York, 2008; Mehrling, *New Lombard Street*.

40. Robert McCauley, "Safe Assets: Made, Not Born," BIS Working Papers 769, February 2019; Paul Krugman, "Fannie, Freddie and You," *New York Times*, July 14, 2008.

41. Securities and Exchange Commission, "The Counterfeiting of Shares of Fannie Mae and Freddie Mac," September 17, 2008.

42. Gabor, "(Impossible) Repo Trinity."

43. Poulantzas, *State, Power, Socialism*, 171.

44. Lazonick, "Profits Without Prosperity"; Lazonick, "Financialization of the U.S. Corporation"; Lazonick and O'Sullivan, "Maximizing Shareholder Value"; Krippner, *Capitalizing on Crisis*.

45. Brenner, *Boom and the Bubble*; Michael Roberts, *The Long Depression: How It Happened, Why It Happened, and What Happens Next*, Chicago: Haymarket Books, 2016; Andrew Kliman, *The Failure of Capitalist Production: Underlying Causes of the Great Recession*, London: Pluto Press, 2012; David Harvey, *Enigma of Capital*; Paul M. Sweezy and Harry Magdoff, *Economic History as It Happened Volume IV: Stagnation and the Financial Explosion*, New York: Monthly Review Press, 1987; John Bellamy Foster, "*Monopoly Capital* at the Half-Century Mark," *Monthly Review*, July 1, 2016; John Bellamy Foster and Robert W. McChesney, "Monopoly-Finance Capital and the Paradox of Accumulation," Monthly Review, October 1, 2009. The idea that Marx demonstrated a coherent "law" of the tendency of the rate of profit to fall has been refuted by Michael Heinrich. See Michael Heinrich, "Crisis Theory, the Law of the Tendency of the Profit Rate to Fall, and Marx's Studies in the 1870s," *Monthly Review*, April 1, 2013.

46. Durand, *Fictitious Capital*; David McNally, "Slump, Austerity and Resistance," in Leo Panitch, Greg Albo, and Vivek Chibber, eds., *Socialist Register 2012: The Crisis and the Left*, London: Merlin Press, 2011.

47. Panitch and Gindin, *Making of Global Capitalism*.

48. Sean Campbell and Josh Gallin, "Risk Transfer Across Economic Sectors Using Credit Default Swaps," *FEDS Notes*, Federal Reserve Board of Governors, September 3, 2014.

49. Satyendra Nayak, *The Global Financial Crisis: Genesis, Policy Response and Road Ahead*, New York: Springer, 2013.

50. Gary Gorton and Andrew Metrick, "Securitized Banking and the Run on Repo," *Journal of Financial Economics* 104: 3, 2012, 425–51.

51. Pozsar, Adrian, Ashcraft, and Boesky, "Shadow Banking."

52. Adam Tooze, *Crashed: How a Decade of Financial Crisis Changed the World*, New York: Viking, 2018.

53. This was how Senator Evan Bayh subsequently summarized Bernanke's position. Dave Weigel, "Why Glenn Beck Is Like Evan Bayh," *Slate*, December 13, 2010.

54. Les Christie, "Foreclosures Up a Record 81% in 2008," *CNN*, January 15, 2009; Les Christie, "Record 3 Million Households Hit with Foreclosure in 2009," *CNN*, January 14, 2010; Susanna Kim, "2010 Had Record 2.9 Million Foreclosures," *ABC News*, January 12, 2011.

5: The New Finance Capital and the Risk State

1. Our notion of the "risk state" owes a substantial debt to the work of Daniela Gabor. However, our theorization of this differs in significant respects. See Daniela Gabor, "The Wall Street Consensus," *Development and Change*, March 26, 2021.
2. The concept of "statization" was originally developed by Nicos Poulantzas, albeit in a very different application. See Poulantzas, *State, Power, Socialism*.
3. Mehrling, *New Lombard Street*.
4. Marcelo Rezende, Judit Temesvary, and Rebecca Zarutskie, "Interest on Excess Reserves and U.S. Commercial Bank Lending," *FEDS Notes*, Federal Reserve Board of Governors, October 18, 2019.
5. George W. Madison, Michael E. Borden, and David A. Miller, Sidley Austin, "FSOC Designation Treasury Report: A Fundamental Shift," *Harvard Law School Forum on Corporate Governance*, February 4, 2018.
6. Brendan Greeley, "The Fed's Balance Sheet Is Normal and Political," *Financial Times*, April 29, 2022.
7. Lizzy Gurdus, "Fed Calls for More Fiscal Stimulus. Four Market Analysts on What's Ahead for Stocks," *CNBC*, September 23, 2020; Kasia Klimasinska, "Fed's Evans Calls on Fiscal Policy Makers to Help Boost Growth," *Bloomberg*, April 8, 2014.
8. Jerome H. Powell, "New Economic Challenges and the Fed's Monetary Policy Review," Speech at *Navigating the Decade Ahead: Implications for Monetary Policy*, Federal Reserve Bank of Kansas City, Jackson Hole, Wyoming, August 27, 2020; Federal Reserve Board of Governors, "2020 Statement on Longer-Run Goals and Monetary Policy Strategy," August 27, 2020.
9. Lapavitsas, *Profiting Without Producing*, 255.
10. Scott Longley, "Should the ETF Industry Be Concerned About BlackRock's Role with the Federal Reserve," *ETF Insight*, June 1, 2020.
11. Kevin McDevitt and Michael Schramm, "Morningstar Direct Fund Flows Commentary: United States," Morningstar, 2019; Amy Whyte, "Active Managers Kept Losing Out to Passive, Even After Markets Crashed," *Institutional Investor*, January 25, 2021.
12. Towers Watson, *The World's 500 Largest Asset Managers*, 2010.

13. Dan Weil, "BlackRock Hits $10 Trillion Assets Under Management," *The Street*, January 14, 2022; Barbara Friedberg and Benjamin Curry, "Top-10 Robo-Advisors by Assets Under Management," *Forbes*, July 9, 2022; "State Street Global Advisors AUM Hits $4.1 Trillion in Q4; CEO Confirms Planned Retirement," *Funds Europe*, January 20, 2022.

14. BlackRock Annual Report, 2020.

15. Benjamin Braun, "Fueling Financialization: The Economic Consequences of Funded Pensions," *New Labor Forum* 31: 1, 2021, 70–9; Braun, "Asset Manager Capitalism"; Maher, "Stakeholder Capitalism, Corporate Organization, and Class Power."

16. BlackRock Annual Report, 2020.

17. Johannes Petry, Jan Fichtner, and Eelke Heemskerk, "Steering Capital: The Growing Private Authority of Index Providers in the Age of Passive Asset Management," *Review of International Political Economy* 28: 1, 2021, 152–76.

18. "Indexes A to Z," *MarketWatch*, July 12, 2022; "There Are Now More Indexes Than Stocks," *Bloomberg Businessweek*, May 12, 2017.

19. Petry, Fichtner, Heemskerk, "Steering Capital."

20. Dawn Lim and Justin Baer, "BlackRock to Move $2tn Away from State Street as JPMorgan, Citi, and BNY Set to Benefit," *Financial News*, December 8, 2021.

21. Jeanna Smialek, "Top U.S. Officials Consulted with BlackRock as Markets Melted Down," *New York Times*, June 24, 2021.

22. Katrina Brooker, "Can This Man Save Wall Street?," *Fortune Magazine*, October 29, 2008.

23. Richard Henderson and Owen Walker, "BlackRock's Black Box: The Technology Hub of Modern Finance," *Financial Times*, February 23, 2020.

24. Ibid.

25. Benjamin Braun developed a similar chart to illustrate this process in "Asset Manager Capitalism."

26. Data from Macrotrends.

27. Authors' calculations based on data from Macrotrends and Ycharts.

28. "BlackRock's Acquisition of Cachematrix Should Strengthen Its Cash Management Unit," *Forbes*, January 28, 2017; "Why BlackRock for Cash Management", BlackRock, March 31, 2022.

29. Marx, *Capital: Volume III*, 567.

30. Davis, "New Finance Capitalism?," 12.

31. Braun, "Asset Manager Capitalism."

32. Hilferding, *Finance Capital*, 109.

33. Mike Scott, "Passive Investment, Active Ownership," *Financial Times*, April 6, 2014.

34. *BlackRock Investment Stewardship Report*, 2021; *Vanguard Annual Investment Stewardship Report*, 2020.

35. *BlackRock Investment Stewardship Report*, 2020.

36. *Vanguard Annual Investment Stewardship Report*, 2020; *BlackRock Investment Stewardship Report*, 2021.

37. Braun, "Asset Manager Capitalism."

38. Ibid., 273.

39. The term "ephemeral form" was coined by David Harvey to describe a concept developed in volume 1 of *Capital*. See David Harvey, *A Companion to Marx's Capital*, London: Verso, 2010, 168; Karl Marx, *Capital: Volume I*, trans. Ben Fowkes, London: Penguin Books, 1976 [1867], 436.

40. Braun, "Asset Manager Capitalism," 292.

41. "Everything Is Private Equity Now," *Bloomberg*, October 3, 2019.

42. Christine Idzelis, "The World's Dominant Investors in Private Equity," *Institutional Investor*, November 6, 2020.

43. Jason Philips and Dhruv Vatsal, "Private Equity Operating Groups and the Pursuit of 'Portfolio Alpha,'" McKinsey & Company, November 6, 2018.

44. Robert Kuttner, "It Was Vulture Capitalism That Killed Sears," *The American Prospect*, October 16, 2018.

45. Joseph A. Schumpeter, *Capitalism, Socialism and Democracy*, London: Routledge, 1994 [1942], 82–3; Karl Marx, *Grundrisse: Foundations of the Critique of Political Economy*, trans. Martin Nicolaus, New York: Penguin Publishing, 1973, 750; Harvey, *Limits to Capital*, 200–3.

46. "The Median Length of Time That These Funds Hold Portfolio Companies," *Private Equity Insights*, April 25, 2021; *Global Private Equity Report 2019*, Bain and Company.

47. "The Life Cycle of Private Equity," Blackstone, August 2020.

48. Chris Schelling, "The Troubling New Trend in Private Equity," *Institutional Investor*, July 25, 2018.

49. Guillaume Cazalaa, Wesley Hayes, and Paul Morgan, "Private Equity Exit Excellence: Getting the Story Right," McKinsey & Company, August 1, 2019.

50. Braun, "Fueling Financialization."

51. Jakob Wilhelmus and William Lee, *Companies Rush to Go Private*, Milken Institute, August 2018; Bethany McLean, "Too Big to Fail, COVID-19 Edition: How Private Equity Is Winning the Coronavirus Crisis," *Vanity Fair*, April 9, 2020.

52. Wilhelmus and Lee, *Companies Rush to Go Private*, 2.

53. Laurence Fletcher, "Hooked on QE: Hedge Funds See Dangerous Addiction," *Wall Street Journal*, December 9, 2016; Annie Pei, "The Fed's to Blame for

Hedge Funds' Pain: CIO," *CNBC*, June 8, 2016; Mona Dohle, "Hedge Funds Hit by QE Policies," *International Investment*, November 19, 2015.

54. Sullivan & Cromwell LLP, "Review and Analysis of 2018 U.S. Shareholder Activism," November 6, 2019; Sullivan & Cromwell LLP, "Review and Analysis of 2018 U.S. Shareholder Activism," March 14, 2019.

55. Sullivan & Cromwell LLP, "Review and Analysis," March 14, 2019, 13.

56. Sullivan & Cromwell LLP, "Review and Analysis of 2017 Shareholder Activism," March 26, 2018; Sullivan & Cromwell LLP, "Review and Analysis of 2020 US Shareholder Activism and Activist Settlement Agreements," December 2, 2020; Sullivan & Cromwell LLP, "Review and Analysis of 2021 US Shareholder Activism and Activist Settlement Agreements," December 20, 2021.

57. Sullivan & Cromwell LLP, "Review and Analysis," November 6, 2019, 20.

58. *Vanguard Annual Investment Stewardship Report*, 2020; *BlackRock Investment Stewardship Report*, 2021; *BlackRock Investment Stewardship Report*, 2020.

59. Svea Herbst-Bayliss and Ross Kerber, "BlackRock's Fink Learns to Live with Activist Investors," *Reuters*, November 13, 2017.

60. Ian R. Appel, Todd A. Gormley, and Donald B. Keim, "Passive Investors, Not Passive Owners," *Journal of Financial Economics* 121, 2016, 111–41.

61. Tom Lauricella and Leslie Norton, "How Facebook Silences Its Investors," *MorningStar*, October 7, 2021; Emily Stewart, "Mark Zuckerberg Is Essentially Untouchable at Facebook," *Vox*, December 19, 2018.

6: Crises, Contradictions, and Possibilities

1. Cezary Podkul and Dawn Lim, "Fed Hires BlackRock to Help Calm Markets. Its ETF Business Wins Big," *Wall Street Journal*, September 18, 2020; Matthew Goldstein, "The Fed Asks for BlackRock's Help in an Echo of 2008," *New York Times*, March 15, 2020; Annie Massa, "BlackRock Becomes Key Player in Crisis Response for Trump and the Fed," *Bloomberg*, April 17, 2020.

2. Gabor and Vestergaard, "Towards a Theory of Shadow Money."

3. Adam Tooze, *Shutdown: How Covid Shook the World's Economy*, New York: Viking Press, 2021; Adam Tooze, "Finance and the Polycrisis [3]: US Treasuries—How Fragile Is the World's Most Important Market?," Chartbook no. 172, 2022.

4. Riley and Brenner, "Seven Theses on American Politics"; Brenner, "Escalating Plunder."

5. Sam Gindin, "Inflation: Reframing the Narrative," *The Bullet*, April 5, 2022; James Meadway, "It's Time to Stop Kidding Ourselves the Bank of England Can Control Inflation," *New Statesman*, November 3, 2022.

6. Braun, "Asset Manager Capitalism."

7. Joe Morris, "Vanguard on Track to Lead US ETF Sales in 2022," *Financial Times*, December 22, 2022.

8. Daniela Gabor, "Revolution Without Revolutionaries: Interrogating the Return of Monetary Financing," *Transformative Responses to the Crisis*, Finanzwende and Heinrich-Böll-Foundation, Berlin, 2020; Pozsar, "Shadow Banking."

9. Braun, "Asset Manager Capitalism"; Madison Condon, "Externalities and the Common Owner," *Washington Law Review* 95: 1, 2020, 1–82; Jan Fichtner and Eelke M. Heemskerk, "The New Permanent Universal Owners: Index Funds, Patient Capital, and the Distinction Between Feeble and Forceful Stewardship," *Economy and Society* 49: 4, 2020, 493–515.

10. Madison Condon, "Externalities and the Common Owner," *Washington Law Review* 95: 1, 2020; Braun, "Asset Manager Capitalism," 284; James Mackintosh "A User's Guide to the ESG Confusion," *Wall Street Journal*, November 12, 2019.

11. Kevin Liptak, "Biden Hails a Change in 'Paradigm' as He Celebrates Relief Bill," *CNN Politics*, March 21, 2021; Adam Hilton and Amelia Malpas, "Biden's Democrats Want to Roll Back the Reagan Era. Are the Party and the Country Ready?," *Washington Post*, March 19, 2021.

12. Annie Massa, "BlackRock CEO Fink Told Trump U.S. Needs Infrastructure Spending," *Bloomberg*, May 14, 2020.

13. Brian Deese, "Biden's Vision for a Twenty-First-Century American Industrial Strategy," Atlantic Council, June 23, 2021; Brian Deese, "Remarks on a Modern American Industrial Strategy," Economic Club of New York, April 20, 2022.

14. Samir Sonti, "The Crisis of US Labour, Past and Present," in Albo, Panitch, and Leys (eds.), *Socialist Register 2022*.

15. *BlackRock 2021 Global Outlook: A New Investment Order*, BlackRock Investment Institute, 2020.

16. Matt Egan, "US Economy Can 'Definitely' Withstand Tax Hikes, BlackRock's Rick Rieder Says," *CNN*, March 17, 2021; "Business Roundtable Starts Major Ad Campaign Opposing Tax Hikes," *Bloomberg,* April 12, 2021; Brian Schwartz, "Major Business Groups Prepare to Fight New Democratic Tax Proposals for Biden Social Bill," CNBC, October 27, 2021; Karl Evers-Hillstrom, "Manufacturers' Group Airs 7-Figure Ad Campaign Opposing Tax Hikes," *The Hill*, October 27, 2021.

17. Sonti, "The Crisis of US Labour, Past and Present."

18. Mariana Mazzucato, "Build Back the State," *Project Syndicate*, April 15, 2021; Mazzucato, *The Entrepreneurial State*.

19. Saqib Iqbal Ahmed, "BlackRock CEO Fink Does Not See Inflation as Transitory," *Reuters*, July 14, 2021; Brian Stewart, "BlackRock's Larry Fink: Higher Interest Rates Will 'Help a Lot of Savers,'" *Seeking Alpha*, January 18, 2022.

20. BlackRock, "2022 Climate-Related Shareholder Proposals More Prescriptive Than 2021."

21. Silvia Amaro, "BlackRock's Former Sustainable Investing Chief Now Thinks ESG Is a 'Dangerous Placebo,'" *CNBC*, August 24, 2021.

22. *MSCI ESG Ratings*, MSCI, 2020.

23. Cam Simpson, Akshat Rathi, and Saijel Kishan, "The ESG Mirage," *Bloomberg*, December 10, 2021.

24. Nancy Fraser, "Contradictions of Capital and Care," *New Left Review* 100, July/August 2016.

25. Maher and Aquanno, "From Economic to Political Crisis."

26. Zachary Levenson, "An Organic Crisis Is Upon Us," *Spectre*, April 20, 2020; Ashley Dawson, "Capitalism's Organic Crisis," *Verso* blog, December 20, 2018.

27. Daniela Gabor, "Private Finance Won't Decarbonise Our Economies—But the 'Big Green State' Can," *The Guardian*, June 4, 2021.

28. Kate Aronoff, Alyssa Battistoni, Daniel Aldana Cohen, and Thea Riofrancos, *A Planet to Win: Why We Need a Green New Deal*, London: Verso, 2019; Leo Panitch and Sam Gindin with Stephen Maher, *The Socialist Challenge Today: Syriza, Corbyn, Sanders*, Chicago: Haymarket, 2020.

29. Matthew T. Huber, *Climate Change as Class War: Building Socialism on a Warming Planet*, London: Verso, 2022.

30. Hilferding, *Finance Capital*, 368.

31. Leo Panitch, "On Revolutionary Optimism of the Intellect," in Leo Panitch and Greg Albo, eds., *Socialist Register 2017: Rethinking Revolution*, London: Merlin Press, 2016.

Index

Page numbers in **bold** refer to charts/figures